BLISSED OUT

BLISSED OUT

the raptures of rock

Simon Reynolds

SERPENT'S
TAIL

Library of Congress Catalog Card Number: 90–60291

British Library Cataloguing in Publication Data
Reynolds, Simon
  Blissed out.
  1. Rock Music
  I. Title
  782.42166

  ISBN 1-85242-199-1

First published 1990 by
Serpent's Tail, 4 Blackstock Mews, London N4

set in 9½/14pt Garamond by AKM Associates (UK) Ltd., Southall, London
Printed in Great Britain by
WBC Print Ltd

CONTENTS

THE END OF MUSIC

ACKNOWLEDGEMENTS

Friendship and continual inspiration: David Stubbs, Paul Oldfield, The Stud Brothers (Ben and Dom).

Spiritual and material assistance: Joy Press.

Allowing and/or encouraging me to write: Steve Sutherland, Allan Jones, Malcolm Imrie, Jon Savage, Simon Frith, Frank Owen, plus Angela McRobbie, who suggested the idea of this book to Serpent's Tail in the first place.

Most of the pieces first appeared in *Melody Maker*, and have been revised for this anthology. Parts of some essays are taken from articles printed in *New Statesman*, *National Student* and *Monitor*.

INTRODUCTION

This book is written in the conviction that what excites people in pop, and what they manage to articulate of those feelings are generally two very different things. A fissure between experience and explication has been intrinsic to rock writing since its inception, in the mid sixties. By the mid eighties, and especially in Britain, this gulf between rock music and rock discourse had grown so wide it was deleterious to the music.

What rock discourses attempt to do is transform the heterogeneous dissensions and desires thrown up in periods of chaotic creativity (like the counter culture or punk) into a unity of alienation/aspiration. Rock criticism's drive is always to establish the 'we' of mass rhetoric as a plausible proposition. All this is for the consolidation and articulation of a culture: a counter culture is a home from home. For Roland Barthes the reward of belonging to a culture was *plaisir*: the satisfaction and secure enjoyment of identity through time. 'Plaisir' he saw as the opposite of 'jouissance' (bliss, convulsive ecstasy, a 'little death' of the individual and of meaning). The rock discourse has always functioned by the fixing of the chaotic and inchoate elements in music, and their articulation in a lasting scheme of value. But, as we all know in our hearts, the most exhilarating moment is that gap when an old musical order is dis-established but nothing stable has yet taken its place. Furthermore, I'd argue that the interesting things in rock are invariably those initiatives that confound the systems drawn up by the rock discourse, that play havoc with its tidy schemes.

This contradiction — rock criticism always kills the thing it loves, by transforming volatility into orthodoxy, jouissance into plaisir — is intrinsic and inescapable. It stems from the schizoid position that rock critics occupy: as cultured, educated individuals who nonetheless love what the parent culture stigmatizes as juvenile, trivial and empty. Burning with an inferiority complex toward the 'high' culture in whose discourse they are themselves fluent, their overweening concern is to validate pop culture. This they have done by bringing to bear on it all the gamut of 'high' cultural tools and terms.

And so the premises and values of literary criticism, political theory, and more recently, cultural studies, are appropriated in an attempt to locate 'content' and 'depth' in something still generally dismissed as inane and shallow. What counts as 'content' varies: in the case of Lit Crit it's an 'authentic' account of the human condition; in the case of the politico, it's social comment or an expression of collective agency; for the cultural theorist, the quest is for the ghost of 'subversion', of unconscious resistance to the status quo as inscribed/coded in style. What all these approaches have in common is that their activity takes the form of interpretation and judgement.

But the rock discourse has, from its inception, been host to a renegade tradition. Instead of arbitration, these writers opt for exaltation. Instead of interpretation and elucidation, they seek to amplify the chaos, opacity and indeterminacy of music. Instead of reading and writing, they prefer rending and writhing. Instead of legibility/legitimation, they prefer the illegible and illicit. Instead of seeking to align rock music with constructive ends, they prefer deconstruction/destruction, the sheer waste of energy into the void. This counter-tradition would include figures like Nik Cohn, Lester Bangs, Paul Morley and Ian Penman, Barney Hoskyns and Chris Bohn.

The renegades' fascination has been with what eludes content analysis. Its guiding conviction, which I share, is that the power of pop lies not in its meaning but its noise, not in its import but its force. And that rock, at its best, should be confused and confusing. Certainly, my own critical experiences of pop have been ones of perplexity — hearing the Sex Pistols for the first few times, seeing The Associates or The Smiths on *Top of the Pops*, being scared by Marc Bolan as a nine year old — moments when the mouth and mind gapes, when you've yet to sort out your responses, or get a firm grip on what a group is 'about' or 'is trying to say'. Moments of powerlessness, of subjection to pop's power. And the renegade writers have looked for this power in all the non-signifying, extra-linguistic elements that defy 'content analysis': the grain of the voice, the materiality of sound, the biological effect of rhythm, the fascination of the star's body.

When I entered the music press, rock music and rock discourse seemed at their most fallow. The music was overdetermined by what was written, just at the point when writing had lost its nerve, was in retreat — to safe notions of what music was for, what it could do. It's quite common for artistic or critical epochs to suffer from an overbearing feeling of lateness (and relatively rare for there to be a sense of being on the brink of a new order), and in 1985/86 there was a powerful sense of having missed the boat, the last big rave-up (punk, or the 'new pop' explosion, depending on where you sat). In sheer desperation, rock discourse had turned away from its void and directed its attention to soul, or jazz, or world music, in search of the ghost of punk (some kind of subversive edge or 'validity').

Rock was despised, denigrated, written off as dead. Rock suffered a neglect that allowed it to breathe again. So around the turn of '87, it became clear that a miraculous turnabout had taken place. Everything that was most suffocatingly stable and stabilizing, drearily coherent, and anxiously worthy about 'rock' discourse had taken hold of pop (Band Aid was the culmination of this maturation). And all the glorious incoherence and Dionysiac gratuitousness that Nik Cohn had first divined in pop, had somehow resurfaced in rock , with a spate of brilliant groups, of which The Young Gods, Throwing Muses and A.R. Kane were the most glaring examples.

This book, then, is the tale of that strange Indian Summer of rock. Without it, 'we' — me and my comrades on *Melody Maker* — might have frittered away our youth in griping and wistful retrospection. Instead we were granted a fortune, allowed to invent our own time as an adventure. We illuminated and sacramentalized the music: the music substantiated our reams and ravings.

That period looks now like a supernova. All the wealth of a past that was fully available to rock as never before, became fuel for a single, giant flare-up of possibility. Bands joined the dots between previous peaks of intensity, made unprecedented connections, fused extremes, took effects and raised them several powers.

And just as an ultimate rock had become possible, so too had an ultimate rock criticism: one that drew on illustrious antecedents — the Nik Cohn/Fred and Judy Vermorel celebration of pop as hysteria, Penman and Morley's ludic labyrinths, the diseased intelligence of Hoskyns and Bohn, Lester Bangs's thirst for headfuck, the Simon Frith/Jon Savage/Greil Marcus school of penetration — and aggregated their most useful aspects.

To an extent, it was simply a question of taking on the old tools that rock criticism had borrowed from high culture and bringing them into line with the modern developments they lagged behind: forcing the humanist version of Lit

Crit that poor rock criticism was founded in, to take on the discoveries of deconstruction, the new awareness of the literature of the fantastic etc; to broaden rock crit's narrow notion of 'politics' so as to include the occult and obtuse politics of gender, desire, the body; and as for the subcultural theory that some rock writing essayed, simply inject a little irrationalism into its scheme, ask whether people really do have ordered desires that are expressed clearly through style or 'passionate consumption'. (Do people *know* what they want?)

And just as rock recovered for itself certain lost powers, so 'we' writers discovered, for ourselves, certain ancient truths. In particular the truth discovered, separately, by Wittgenstein and Bataille, among others: that thought is a ladder you ascend only to pull up behind you and abandon; that it is only through language that you can reach that which lies beyond language's reckoning. In other words, the only way for rock to live again was if the rock discourse could somehow manage to *end* itself — again and again. Enter gladly into an endless end. And so we directed our enmity towards 'meaning', and in particular, against punk. Or rather what punk had turned into, had bequeathed to British rock culture: a stifling fixation on the text, an overbearing neurosis for meaning and relevance, an urge to totalize, and a gamut of taboos and inhibitions about what was sonically permissible. Rather than continue to probe rock for its 'spirit', it felt more like fun to rub against its 'skin'. Rather than respond to rock as a series of 'statements', it seemed more exciting to be swept up in its incoherence. For a change. As a way of staying interested.

> It is the sure sign of the death of a religion when its mythic presuppositions become systematized, under the severe, rational eyes of an orthodox dogmatism, into a ready sum of historical events, and when people begin timidly defending the veracity of myth but at the same time resist its natural continuance — when the feeling for myth withers and its place is taken by a religion claiming historical foundations.
>
> Nietzsche, *The Birth of Tragedy*

In 1987, to believe that rock could have, was having, a Second Coming was practically a heresy. The rock discourse does operate like an organized religion; it channels the mystical impulses of rock fans into orderly, doctrinal adherence. As adepts of the renegade tradition, we preferred the singular moment of awe to the rock discourse's investment in a long-term scheme of amelioration; we celebrated the pagan fascination for the icon or thing-in-itself to the devout believer's search for the Essence; chose the epiphany over faith.

Our enemies were both the churchy highmindedness of the rock discourse, and the agnostics, with their camp abnegation of seriousness, their won't-get-fooled-again cynicism of lapsed believers, who had secretly slipped back into their parents' belief in the ultimate triviality of rock.

Our search was for a new, more credible seriousness, as against the discredited sanctimoniousness of those — U2, Simple Minds — who still believed rock could save the world. We imagined a *local* seriousness, the serious-as-your-life of the ecstatic moment. A seriousness that would not repeat the old mistakes of rock discourse, and fall into systematization, dictation, legislation, over-determination.

This book is an argument about bliss; it is an argument about noise; above all, it is an argument that 'bliss' and 'noise' are the same thing — a rupture/disruption in the signifying system that holds (a) culture together.

It is about noise in the most elastic sense: as well as simple dissonance, it is about many other forms of code jamming — 'the noise of the body', the 'visual noise' of certain kinds of flamboyance, brio, effervescence, élan (Bolan, Prince, Morrissey); the discordant chaos of contradictory desires, as they escape in the form of impossible reproaches and demands upon life; 'political noise', the uproar that occurs when desire is not articulated as a programme of demands, but is vented as pure *demand*, blank and intransitive (the 'nonsense' of 'don't know what I want but I know how to get it' and 'we want the world and we want it now'); the geyser gush of glossalalia (Morrissey's falsetto, Prince's scream, the Pixies' holler).

It is an argument that borrows freely, impartially and indiscriminately from the gamut of definitions of 'jouissance': Julia Kristeva's irruption of the semiotic into symbolic language, Hélène Cixous's serenity, Barthes's 'void of bliss/degree zero', Lyotard's notion of the 'sublime' (all that promises our defeat and death).

The contradictions of trying to write 'bliss' are manifest, but intrinsic and vital. What is involved is a writing that fervently seeks out its own limits, endeavours to expose and amplify its silences, reach its own end.

Barthes writes in *The Pleasure of the Text*, of how 'criticism is always historical or prospective . . . the presentation of bliss is forbidden it: its preferred material is culture, which is everything in us except our present.' I'm not sure if I succeed in capturing the apocalyptic now of the music celebrated in *Blissed Out*. But the tense is at least that of the immediate past, the *just now*: the grave tone of the autopsy, of an inquest into a recent fatality. For that's what the music has done for and to me. I fell. I was void.

MISERABILISM

morrissey

I think I've met them all now. For me, there are no more heroes left. And no new ones coming along, by the look of it. It could be that this is a time marked by a dearth of characters, or that the smart people in rock aren't interested in self-projection but in obliterating themselves in noise. But really, I think, it's the case that, in this job, you don't have time to develop obsessions, what with the insane turnover, and all the incentives to pluralism.

The heroes you have kind of linger on from a prior period when only a few records passed through your life, when you had the time to get fixated, spend weeks living inside a record. It's a real effort to click back to that frame of mind, which is bad because fanaticism is the true experience of pop, not discrimination and broad-mindedness — I think of the splendid devotion of all those boys and girls, who as soon as they've got hold of the new Cure or New Order or Bunnymen record, immediately set to learning the lyrics by heart, then spend days exhaustively interpreting the Tablets From on High, struggling to establish some fit between their experience and what is actually some drunken doggerel cobbled together in a studio off-moment.

Seriously, I approve. I approve the deadly seriousness, the piety, the need for something sacred in your life. However 'deluded'.

It's become a reflex for critics to castigate the readers for being partisan, for being sluggish and single-minded in their choices. We exhort you to disconnect, discard and move on, acquire a certain agility as consumers. But maybe this ideal state of inconstancy we advocate only makes for fitter participants in capitalism. For the one thing that makes rock more than simply an industry, the one thing that transcends the commodity relation, is fidelity, the idea of a relationship.

There are voices you turn to as a friend, and you don't just turn your back on your friends if they go off the rails. You hang around. You give them the time of day. So — in the year in which we've forced the text-centred discipline that is rock writing to incorporate everything that it has excluded for so long (the relationship between the star's body and the fan's, the voice, the materiality of music) — maybe it's time to make criticism grapple with what undoes it, 'the uncritical' itself.

When I meet Morrissey, at the Hyde Park Hotel, he's dressed from head to foot in black. So am I. The whole tableau is idol meets fan to an embarrassing tee.

Happily, my finally getting to meet him coincides with the release of one of Morrissey's great records (they seem to alternate quite evenly with duff ones), so there's no awkward rub between the fan's loyalty and the critic's 'responsibility' to the 'truth'.

Viva Hate! feels implausibly fresh: the music's breathing again, free of a certain stuffiness and laboriousness that had set in seemingly irreversibly in The Smiths' twilight period. All due respect to Johnny Marr (though the haircuts never get better . . .) but, like most people 'blessed' with skill, there was a tendency to be used by one's versatility rather than use it. Songs were getting written to accommodate guitar conceits, pointless feats and smotheringly unnecessary elaboration. And I never much cared for the bumptious, muscular side of The Smiths, so I welcome the spaciness Vini Reilly brings as new guitarist, whether it's the lurid wig-out of 'Alsatian Cousin' or the dew-and-moonbeam iridescence of 'Late Night, Maudlin Street'.

In American teen slang, Vini is a 'space' — a dreamer, someone not all there. Hailed by Paul Oldfield as 'the missing boy of pop', someone whose resistance takes the form of an absenteeism from life, it strikes me that Reilly's mystical anorexia is unusually suited to Morrissey's neurasthenia, his supine delinquency.

Viva Hate!, unsurprisingly, returns again and again to the Englishness which obsesses Morrissey. For instance, 'Everyday Is Like Sunday' pores over the drab details of some benighted seaside resort: 'Hide on the promenade/How I dearly wish I was not here . . . trudging slowly over wet sand . . . win yourself a cheap tray . . . share some greased tea with me . . .' Typically, Morrissey seems to cherish the very constraints and despondency of a now disappearing England, fetishize the lost limits. What is this love/hate relationship you have with Englishness?

'There are very few aspects of Englishness I actually hate. I can see the narrowness, and love to sing about it. But I don't hate Englishness in any way. All aspects of England, whether it be underclass, or extreme affluence, I find very interesting and entertaining. And it's still, I feel, cliché as it may seem, the sanest country in the world.'

But there is the echo of Betjeman-on-Slough in the line 'come! come! come! — nuclear bomb!' I mean, if it was such a rotten holiday, why hark back to it?

'That never really occurred to me. The pleasure is getting it out of your system, saying "never again" instead of "same again next year". And the British holiday resort is just like a symbol of Britain's absurdity, really. The idea of a resort in Britain doesn't seem natural.'

Again, on 'Late Night, Maudlin Street', you say: 'I never stole a happy hour around here' — but the whole effect of the song, the way your murmured reveries drift in and out of Vini's entranced playing, just makes the whole time and place seem magical, otherworldly, and incredibly precious . . .

'It is a trick of memory, looking back and thinking maybe things weren't that bad, but of course, if you concentrate, you realize they were. But I don't want to sing about football results or importune people to dance. There are too many other people doing that, and I feel sad there aren't people making serious statements. I feel slightly let down. I feel I should look about and see streams of groups being angry and hateful — but it's just not happening at all.'

For me, this song is the centrepiece of the album. But you seem not so much angry, as succumbing to memories, drowning in them, leaving this world behind. . .

'But, I think, finally exorcising the ghost of that past and those small times.'

It reminded me of the comparison the Stud Brothers made between you and Sinead O'Connor: the 'rigorous autobiography', the way both of you seem to have stopped living in order to document more completely your adolescence.

'But my life never really started at any stage — which I know you won't believe, but it's true — so it never really got stopped at any point. But obviously the past is what makes any person. It's because of your past that you're sitting there now, with your list on your knee. I can't help thinking about the past.'

The line 'women only like me for my mind' is clever . . .

'It's the final complaint, I suppose, in the long list of complaints about the past.'

It's still not widely appreciated that men can want to be objects, as much as agents, of desire.

'But I think men are seen like that, actually — now. Men are aware of their sexuality in a way they previously weren't, or weren't supposed to be. I think women have become very open about their needs and desires, and this was entirely due to feminism. By women being open about sex, it made life much easier for men. And this is why feminism helps everybody, to be slightly more relaxed about life.'

Mindful of Morrissey's Jean-Genet-like interest in ruffians, as evinced by 'Suedehead', I ask: have you always been drawn to people who are tough and streetwise and unlike yourself?

'I'm enormously attracted to people who can look after themselves. I'm obsessed by the physical, in the sense that it always *works.* It's a great power to be very physical, to be able to storm through life with swaying shoulders, instead of creeping and just relying on your thesaurus. That doesn't work! I've had so many conversations with people trying to convince them of a particular point, and although I find words central to my life . . .'

You'd like to be capable of violence . . .

'Nothing shifts or stirs people like a slight underhand threat. They jump. But most of the friends I have are very verbal and cross-legged individuals and not very demonstrative in any way. So I've never belonged to any physical set. The song "Break up the Family" is strongly linked with "Suedehead" and "Maudlin Street", that whole period in 1972, when I was twelve, thirteen. "Break up . . ." is about a string of friends I had who were very intense people and at that age, when your friends talk about the slim separation between life and death — and you set that against the fact that this period of your youth is supposed to be the most playful and reckless — well, if you utilized that period in a very intense way, that feeling never really leaves you.'

Did you all consider the family a bad institution?

'No, we didn't feel that at all. The family in the song is the circle of friends, where it almost seemed, because we were so identical, that for anybody to make any progress in life, we'd have to split up. Because there was no strength in our unity. And that's what happened, we did all go our separate ways, and quite naturally came to no good'.

And your gang, were you outcasts, victimized by 'The Ordinary Boys'?

'Yes, but half of it, I have to confess, was the effect of deliberate choosing. We chose to reject the normality of life, and be intense and individual.'

Do you think, in ten or twenty years, your life will still be structured around these playground antagonisms?

'Yes. People don't really change, do they? They don't change. And the playground antagonisms are replaced by other . . . more adult antagonisms.'

Office antagonisms.

'Yes. Canteen antagonisms . . . getting heavily antagonized while you're queuing up to purchase a doughnut. But surely you have a happy question?'

The last track on *Viva Hate!* is a rueful little ballad with the self-explanatory title 'Margaret on the Guillotine', which describes 'the wonderful dream' (i.e. the gory and spectacular public execution of our PM) that all 'the kind people' harbour. The chorus, repeated five times, is the plaintive, rhetorical question: 'when will you die?' You realize all this will cause you no end of trouble?

'Anything that's very clearcut and very strong causes difficulty, doesn't it? But why should it? I'm not looking for attention. In this case, attention is the last thing I really need. I don't want to be in the *Daily Mirror*. There is something in this above controversy and outrage and all these over-familiar words. It's too easy to be controversial.'

So you mean it? You'd like to see her dead?

'Instantly.'

In a cruel, bloody sort of way?

'Yes.'

Would you carry out the execution?

'I have got the uniform, ready.'

One line in the song seems to me to be very revealing: when you say you want to see her killed 'because people like you/make me feel so tired . . . so old inside.' If you compare The Smiths with the previous Great White Hopes of preceding eras, it's clear that the rebellion of the Stones, Who, Pistols, Jam, was based in some kind of activism or at least action, an optimism about the potential of collective or individual agency. But The Smiths' rebellion was always more like resistance through withdrawal, through subsiding into enervation.

The fantasy in 'Margaret on the Guillotine' is more like wishful thinking, than the resolve to do violence, or even personify violence theatrically. Isn't the effect of 'Margaret . . .' just to encourage wistful resignation?

'Maybe, but I do also firmly believe in action. But also there's a great sense of doorstep rebellion, and stamping of feet. I think, above all, that dealing with people's manipulations *is* very tiring. You grow old very quickly when every day of your life you're trying to win arguments. Politically, I do feel exhausted. I do feel there are no more demonstrations, no more petitions to be signed. I think those things, and group meetings and crêches, are completely boring and a waste of time. I do feel a sense of apathy.'

I'm interested you talk about 'stamping of feet', because this fantasy of offing Mrs Thatcher, as though this would somehow solve everything, as if the 'evil' in this country weren't a lot more structural and entrenched — well, there's something a bit childish and petulant about it.

'Believe me, I'm totally aware of that. But there's also something important about it. The song is silly, it's also very heavy, and it's also very brave. And I sit back and smile. Surely you can see that the very serious element in it puts the straightforward demonstration "Maggie Maggie Maggie Out Out Out" protest song, in its place and makes it seem trite and a little bit cosy?'

The thing with protest songs is that pop's always been about the immediate, spontaneous and puerile, it hasn't the patience to slog through sub-committees and lobbying and making orderly demands through the proper channels. Pop isn't programmatic, it won't negotiate, it wants the world and it wants it now, and it's much more satisfying to hear about your enemy being slaughtered. Even if it's just a fantasy . . .

'Is it? You obviously haven't listened. I think it's possible. The times are quite ropy. Things are touch-and-go. You don't believe me? There's a lot of organized suffering in England right now.'

Petulancy is Morrissey's forte: petulancy and POIGNANCY. They're the reason why he's been vilified as regressive, maudlin, self-martyring. Underneath the scorn, the subtext is that Morrissey's art lacks a vital virility. Female artists are allowed to be vulnerable, frail, because this corresponds with the idea of woman as lack. But in a man, such qualities merely indicate a repugnant limpness of being. Poignancy spells NANCY.

Not that the accusations are inaccurate. Morrissey is regressive. He can't grow, as an artist or a person, because he's addicted to his own neurosis, addicted to poignancy — which is, after all, the sublime taste of your own defeat, your own incompleteness.

Poignancy (and this is why its domain is the minor key) is the exquisite meshing of two contradictory feelings. It's a piercing beauty, or a sweet sorrow. Anyone who's ever treasured their pain, tried to prolong it, toyed with exacerbating it or been driven to dwell on inside it long after recovery was an option, preferring the company of ghosts to the dreamlessness of everyday sociability — that person understands poignancy.

Morrissey has always lived and breathed poignancy, always secretly treasured the gulf between himself and the loved one, the difference that makes love possible but makes possession illusory, a delusion, so that, in the end, we are all unrequited lovers. And poignancy is why he obsessively prizes and keeps open ancient wounds.

But poignancy isn't just retrospective, it's also the rapture that's the same as grief, a radiant apprehension of death. In its own, gentle way, poignancy is as profound an intimation of the contradictions of being, as any of the mindfuck experiences or headlong plunges into the horror-of-it-all that the anti-Morrissey brutalists advocate.

A lot of people — including the singer himself — see the point and appeal of Morrissey as 'authenticity'. There's a simplistic notion that his fans identify straightforwardly with the scenarios in the songs. But how do they connect with such a statistically-remote calamity as 'Girlfriend in a Coma?' Isn't there something almost aspirational about their identification with such irregular forms of martyrdom? A craving for the hardest hit of self-pity?

'I don't feel they're extreme. If anything, I feel they're understated. I think people live very urgent lives. I don't feel I'm in any sense vaudevillian or melodramatic.'

On 'Rubber Ring' you seemed aware that, for many of your fans, the relationship is going to be a temporary if intense, even lifesaving one. Do you think that maybe most of your fans are going through a phase, and that most of them will emerge the other end and leave you behind?

'Well, it probably is a phase. But if people move on, it's understandable. In the event that everyone moves on, and I'm left dangling in the recording studio — then it would seem to confirm everything I've ever thought about the cruelties of life.'

It seems to me the only people who do persist in that phase and make something tenable out of an unsatisfied, unsettled life, are rock musicians, and rock critics. But has satisfaction ever threatened to descend on your life?

'It's never been something I've been immediately faced by. It's definitely a possession of other people. I have a very long list of things I want to do.'

Artistic or personal?

'Artistic. Nothing else counts.'

Does a notion of 'artistic growth' have any place in your scheme?

'Not really. Can you give me an example of where that's happened?'

You're right — in rock and pop, it seems that people just have their thing.

'And they hone it. Or they start bad and merely get better. Artistic growth? I don't really have any ambitions to change in any drastic ways. I'm quite satisfied with how I am.'

You're satisfied with your dissatisfaction?

'Totally. I couldn't be happier. I don't want anything to interfere with this state of dissatisfaction.'

And there'll be an endless-renewed harvest of dissatisfied young souls filling up this phase which is your constituency, a.k.a. adolescence.

'But I don't consider it to be adolescent. I am not adolescent. I'm twenty-eight. It's something quite beyond and more complicated than "adolescence", something that hasn't been thought out yet, but shouldn't be dismissed as "adolescent".'

I'm just using 'adolescent' as a handy signifier for a life of restlessness, impatience and insatiability. But would you prefer 'a questioning life', maybe . . .?

'Yes, something like that . . . and that's something that can only aid and assist.'

And you'll grow old (but not up) gracefully . . .

'Disgracefully. I grow old disgracefully!'

Why were The Smiths 'important'? Because of their misery. Never forget it. Around *Meat is Murder* the critics suddenly discovered Morrissey's humour — George Formby was trundled out as a reference point. If you ask me, The Smiths could have afforded to be more humorless. The Smiths' finest moments — 'Hand in Glove', 'How Soon is Now?', 'Still Ill', 'I Know It's Over' — were moments of reproachful, avenging misery, naked desperation, unbearable reverence — free of the 'saving grace' of quips and camp self-consciousness. If there was laughter it was black, scornful, scathing. If the Smiths had only produced sunny, cuddly stuff like 'Heaven Knows', 'Ask', 'Vicar in a Tutu', they would have merely presaged the perky negligibility of The Housemartins, the sound that grins itself to death. The Smiths were heroic party-poopers at the *Top of the Pops* office do, glowering at the forced jollity; they were like those gauche youths who turn up to house parties only to cling to the dark corners in chaste disdain, driven by the naïve, vaguely inhuman conviction that all merriment is a lie.

And The Smiths were important because of their extremism, their unbalanced view of the world, their partiality. Morrissey is a character in a pop era of nonentities, and characters are always lopsided, contrary, incomplete, the sum of wounds and bigotries. Morrissey is 'half a person', his very being constituted around lack, maladjustment — this is the vantage point from which he launches his impossible demands on life, his denial **of the reality** principle. Satisfaction and adjustment could never enter The Smiths' picture, for this would breach their identity.

This is why Morrissey can't 'develop' as an artist. How could he grow when his very being is constructed around the petulant refusal — 'I won't grow up'? The refusal to be responsible and motivated, to get a job, to take on the brutalization and disenchantment entailed in 'gainful' employment. The refusal to collude in the state of dreamlessness that is adulthood, even to the Pyrrhic point of clinging stubbornly to the state of being unsatisfied, forever. Having perfected this petulant stance, all he can do is reiterate it — with a self-deprecating acknowledgement of the onset of self-parody: 'Stop Me if You Think You've Heard This One Before', 'Sweet and Tender Hooligan', where the chorus is simply 'et cetera, et cetera' . . .

Not that Morrissey's misery is something we simply identify with. What The Smiths were about was narcissism, damaged, exploding back with a defiant fantasy of martyrdom. The Smiths seduce us into aspiring to the same heroic pitch of failure and exile. The tragedy of The Smiths is that Morrissey could only become the victim of the perfection of his style. Like Jagger, like Rotten, he is condemned to live out its pantomime forever.

When The Smiths first appeared they seemed to be a reaction against the opulence/corpulence of nouveau riche new pop. Really, they were a return to a different vision of 'new pop', the Postcard ideal. The Smiths were the second coming of Postcard — the whiter-than-white 'pure pop': the sexual ambiguity; the Luddite insistence on guitars: Edwyn Collins's avowed rating of romance over sex; the swoon instead of the earthy R&B rasp; the flustered undance-ability.

What The Smiths returned to the charts was something that pop had seemingly left behind — adolescence. New pop had rapidly lost its mischief and settled down into a post-rock, post-teenage maturity, peddling naff fantasies of sophistication to a new generation of moneyed teeny-boppers whose only desire was to grow up as soon as possible. The Smiths, on the other hand, provided fantasies of innocence to those in the process of leaving behind their adolescence. Their constituency was the silent majority of music paper readers that critics love to sneer at: students, ex-students, and those destined to be students (sixth formers and fifth formers). The pale skinny boys identify with Morrissey because he lives out their quandaries. Morrissey is a paradigm of a certain kind of ethereal, inhibited masculinity that would rather live in dreams than risk being disappointed by reality. (Morrissey invests his emotion in pristine idols, preferably dead, like James Dean, rather than deal with the mess and awkwardness of any real close encounter.)

Situated in the space between the constraints of childhood and having a career, these are people who dream for a while of wanting a vague something more from life, yet are saddened by these dreams because they know deep down they'll probably relinquish them, buckle down to a life of mediocrity. When this happens, the records get harder to listen to, the music gets to be like a reproach, stirring up the taunting ghosts of prematurely foregone dreams. Nagging 'but . . . you've got everything now', 'please save your life/because you've only got one' . . . which is why people give up pop music, in the end.

New pop, far from being a bright new beginning, turned out to be merely the inauguration of global designer-soul, the soundtrack to the new yuppie culture of health and efficiency. In the face of the benign totalitarianism of leisure capitalism and its off-the-peg self-improvement, The Smiths glamourized debility and illness, advocated absenteeism, withdrawal, the failure to meet quotas of enjoyment. The profound embarrassment of Morrissey's dancing turned the lack of oneness with your body into glamour. All the self-squandering and deficiency of lifeskills that animated The Birthday Party and The Fall, The Smiths turned into brilliant, glamorous, consumable pop, two minute bursts of otherness in the heart of the charts.

They were meant to be The Rolling Stones of their time. If The Stones' camp appropriation of black R&B sexuality was the supremely relevant response to straitlaced, petit bourgeois English suburbia, then The Smiths' refusal of the travesty of healthy sexuality that black pop degenerated into, was the appropriate response to eighties 'liberated' suburbia. The Smiths deployed the imagery of provincial northern life, the residues of a lost Englishness, as a weapon against the cheap hedonism of an Americanized southern England. The very parochial stuffiness that the Stones reacted against had somehow become an alluring and reproachful memory. 'As grey and repressive as this lost world was, the inchoate colourific eighties is worse. At least then you stood out, if only to be beaten up . . . Morrissey is needed, not as an ombudsman, or a figure of the eighties, but as a horrified figure *against* the eighties, who has turned his back on the march of pop time as the last keeper of the sanctuary of self-pity, apartness, exile' (David Stubbs).

For the Stones, desire was obviously the enemy of materialism, work and a planned life. But today desire has become incorporated as one element in a life's work. Getting in touch with your body, getting in touch with your soul, has become a humanist work-out. 'Satisfaction' has become feasible, something you can plan for. The Smiths, hooked on the glamour of the misfit, could only occupy an IMPOSSIBLE position, attempt to create a rock music where aggression was replaced by vulnerability, hedonism by asceticism.

From the private pain, the furtive 'minor language' of unrequited obsession, that they began with, The Smiths went public, became the rock band, the pollwinners, ombudsmen for wider grievance. Whether speaking out for the silent rock majority against the soulboy mediacrats, or representing The Smiths as media martyrs. Morrissey ascended a paranoiac spiral of statesmanship (paranoia is inverted narcissism) — check the progression from 'Panic' through *The World Won't Listen* and *Louder Than Bombs*, to *Strangeways, Here We Come*.

'Did that swift eclipse torture you?/A star at eighteen and then — suddenly gone/ down to a few lines in the back page of a teenage annual/oh but I remember you/I looked up to you' — 'Little Man, What Now?'.

'Fame, Fame, fatal Fame/It can play hideous tricks on the brain' — 'Frankly Mr Shankly'.

One of the best tracks on *Viva Hate!* is 'Little Man, What Now?', an eerie, enchanted, rather chilling song, in which Morrissey ponders the fate of a young TV actor ('a real person — but I don't want to name names') he remembers from 'Friday nights 1969', briefly elevated to the level of minor celebrity before being abruptly dispatched back into obscurity, never to return — except for an afternoon TV nostalgia show, where the panel 'couldn't name you'. It's another example of Morrissey's unusual awareness of the trajectories of fame, and the ways in which fans use and are used by stars.

'Fame is the most fascinating subject in the world and I'm keenly interested in speaking to certain people who've had fame and then lost it.'

Did you always crave fame?

'I always had a religious obsession with fame. I always thought being famous was the only thing worth doing in human life, and anything else was just perfunctory. I thought anonymity was easy: it was easy to be a simple, nodding individual who got on the bus. I wasn't terribly impressed with obscurity.'

Did you have a rich sense of destiny and difference?

'I always knew something, shall we say, *peculiar* was going to happen. I think real, true artists do have that instinct.'

From the age of what — nine, ten?

'Much earlier. In some form. I saw a multitude of options and the dilemma was just which one to concentrate on. Obviously, I wrote. At the age of six I compiled a personal magazine every week. I was intensely interested in journalism, and all the things around it, whether it was performing or actually playing records. I intensely envied DJs. To simply sit on this cushion at the BBC day after day and flip on anything they thought was moving — well, I thought that was the most sacred and powerful position in the universe. To me, it was more important than politics.'

You wanted to be a DJ?

'At a tender age, I craved that power — to impose one's record collection on people in launderettes and on scaffolding. But now I think it's such a terrible job that DJs deserve to be the highest paid people in the country. To have to sit in an office all day playing the same records — all of which are awful — over and over and over again — well, it's not funny, is it? We shouldn't pick on these people. We should send them parcels!'

About this early magazine . . .

'I was only six, so the art direction let it down a bit, really. It was simply the Top Ten, then certain pin-ups of artists of my personal choice. . . sketched, in fact, by the editor himself.'

What kind of circulation did it have?

'There was just the one copy, which limited readership somewhat.'

You quickly became an avid reader and writer?

'I very quickly became obsessed by music papers and pop journalism, and collected them ravenously.'

Did you turn to music as an avenue for writing, or were you driven by musical instincts?

'By staunch instincts of very brittle criticism. Developed through having had this magazine of my own since the age of six, and listening to the Top 30 every Tuesday only to run off instantly to the typewriter in order to compile my own personal Top 30 which totally conflicted with how the world really was. But in my sense, my Top 30 was how the world should have been. It was a Top 30 of contemporary records, but the new entries were very unlikely, and obviously I favoured certain musicians, like T. Rex.

'I can remember writing an extravagant critique of "Cinderella Rockefeller". I was always a totally dissatisfied consumer, aflood with complaints. It seemed to me that the world of pop music, which I worshipped, was there to be altered and corrected.'

this other people's stuff — has been an abiding acrimony on the rock 'left' for some fifteen years or more. (Punk had very little impact on the charts, on what sold.) So Morrissey's infantile gainsaying of pop reality was the chrysalis for indiepop's current wistful, wishful fantasy of a 'perfect pop' returning to oust the impostors in the hit parade.

'I think we have now reached an unthinkable state, where things are orchestrated entirely by unsympathetic and unmusical hands and ears. The people in key positions are people who don't consider pop culture to have any serious importance whatsoever.'

You believe pop is or can be art, but that belief is sustained by only very rare instances. You seem to have very specific ideas about what those are. The other day it occurred to me that there are maybe two kinds of intelligence in the world: one that's very open, that tries to take on everything, and accordingly gets paralysed by choice: another kind that's narrow, that finds strength focusing on some things and excluding most everything else . . .

'If I liked everything, I'd be very hard to understand. I always found the idea of people who were very hard to please, including journalists who were very critical — I always found they were almost always right when they found something praiseworthy. I find people who are unbudgeably fair quite time-consuming. I find agreeable people immensely disagreeable.'

Is that the idea of *Viva Hate!* that we need bigotries in order to make sense of the world, in order to act? (The hankering for a punk-style commotion is precisely for such an illiberalism, a taking of sides, a new order.)

'Sadly, a lot of people need to be told, rather than asked. Also, I often feel I gain from venomously critical views of me as an artist, more than from dithery, sloppily fawning, supportive views.'

Going back to fame, to your intimate knowledge of the processes of identification and obsession . . . having been through various manic fixations, you have progressed to being a star, the subject of fixation yourself. Most of your fans though, will remain condemned in a lonely monologue with their distant idol . . .

'Condemned sounds a bit rough. . . But, nonetheless, I can't help but agree.'

You encourage the obsessiveness, though, don't you? I remember you once saying you were delighted people sent you underwear, or demands for underwear . . .

'Yes, both! I do gets lots of very fascinating and fascinated letters, and lots of fascinating gifts. I can very clearly understand obsessiveness, and the people who write to me see that I understand obsession and preciousness. And I respond in the same way. I still get very nervous when I meet people who I admire . . .'

What does it feel like to see your image about, on hoardings, in magazines, to hear your voice on the radio?

'It's very odd. I was in a shop once, buying scented candles, and on the radio came Steve Wright with a collage of Smiths' songs, and I got a distinct chill, almost as though the hand of death was tapping me on the shoulder, saying: "put yer candles down, it's time to go!"'

The Smiths were prime movers in what you could call the depoliticization of personal life, after punk's initial demystification. Remember 1980: 'personal politics' was the phrase that tripped off every lip, groups like Gang of Four ('Love Like Anthrax'), Delta Five, and Au Pairs worked towards their notion of the equal relationship, liberated from the veils of romantic false consciousness. A 'radicalism' that was barely distinguishable from the pragmatism and 'common sense' of therapists' and counsellors' discourse, with their notion of love as contract.

Then 1982: attention shifted to the public language of love, to pop's sexual iconography — the buzzwords were the 'language of love', 'the lexicon of love', 'the lover's discourse'; demystification was superseded by deconstruction and ambiguity.

Finally, with Nick Cave's misogynist agonies, the Jesus and Mary Chain's candyskin classicism, and The Smiths' eternally unrequited gaze, came the return of romanticism in all its purity and privacy. Pop had returned to what it had always been about: the personal as the realm in which the meaning of your life is resolved. Romanticism — the dream of the redemptive love that will bring heaven-on-earth, resolve all difference, end alienation — has in the twentieth century replaced religion as the opium of the people.

But it's the dream that continues to speak most deeply to us. Maybe the superstition of love is our last reservoir of spirituality in the face of those 'specialists of the soul' who would seek to reform relationships in accordance with their ghastly notions of 'negotiation', 'support', 'partnership'.

I always come back to the Stones when I think of The Smiths, because of the camp, but mainly because of the way each band illuminates their era for us. For the Stones, satisfaction was the goal: everything would be all ALL RIGHT if we shed the inhibitions that held us back and down. Revolution meant good sex on the 'morrow.

But the Stones were the product of expansive times. The Smiths the product of contracted and beleaguered times. With The Smiths it was a question not of desire but of longing — the yearning to belong to or with someone, to belong somewhere. The dream that two 'half-a-persons' can make a whole, fit 'hand in glove'. The Stones and their time were all about leaving home; The Smiths and our time are about pining for a home.

Morrissey is the first major teen icon whose aesthetic is based around the conviction that rock'n'roll's best years are (in the) past, that the premises of youth culture have been outflanked ('I Know It's Over'). The first major teen icon whose work is grounded not in anticipation and impatience, but vacillation, resignation and looking back.

These feelings — homesickness for a place you couldn't wait to leave (Manchester), nostalgia for a time that was never any good in the first place (adolescence) — were why the music of the Smiths refracted the quandaries of the eighties like no other. It's a sign of the times that pop-as-reinvention-of-the-self is something that resonates for fewer and fewer people in the world that is the music press readership. That the pollwinner, the figure most identified with is Morrissey: victim of his past, chained to his memories, only able to imagine being eternally unrequited by life.

And as he says, artists don't really 'develop', they have their act, gift, whatever, and stick with it. That peal of exile first heard in *Hand in Glove* still rings true in moments on *Viva Hate!*, and no doubt always will, no matter what follows, in the same way that traces of wantonness persist in Jagger's voice, beneath all the mannered overlay of time.

As I neurotically double-check if the tape is running, I mutter by way of apology, 'I've had some bad experiences with tape recorders.'

'Oh, I've had some bad experiences with people actually . . . you're very lucky.'

(1988)

throwing muses

The last thing I want to do is break the spell. The last thing I want is to impale this dancing, living creature upon the stake of meaning. Is it possible to write about Throwing Muses without confining their strange and terrible beauty, taming it, making it easier to live with?

The music of Throwing Muses has inhabited my flesh like a cold flame these past six months. A kind of traumatized folk-punk, shifting fitfully between grace and frenzy, extremes of heat and cold, their debut album is the choreography of a body possessed and scattered by dread: as The Stud Brothers put it, music like 'a punch, accentuating and projecting every hiss, mutter and scream . . . so exact and punctual it's simply sublime.'

This is an exceptional band — David Narcizo on drums, Leslie Langston on bass, Tanya Donelly a talented singer-songwriter in her own right — but the star here is Kristin Hersh. She writes the words: arresting images (lives that go in circles 'like a pigeon on a tyre'), moments of disturbing lucidity amid inscrutable dream-imagery ('give me what I want/ And all I can think about is losing it'; 'why can't you do to my insights/What you do to my insides?'; 'I'm in a deep hole I dug by being deep').

But what pierces and transfixes is the rendition; the rending of the text, by Kristin's voice, its violence and daring. A voice that moves somewhere midway between Stevie Nicks and Diamanda Galas, that goes places there aren't words for. On 'Finish', mid-syllable, a hiccup of desolation that'll turn you inside out. Kristin's voice is gratuitous — so much more happens than is needed to get across the 'meaning': an endless haemorrhage of semiotic material, released in sobs, moans, sudden gales of rage, a luxury of grief. What is conjured is the apparition of someone falling apart before your eyes.

But more than anything she 'does' with her voice, it's something clotted, intractable, something inconsolable within its fabric, that holds and entrances. Kristin is blessed or cursed with the voice of a body congested with tears, torn inside.

Shivers down the spine? Glaciers.

'The first time I heard my own voice? We were recording in a mobile unit in this street, because I'd broken my leg. The song was pretty and harsh. Then they played it over these big speakers, and the doors of the van were open, so my song was booming out into the neighbourhood. And I realized that when you record a song it's not yours anymore, it has a life of its own. And suddenly hearing something that is part of your body, out there, beyond your control, entering other people's lives — it was too much for me, I just collapsed, crying, everyone had to hold me up . . .'

Strange talking to Kristin Hersh, trying to connect this sweet, funny girl and her rich, throaty laugh, with the haunted and haunting vinyl presence. Drinking blackcurrant juice from a plastic beaker, her hair in a bob that looks as though she did it herself with kitchen scissors, she looks like a child. At other times, she looks spinsterish, in cinder-coloured skirt, tatty shoes and (most mindblowing), a kind of denim tanktop. Actually, she's twenty, and a mother.

'When I discovered I was pregnant, it was at a time when I was very manic about the group, I felt it was my mission. And I also felt about twelve years old. But I came to feel it would be a step backwards for me to abort the pregnancy, that it wouldn't be moving my life forward. And, anyway, doing the band had become less of a time thing, more a psychological matter of getting down to writing. Having a child is an enriching thing as regards that. It's given me an incredible new perspective on what life is, and what it's worth. I had been very anti-body before. I couldn't figure out why our spirits were supposed to have bodies and exist in the physical world of cars and houses. And then Dylan came along, and he didn't have to do anything, he just was.

'And all the incredible holes he puts in me, all the fear he creates in me, has given me such an awesome respect for life. He's just a raw nerve. If something happened to him, my whole life would be crushed.'

Wandering around the Muses' hometown, Newport, Rhode Island, I begin to believe this could be heaven — beautiful colonial architecture, quaint, toytown paint-schemes, big gardens, porches, wide, empty streets. So how has this suburban paradise spawned something like Throwing Muses? The mystery deepens when I learn that the band's background isn't even affluent-but-screwed-up middle class, but liberal and permissive and caring. Their parents are philosophy professors and learning-disabilities therapists and guidance coun-sellors and physical therapists. Tanya and Kristin spent their early childhood in communes.

'But there's also been a lot of divorces, remarriages . . . there's certainly been turmoil. And remember — when you're adolescent you can make a lot of trouble for yourself.'

Adolescence. Adolescence is what pop has forgotten or betrayed. Throwing Muses are one of a handful of groups who write about adolescence as a period of maladjustment and withdrawal, who resist the now-pop version of youth as healthy, extrovert, unproblematic hedonism.

Compare The Smiths with Throwing Muses. Both Morrissey and Kristin Hersh work with and within the flux of adolescence – the vacillation between agoraphobia and claustrophobia, possibility and constraint; the feeling that one's body, and the cultural meanings attributed to it, are a cage.

Morrissey represents that flux, turns it into couplets, quips, aphorisms, insights, a wisdom we can draw comfort from. Hersh reproduces that flux, her voice *is* flux. The Smiths are a synopsis of pain, a resolution — awkwardness and alienation ennobled, given poise. Hersh is the presence of pain; her voice, the intolerable stress it inflicts on the words, is the sound of the inconsolable wrestling with the insoluble. The difference is between commentary and embodying. It's the reason why The Smiths are more powerful as a pop institution, and why Throwing Muses are more powerful as art.

'The songs on the first album stem from a period a year and a half ago that was the emotional and physical hole of my life. It was as dark as the record suggests. I was very unhappy, physically and psychologically ill. If I was to describe the symptoms that would limit the songs too specifically for the listener.'

I tell Kristin about how, a while back, somebody invented the term 'miserabilism'. The people who used this vile slander seemed to believe that any kind of troubled, troubling music, anything introspective or tragic, was self-indulgent wallowing. Pop music, it was argued, ought to address itself to the 'real' problems — unemployment, racism, etc etc.

'That's strange, because I think of our music as very political. Politics has to start from the insides. If you just deal with politics at a surface, organizational level, you never understand how things have got to be this way. I tend to see people as walking garbage cans, full of all this mess they don't know how to deal with.'

Or, as she said in an interview with Paul Oldfield: 'Throwing Muses go so far into people's inner dreams, their family lives, that you find what appear as outside problems.'

Kristin continues: 'A lot of the songs deal with the agoraphobia versus claustrophobia dilemma: the problem of what a home is, when do you leave it, how are you going to make yourself a home. The problem is that where there's security, there's also entrapment.'

Whereas adolescents' problem is that they're between homes, they don't have that shell, so they're free but also vulnerable.

'Teenagers are very open to the world. They're trying to figure out what's going on, what they're going to grow into. They take on the whole world, but they've got no patterns with which to deal with all that experience.'

Because growing up involves making your mind up, making up an identity for yourself. And identity really means limits, a refusal of choices and possibilities, a kind of protective blindness.

'Exactly. Adolescents have no defence like that to cut off experience, they have wide-open eyes, and they take it all on. It's obvious from the record that I was weighted down by an incredible burden I didn't know was mine or not.'

But, as you say, a fixed identity, a shell, is also a trap, is no solution. I'm reminded here of the ideas of Julia Kristeva. She believes the mistake psychoanalysis has made hitherto is aiming to shore up a kind of finished and defined ego. Instead, she imagines a kind of lifelong therapy, a continuous flow of repressed material, liberated through art and fantasy, pushing back the borders of the self.

'That sounds wonderful. That's my whole argument with the self-actualization movement, this idea of a fixed and tidy self. It's like when I finished those songs, I felt an incredible sense of boredom, "Oh, now I'm done." I actually wanted to be upset again.'

One of the things I feel about Throwing Muses music is that it's visceral, sexual, but not sexy. The sexuality in the record is troubled, mind and body are not at one with each other.

'It's the same with 90 per cent of adolescents, I guess. But especially right now. They're not sure what they're supposed to want or be. David (Narcizo) always says that we trust this music more than we trust our own bodies. The thing is that, when you're not in touch with your body, you're not in touch with the earth, with our reasons for being here. A lot of that album is about feeling that your body is a cage, that your physicality boxes you in, could betray you.'

Why women especially?

'Women today are presented with too many choices, not enough choices. We're still limited by sexism, but at the same time we're bombarded with images telling us that we have to achieve a lot. Women are still judged so much by their appearances, so we feel we have to get that perfect first, before achieving anything.'

I think we're talking about anorexia here, aren't we? Something you've been through?

'Yes. "America (She Can't Say No)" was from that period. It's about how America is a land of excess. Obesity is a huge problem here, but so is anorexia. People don't appreciate the material belongings that surround them, they just buy things and then chuck them away, they consume and consume and get more and more lost. And when I was fifteen I had to take all this craziness on my shoulders, there was so much imbalance out there, so much excess. I had to go to the other extreme, I couldn't be balanced myself.'

Another thought — love in Throwing Muses is not the vision of mutual support, of exchange and negotiation, that pervades yuppie consciousness, but love as being devoured and possessed and controlled . . . The mood of the music is sometimes murderous, homicidal: its subtext could almost be 'men! can't live with 'em, can't live without 'em!'.

'Well, that's because love and fear are really inseparable. Being in love leaves this huge hole in your self, and if you're adolescent, and don't have a clear concept of yourself, then you are just a hole, an outline. And if anything happens to the person you depend on, your whole being is just this lack. That's real scary when you're struggling to create yourself.'

I've read that you feel that the music comes from outside of you.

'What happens is that maybe I'll just see the shape of some chords, or where my fingers should be on the frets. Or songs will come about because of the sound of the words. It really does sometimes feel like someone's playing a trick on my head. For instance, I was writing a new song and it was making sense and suddenly these words came into my head: Once there was two Mexican women/ran over the hill/ripped off their skin/and ate it up. And I was going: "C'mon! Don't make me say that! They're going to hate me!" But . . . when I sat in the middle of the song, it worked.'

*

Women in rock are forced to speak as women. Men are allowed to assume a neutrality, to wield truth on behalf of everybody. But maybe Kristin Hersh will be one of the first female artists whose alienation transcends gender. She'd hate to be thought of as a seer, but maybe she is destined to be a figure like Morrissey or Ian Curtis, someone whose vision of adolescence comes to represent all our experience. And with this would come a second liberation for women, the freedom to transcend the roles set up by figures like Annie Lennox and Janet Jackson, and to recover the right not to be strong, independent, immaculately in control. The right to be as fucked up as men.

'Or even not to be fucked up, just to be regular. That would be an incredible relief.'

But what if motherhood, fulfilment, her committed relationship, turned out to be an abrupt end to the productive misery of adolescence?

'I've been worrying about this. When I didn't have any way out, I felt like songs were a tunnel and if there was any mess I could just funnel it out and it would become a beautiful picture at the end of the tunnel. But now I'm more together, I've a whole lot of other areas in which I can express my feelings, I just hope the songs won't lose anything. What I've found is that there's a lot more complexity and problems in happiness, many more layers, than I'd imagined. I doubt I'll ever be fulfilled, but I'm less manic. The darkness hasn't necessarily gone, but now I can live with it, instead of inside it.'

(1987)

LESS IS . . . LESS

regressive rock

At the end of 1986, John Peel described that year's Festive 50 — his audience's annual poll of favourite records — as the most staid and conservative since 1975, the nadir of progressive rock. For more than a decade, the spectre of the return of the hippy, of progressive rock, has haunted music-making. But it's clear that it's hardly plausible to account for the current indie mire in those terms, as a problem of indulgence, pretentiousness, over-inflated ambition and gross-out. Fact is, it's precisely the too-thorough internalization of punk's dread of the hippy and the resulting strategy of self-limitation that has led to a wholly different kind of dire stasis. REGRESSIVE ROCK: the enemy is not a new breed of post-punk dinosaurs, but of post-punk mice, or voles.

1967

And what better time to consider this dead end than the twentieth anniversary of 1967, that pivotal point at which sixties beat music leapt into the beyond, and the very notion of 'the progressive' was born. 1967: minds were blown; dance was left behind as beats stretched out into timelessness; rock acquired a whole new chromatic and spatial vocabulary, as new kinds of instrumentation were added and the studio itself became an instrument; the first dabblings with stage effects and multi-media experience were made.

Current indie music refuses this leap into the beyond. Burdened by hindsight, by a chronic fear of becoming bloated and self-indulgent, this indie generation tries to freeze-frame development at the point just before 'it all went wrong', and so turns its back on the few things that went right. Time and time again, indie music chooses The Byrds of 'All I Really Want to Do' over 'Eight Miles High' or

'Younger Than Yesterday', chooses the Velvet Underground of 'There She Goes Again' over 'Venus in Furs', the Pink Floyd of 'See Emily Play' over 'Interstellar Overdrive'.

1979

To 1967, I'd add another year, an equivalent point of take-off — 1979 (punk energy making its first altercations with black dance production, dub and funk, its first trysts with electronics, its first stabs at multi-media performance). Current indie pop refuses the dizzying possibilities of 1967 and 1979, attempts a deliberate retardation of development. 1966 and 1978, Byrds and Buzzcocks, are merged into a 'pure pop' limbo. The desire to be sixteen forever has caused the sound of being sixteen —noisy guitar primitivism with no added knobs or frills — to become fetishized, petrified. But this 'perfect pop' is regressive rock because it is a rock idea of pop, a fantasy dreamed up within music paper discourse. The real 'perfect pop' of 1987 is most likely Mel and Kim, Jam and Lewis productions like Janet Jackson, Stock Aitken Waterman, etc.

Paralysed by fear of 'the progressive', this stunted generation have chosen to take as their inspiration the sprightly, cramped insistence of The Monochrome Set, The Undertones, Girls at Our Best, rather than the stealth and reach of Can, Tim Buckley, Hendrix, Talking Head's *Remain in Light*, PIL's *Metal Box*, chosen to explore an emotional climate of suave nonchalance or at best pensive mawkishness, rather than denser and more elusive feelings; chosen to prefer the banal clarity of 'communication' over the glare of revelation and the clouded vision of horror.

INVERSIONS

Regressive rock is an exact inversion of progressive rock: both started with a commotion (punk, psychedelia) and slavishly followed through its principles and logic, ending up a remote travesty of the original. Look at the parallels-in-negative.

Progressive rock followed through psychedelia's cosmic ambitions and became BLOATED and meandering. Regressive rock is ANOREXIC, reduced and confined by its anxious deference to punk's creed of minimalism and under-production.

Progressive rock was GLOBAL, selling hugely, gawped at in stadia (the 'ant-like figures onstage'), disseminated so broadly as to be rootless and meaningless. Regressive rock's meaning is diminished because hardly anyone at all is into it;

the scene is claustrophobically LOCAL, a parochial huddle — its problem is not one of dehumanized distance but of an overdose of intimacy. That's because psychedelia privileged the 'far out', punk privileged the grass roots.

Progressive rock believed in FUSION, the grafting on of new musics. Regressive rock is obsessed with PURISM: there's a steadily more depleted and over-stretched gene pool of approved 'pure pop' traces, resulting in ever more grotesque and gormless breeds. (Like pedigree dogs.) Can you imagine what the offspring of the BMX Bandits will be like?!

Progressive rock fetishized the VIRTUOSO. Regressive rock fears accomplishment, privileges INCOMPETENCE, or at least demands the active concealment of skill.

Progressive rock was OVER-CONCEPTUAL, made risible attempts to sum up all the riddles of existence on a single (or triple) LP, extended these pompous didactic ambitions on to the stage with all manner of theatrical set pieces. Regressive rock's sin is its lack of conceit, its cultivation of EMPTYHEADEDNESS and naïveté, its refusal to stretch beyond a shallow delving into the slight pangs of mundane love and small sadness.

Progressive rock was over-dressed, the music of a leisured rock aristocracy, who possessed the money to lavishly construct a LUXURIOUS palace of sound, and the time to squander in excessively fastidious attention to detail. Regressive rock groups, on the other hand, are stingy with sound; their music is governed by a PURITAN aesthetic of austerity. Records get knocked out in the studio hastily, emerge knock-kneed, spindly, pallid and monochrome.

STUNTED REMNANT

Regressive rock is the attenuated remnant of punk, the substance of punk shorn of its spirit (ambition, anger, artifice). Punk reduced, through shortsighted, dogged adherence, to an anti-hippy tradition: instead of long tracks, pseudo-virtuosity, mystique, complex instrumentation — a self-conscious absence of these things. These are the anti-hippy hippies . . . Close Lobsters, Wedding Present, Miaou, Pooh Sticks, Railway Children, Soup Dragons, Flatmates, Shop Assistants, Mighty Mighty, The Chesterfields, Primal Scream, The Housemartins . . . the list is endless. And if you define 'regressive rock' as deliberately induced arrested development, then you can add the whole Grebo Rock boom to the list (Crazyhead, Zodiac Mindwarp, Gaye Bykers, Batfish, The Cult, Bomb Party etc). You can include a lot of the trad-rock bands in America (Camper Van Beethoven, anything produced by Don Dixon or Mitch Easter, anything influenced by Big

Star, The Feelies or The dB's). Even the cults of Real Soul, Third World Music and Go Go are forms of regressive rock, in so far as they're fantasies generated within rock press discourse, and represent a retreat from the studio and technology in search of roots and 'raw truth'.

Of course, limits can channel brilliance productively, make it blaze all the more fiercely. But instances like the Primitives get rarer and already one feels ashamed for indulging such backward passions. Exactly a year ago, I celebrated the 'new innocence' of 'anorak' groups like The Pastels, James, and The Bodines. But the problem with these groups is not that they're wimps, but that they're runts; not that they're vulnerable or soppy, but that they're flimsy. What's happened is that the perfectly valiant and appropriate refusal to grow up has become a refusal to grow, musically — to take on space, drift, experiment. This petrification of the sound of adolescence has meant a loss of the essential dynamism, fluidity and reach of adolescence, its true pretentiousness.

TRAD JAZZ

Clearly the enemy in 1987 is not some new generation of rock dinosaurs (Banshees, Cure, Cocteaus, Bunnymen) but the puny underachievement and Luddite anorexia of REGRESSIVE ROCK. The choices ahead are as drastic and clearcut as the choice between trad jazz and new jazz. I suggest a total overhaul of values. Instead of sparseness or spareness, a corsetted sound, look for opulence, sprawl, vulgarity even — the ruinous vanity of Prince, the indecently sumptuous Act. Abandon the obsessive search for grassroots, and value music for its distance from them, its floating free and outlandishness. Look for music that takes the plunge into the infinities of outer or inner space, rather than music which paddles through the shallows of everyday feeling.

Reject the exhausted creed of naturalism and prize the far-fetched, the super-or un-natural. Rescue the word 'pretentious' (all it means, after all, is aspiring to something) and turn 'unpretentious' into a pejorative. Rehabilitate the notion of 'art-rock', and raze the self-limiting horizons of 'power pop'.

THE MOON

The spaces of pop (the disco, venue, pub, party) are social spaces — packed, bustling, sweaty, normative. The only escape is to be found in the anti-social (the alien within, the heart of darkness) or the extra-terrestrial (the alien expanse without). It seems to me that there are a number of satellites (labels like 4AD, Mute, Factory, Play It Again Sam, Product Inc, Blast First, plus various hip hop,

house and electro producers whose work has very little to do with the human),
satellites bound to Planet Pop by some kind of gravitational attraction, yet
estranged by the nature of their practices (the lost spirit of '67 and '79). From time
to time they shed meteorites and the odd one will make a small, exotic dent on
the surface of pop. For the most part, it's up to us to follow David Stubbs's advice:
leave and let loose this place, and drift to the moon.

(1987)

indecency
(written with David Stubbs)

There's a consoling belief, one that has always held dull sway over critical and receptive minds, that both rock and pop are fundamentally about Good Songs. 'He may be ugly, but at least he writes good songs.' 'They may not be the future, but they do craft good songs.'

It's an easy platitude, a constant appeal: 'excellent grasp of the song structure', 'well-crafted', 'wry', 'observant lyrics'. Amazingly, 1986 has seen a reappearance of the singer-songwriter, with Peter Case, Stan Ridgway and Andy White receiving more than a smattering of applause. That this should be the case is as much a curiosity as the pop success of Chris de Burgh. Evidently, there are some very decent people out there.

Moreover, a hip consensus of veneration has settled around a canon of lost rock visionaries: Tim Buckley, Alex Chilton, Scott Walker, Dylan, Patti Smith, Nick Drake, Lou Reed, Gram Parsons, the luminaries and seers who shaped truths and made sense. The current mood of retrospection, coupled with reissues and reassessments (another Dylan biography!) all indicate that a sense of lineage and legacy has been established. This is rendered quite conscious not just in the touching veneration of Andy White ('it's in my blood!') but even in the work of Sonic Youth, who apply a sense of legacy to their history of rock extremity. They make references to the Stooges' '1969', to Manson, to Presley's 'Mystery Train' (also the title of Greil Marcus's famous book on the mythology of rock). Far from slaughtering their ancestors ('Kill Yr Idols') Sonic Youth reaffirm their heroic, historic significance.

This inordinate attention to the past arises from both shame and pride. The dust has settled on rock, there are no cloud bursts of white blindness as such, nor any prospects of any. So, a sort of ignominious continuation — Elvis Costello's thirty-third album! There isn't much of a future, but one hell of a past. In this more temperate climate, we can see that rock's estate is a grand one, and it's tempting to tramp its grounds — necessary, perhaps, if only so as to have somewhere to 'go'. It's been a quiet sort of year. A steady year. Not unlike last year. Or the year before that.

Legacy, estate — today's principal activities are alchemy and archaeology. The idea is that, if you pick out the best bits from the past, combine them, mix and match them, dust them down and restore them fondly, then the result will be something better. Take a little Can, pluck out the eyes of Grace Jones, warmed-up Kraftwerk, siphon off the froth of Aretha Franklin's 'passion', snatch a little Glitter leather and smear off a fingerful of Bowie mascara, ignite with the spark of a torch song, and you've got — Eurythmics!

Take the Bunnymen, overlay every cartoon watchword in pop over the past twenty years, and you've got — The Mighty Lemon Drops!

. Scrape the residual platinum off every major jazz, soul and classical efflorescence knowable to pop, melt it down and redisperse it in silver phials and you've got — ZTT!

These people construct their own hierarchies of taste, quite often in the hope of intoxicating us or invading our sensibilities with a violent shock of colour. But the indecency is borrowed — at heart they're workers, tinkers. This is 'perfect pop', pop perfected, finished off.

If it's not Perfect, then it is LEARNED pop, necessarily referential, secretly wistful. Weller, of course, with his stern blackboard of Philly, Stax, Motown and Mod. Of course, pop learnedness can be genuinely clever, helpfully perverse. Nick Cave finds a sort of superfatted theatre of tragedy in the *later* Dylan, the *later* Presley, makes sense of Gene Pitney and the New Seekers, reinvests the Singer and the Blues with a novel, unbearably ironic significance. Or Psychic TV's 'Godstar', their knowingly morbid celebration of the Stones in their most colourful, outlawed years of lurid decay, the angel Brian Jones about to snuff out. Behind Psychic TV exists an occult, disparate breed of hipsters heavily into Gary Glitter, early Sabbath, Arthur Brown, Grateful Dead, just because they know it would scandalize the prevailing arbiters of taste.

If we must have a past, then let's be sure it's molested with this kind of amusement!

Alas, the more orthodox cherish a notion of pop as historical progress. Pete Astor of The Weather Prophets defines his project as 'reactivating and redefining old musical forms', claiming that this was what T. Rex was all about: 'revitalizing Chuck Berry and Howlin' Wolf,' reapplying these ancients in a pop context and embalming their legacy. Revitalizing! T. Rex! The rash combustion, the pyrotechnic spree of the Electric Warrior reduced by the fond stroke of a pen to mere running-boy torch bearer in pop's endlessly unfurling tapestry!

The whole Creation aesthetic seems based in the sad conviction that rock is over, it's been and gone, and all that's left is to uphold the legacy through the Dark Ages of Plastic Pop. The result is bands like Primal Scream: a living, breathing archive of rock gesture. A mere footnote.

As one settles down, then, to a quieter pop life, grows a little older, the more it seems that the 'correct', the 'valid' response to music is the appreciative, the considered and discerning response, the thinking cap doffed to the craftsman. It is hard to think of any British rock, for instance, that's sufficiently ignorant to consist of nothing but screamworthiness alone. An influence here may well be English Literature, with bands and critics adopting the tools of the stuffier sort of literary criticism, the kind that sees the priority of art as being the reaffirmation of human values, art as the search for a stable base, art as something that orders the confusion of experience. Hence, a music that demands to be considered at the level of what the words mean, the coherence of the narrative, the intentions of the artist, biographical input.

Hence Costello, The Triffids, The Go-Betweens . . . well, we're thoroughly partial to all of them, but strongly suspect that they have nothing to do with the rupture, the indecency of pop.

At the moment when conscientiousness sets in, when a conscience is acquired, when you start casting conspicuous glances over your shoulder, this is the moment at which POP becomes ROCK. The difference has nothing to do with the presence or absence of powerchords. Rock is evocative; pop provocative. Pop provokes a restless, alluring, mass response: compulsion as opposed to appreciation. The difference is analogous to that between breakaway Protestantism and Catholicism, as rock was a breakaway from pop. Protestantism concerned itself with the inscription of dogma, attention to the text, was more emphatically scriptural. Catholicism, however gripped the masses by virtue of its incense, its ritual, all quite arbitrary, compulsion without purpose. In the same way, it's the heathen elements of Pop that trouble the sober-minded rock fan, keen to see through the superficial, engage with the depth of an artist.

STARLUST

Pop attracts an abnormal fixation of the gaze, fetishism, voyeurism. Pop, in a word, is fascination versus meaning. The power of pop is situated in so many other places than the good song, or good intention — in the strange, the intolerable, the unattainable, the curiously sexual. While the beaverish construction of good songs continues apace, you'll find the pop kid skiving off, caressing the cornerstone, transfixed by its coarseness.

Rock is about Essences and Ideas. Pop is about the thing-in-itself. Take the voice. Good songwriters often have unremarkable voices: a weather-beaten bleat that denotes experience, maybe, or a finished shine in which meaning can glisten. More often than not, they're no more than a glass through which the all-important text is transmitted. Diction is paramount.

With pop, the voice becomes material, in itself, with a voluptuous quality above and beyond its expressive function. Michael Jackson singing about anything — fish, or socks . . . Need either he, or we, 'say' more? One didn't measure Bolan by his doggerel, but by his pucker. Moreover, Morrissey's falsetto wail soars above and beyond the bad music criticism languishing in his lyrics. Then there was the strangeness of Siouxsie, leading us in circles, nowhere in particular.

This composition of pop suggests occasional rupture and random fun-quake, rather than a benign process of amelioration, or accumulating body of good work. There is a history to be written of the VOICE in pop, the voice that makes present the physicality of the body. Which has its own story: Jagger's lips, Hendrix's cock, Bolan's grin, Prince's tongue, Morrissey's nipple (one of the few options of indecency left, to revel, to splay oneself-as-object, play *thing*).

Even the pop consumer's body has a history. In *Starlust*, Fred and Judy Vermoral suggest a life of pop as a flood of tears, semen, saliva, love-juice, breath, sweat, fantasies of licking whipped cream out of Clem Burke of Blondie's bum. There's a 'truth' of pop music to be found in the wet seats at Beatles or Stones concerts — as much as in the pantheon of Lennon's songwriting, or the vicissitudes of the counter culture.

And do many fans, we wonder, fantasize about being given an enema by Van Morrison?

This lascivious hankering for the impossible, this lusty speculation and mystification, what the Vermorels call 'consumer mysticism', all of this was written off by Punk, which left us with a shame about worship, made it a part of its task to negotiate equal terms between audience and artist.

Finally, pop consists in its own surfaces, as sound-in-itself, rather than instrument of discourse. That's what (once) made The Jesus and Mary Chain pop and Nik Kershaw rock. On 'Never Understand' the song is lost in an aggravated, black hole of noise. Bolan, too, was a buzz and a blur, not a series of compositions.

What this ideal and proven pop amounts to is spectacle, a near-touchable presence from afar. The rock artisans, the good songwriters, are mere messengers, with a modest and inadequate sense of their selves. Poor old Peter Case in his suit! It's as if his actual presence were some kind of inconvenience, like going to the toilet, as if his body were a mere nuisance.

In good songs, the thinking is: 'you reap as you sow!' There's an ecological balance at work. You draw from life and you give back to live. Wisdom! As with folk, it's a natural process, simply reflective. But pop sets itself against nature and abandons wisdom for folly, moments of dissipation. Pop is un-natural, larger than life and insistent enough to make of itself an inevitable part of the landscape, like a motorway, or pollution. (Fantasy has its own reality-effect on behaviour and appetite.) Pop can be sufficient intoxication to induce a different state of being, other than the one in which you exist. Is this extensive egotism preferable to the scheme of collective improvement drawn up by good songs?

Pop is not about schemes but about SELF! SELF! SELF as cartoon, heightened sense of self, self as superman. This striding, Nietzschean self, 'bigger' as opposed to 'better', couldn't be accommodated in any kind of social order, would never really be happy. Morrissey's wounded narcissism is both intolerable and intolerant: driven by an instinctive disgust, he makes a meal out of himself in protest against the mealy-mouthed, constructs a grandeur out of swollen self-pity. 'I'm HERE!'

Compare this to the strenuously managed, balanced sense of self arrived at by the likes of The Eurythmics and Howard Jones. Take note, when we say 'pop' it's to the exclusion of such rock-minded types who happen to occupy prominent positions in the pop charts. This pegged and tapered generation have learned from punk, will never repeat the glaring abuses of an earlier rock aristocracy. They will succumb to neither self-abuse or abuse at the hands of others. Unlike earlier pop stars, they have been careful not to be ripped off — they have a hand in the business side, share production, invest their earnings wisely. They aren't puppets. They know when to just say 'No'. These artists aspire to self-sufficiency, complete control, self-exploitation.

Perhaps it was better in the days when the stars were ripped off, fucked about, had no grip on their affairs. They were exploited, for sure, but their exploits were myth incarnate. These foolish spendthrifts hurtled, flashed and exploded on a clear black sky, crashed their limos into trees, were sensationally naïve. They made martyrs of themselves occasionally — a sorely missed commodity. Not for them, the index-linked pension. Not for them, the twilight appearance on *Pebble Mill.*

The pop hero is uneconomical. He spends his money and himself too quickly, runs up massive bills, gives, gives, gives, takes, takes, takes, fast forwards himself to extremes of bliss, extremes of abjection, invests unwisely in the single love-object, the addiction or the fetish. The results are often catastrophic. Pop creates more problems than it solves. In love, the sensitive, reflective songwriter will treat the issue as a matter for negotiation, a question of exchange, the construction of a partnership. This vision of love as healing or therapeutic, scours desire of its irrational elements, ravenous appetite, inequality, worship, degradation and devouring.

To essences and opposites: decency-rock is conscience, consideration, assessment, education. Pop is vandalism, hysteria, oblivion, truancy . . .

LOVE JUICE OR TOPSOIL?

The demand for good songs occurs when people who have grown up with pop are forced to accommodate their love of pop within their new sense of themselves as responsible adults. Since the sixties, rock and pop have been considered a stamping and breeding ground for burgeoning leftist/liberal sensibilities, a place where dissent is felt and upsurges occur. Rock is pop energy commandeered for protest. . . but pop is *protest-in-itself.*

Morrissey's dissatisfaction may not arise from political constrictions, but from a more profound restlessness at the limits of life. If Bolan is in heaven, he's probably miserable. If he'd been in Eden, he would have probably left apple cores strewn all around the garden.

For sure, The Beastie Boys would have! What's startling about 1986 is the manner in which the pop obsessions of self, want, luxury and aggression, have found their way to the surface of hip hop, with all the softer elements not germane to this violent push ruthlessly edited out. The rupture of hip hop is a quite logical, unsettling upshot. Unsettling, because it cannot be tamed.

Run DMC loathe 'fuckin' faggots', The Beastie Boys say all girls are fit for is menial work and occasional abuse. Schoolly D reckons it's funny the way people squirm when they lie dying of gunshot wounds. This is what happens when the bedrock of decency, the liberal sensibilities and assumptions which we all share, are all that's left to be scandalized.

They're out for us — we sucker-ass liberals are the target. And yet, awkwardly, schizophrenically, these twisted sickos are taken up by the right-on, their cause espoused in the same breath as calls for a better world, the assumption being that the better things in life — hip hop imports, clothes, socialism — would undoubtedly cohabit in utopia.

Well, to embrace both decency and pop in this context, to be a socialist by day and a hip hopper by night after a hard day's campaigning, are quite feasible options, but only in a rotten, free-market society such as our own. It's a privilege, not a proof that a better world would be enriched, or its advent hastened, by pop.

Oh sure, it can be a tonic, and it's useful as glucose if you just want to kick things over, but, come the advent of a newer and more just social order, the one for which we all cry out, there would be no place for the scandal and achievement of pop, for Prince and any foul Beasties.

Plato wrote that the potentially subversive qualities of music were such that it would not be permitted in the perfect state. And so our pop, with its incitement to insatiability, its spiralling creation of new appetites, would have to be, regretfully, abolished. Rap, with its frequent assertions of power, would have to be put down, like some troublesome insurrection, or would no longer be necessary, in the new, egalitarian, ego-supportive state of play. The truth is that pop is of much greater danger to social democracy than it is to capitalism.

Ecologically, too, pop is highly unsuitable. Its courting of chaos, its materialism, its abuse of, and disrespect for, its resources, its spendthrift gluttony would be intolerable in any delicately-balanced and naturally-harmonious social order, the kind of world we need to seek out! (Acid rain is ruining our forests! Our layer of topsoil is diminishing dangerously! Mother Earth is not being respected but raped!)

Pop's power, its danger and its crime, consist in its over-stimulation of desires for pleasure and for self-aggrandizement: desires constructed by capitalism. Pop is hysteria, a neurotic symptom of what may well be the last days of Western capitalism. For each of us, as the apocalypse looms, there's a power struggle within the self, between decency and dissipation. Pop's role in this struggle is to lure us into truancy from our better selves.

Pop or a better world. The choice is yours!

(1986)

prince

Prince wants to be everything to everyone. He wants to be all you could ever need. Musically, he's a pop polymath, flitting between funkadelia, acid rock, deep soul, schmaltz — often within the same song. And his love songs return over and over to the fervent wish to satisfy each and every need, live out all the fantasies of his beloved.

But if Prince pleases, in music, in bed, it's because nothing is ever done just to please. Prince never caters, never serv(ic)es; he's always pleasuring himself first and foremost, following his own wayward impulses. Even the pinnacle of his success to date was free of any taint of pandering: compare 'Purple Rain' with Michael Jackson's 'Beat It', where Eddie Van Halen was dropped plum in the middle as a calculated bid for MTV exposure and the Middle American AOR heartland. But when Prince rocks out it's because that's as much a part of him as the funk strut. He contains within himself all the pop factions (and the racial and social divisions that lie behind them) that record companies try to straddle with strategies of hybridization as maximum market penetration. As Barney Hoskyns put it in his *Prince: Imp of the Perverse* — 'he is where all the desires of pop meet and tangle — their camp cupidon, their locus of signification.' The undeniable 'something for everyone' crossover effect of *Purple Rain* won a huge, variegated audience. But subsequent albums, especially *Sign of the Times* have seen Prince's cultural schizophrenia implode within individual songs. And so sales and profile have dwindled to a fraction of their enormity circa *Purple Rain*. Prince is now demanding listeners as mixed up and variegated inside as himself, and is finding that there aren't that many around.

Prince has a near-pathological desire to escape the confining fixity of an identity. 'Prince' is not so much a person as a persona, a space, in which he can become anything he or we want him to be. His being, his desire, is stretched and broken over sexual/racial divides. So Prince's impulse is always to dissolve differences and borders. The desire to be everything for somebody, the yearning for ultimate closeness, reached its lunatic peak in the sublime schizophrenia of 'If I Was Your Girlfriend': 'if I was your one and only friend would U run to me if somebody hurt U even if that somebody was me?' The song's agony is that of the spirit chafing against the straitjacket of sexual identity. Sex for Prince isn't 'communication' or 'exchange' but something altogether more mystical: the dissolution of the very differences and identities that make communication and sex possible. Like Morrissey, Prince feels trapped by his sex, or rather by the cultural assumptions/expectations vested in it. Prince confounds all this. He will pursue like a panther *and* be coy prey, present himself as rapacious subject of desire *and* fey object of bliss ('Anna Stesia' pleads 'praise me, ravish me'). With 'If I Was Your Girlfriend' he created another identity for himself ('Camille') by subjecting his vocal to studio wizardry that tweaked it up to an androgynous 55 rpm. But maybe that isn't such a departure when you consider that falsetto has always been 'a sexual mask. . . the sound of a woman coming from a man. . . a way to demonstrate to his intended lover that he understands her fears and desires as if he were female himself' (Michael Freedburg).

But there's at least one fantasy Prince can't or won't live out, one role he can't slip into with ease: the black pop statesman. Throughout his career there have been calls on Prince by both the US and UK critical establishment to be a better role model, to make himself accountable to some kind of community, to address himself explicitly to the problems of the day. Even now, there are those churlish souls who mourn the fact that *Lovesexy* is not a *There's a Riot Goin' On* for the eighties. But Prince is either too frivolous or too religious for his flighty fancies to be pinned down to this discourse of responsibility and constructive intervention. His responses to the troubled present are either retreat ever deeper into the infantile security of reclusive hedonism, or especially on *Lovesexy*, a wishy-washy, semi-mystical affirmation of the power of 'positivity'. *Sign of the Times* was like 'What's Goin' On', in that it's a pandemonium of anguish and compassion in the face of the impending apocalypse, devoid of any real critique let alone programmatic approach to change. Protest as a groan of anguish, as the sound of something buckling under pressure, rather than protest as a policy document. Fantastic records both, but like *There's a Riot Goin' On*, they don't fit the erroneous model of 'political soul' that's been constructed by white 'soul-cialists'. It's the songs' incoherence — for who can keep themselves together in a world that's falling apart — that gives them their power: to hurt, if not to motivate.

Along with the bleatings about 'responsibility' and 'growing up' come other carping reservations. A certain schoolmasterly tone enters the prose: 'there is an. . . undeniable talent here, I grant you. . . but it's frittered away in self-indulgence and conceit. If only Prince would acquire a bit of self-discipline, he could channel that talent and produce consistently first-rate soul records.' Pah! As if a steady stream of uncut, top-notch, straightforward soul is what Prince should be striving for! Prince overflows and perforates the category of R&B at so many points, it's barely relevant. Miles Davis has already described Prince's music as jazz; his use of electronics can be a as minimal and futurist as Front 242 or DAF; at other times his intentions are patently psychedelic. Prince doesn't so much build bridges between categories as create music that exceeds each category simultaneously.

But perhaps the best tag for him is 'hippy', in so far as that term has become, for post-punk critic and consumer alike, a cipher for pretension, over-inflation and over-reach. Prince is a hippy! This covers both his penchant for fusion, and his dippy mystic positivism and cosmology of love. Indeed, in his formative years he was influenced as much by Santana, Joni Mitchell, Todd Rundgren and Hendrix, as he was by Sly Stone, George Clinton or Earth, Wind and Fire. (And these black musicians were themselves all shaped by the counter culture and acid rock.) You can hear it in the jazz metal fills in 'Glam Slam' and 'U Got the Look', in the way the West Coast power pop of 'I Could Never Take the Place of Your Man' subsides brilliantly into a brooding meander of acid guitar, in the raga anthem 'The Cross' . . .

Most pop is created in factory conditions, as product made to satisfy specific consumer needs. Prince has been elevated by success to a level beyond that of a musician working for a living. He's often slammed for being a 'spoilt child', which seems to stem from a distrust of the fact that his music is play rather than (good) work. Post-punk criticism is still uneasy about music that isn't tied to a good intention or specific function, that isn't answerable to a community. But Prince has floated free of grassroots or use value, and ascended to an aristocratic, aerial domain of licence and luxury — where he's instigated a promiscuous chaos of stylistic miscegenation.

While his superstar peers make records with one ear cocked in anxious deference to pop currency, Prince alone behaves like an aristocrat, squandering the success he's earned rather than consolidating the estate with cautious measures. (In early 1989 it was revealed that the aristocrat was close to bankruptcy, the *Purple Rain* fortune dissipated in over-lavish stageshows and in supporting the stillborn careers of a seemingly endless series of protégés.) And he demands an aristocratic listener, one prepared to laze and gorge. Prince's adolescence was spent, by his own account, in daydreams (of sex, of fame) in the basement lair where he also learned his multi-instrumental virtuoso skills. This little bubble of unreality has since expanded until it enfolds the entire Paisley Park complex in Minneapolis, with all the technology and all his minions at Prince's beck and call.

This reminds me of two things. The Jesus and Mary Chain's perpetual twilight adolescence, cooped in their bedrooms, steeping themselves in pop and producing, years later, pop of their own, veined (like Prince's) with references and allusions. And Des Esseintes, the aristocrat recluse in Huysmans *Against Nature*, who dedicates himself to the diligent pursuit of ever more rarefied and unnatural means of stimulating the senses. Prince's music makes me think of Des Esseintes's symphony of perfumes: exquisite, heady, overpowering, slightly nauseous.

Prince does to black music what the Butthole Surfers do to rock — survey its whole length and breadth, take whatever seems like a good idea, regardless of its proper place in the narrative of pop, gather then let loose with a supreme incontinence and disregard for modesty. And of course Prince also casts his eye over rock too. What a spree! Prince and the Buttholes both play with sound in the most wanton fashion, disfigure, aggravate and dismember it. There's a gratuitousness of form over content: so much more is done than is 'required' for the purposes of communication, so much flaunting and adornment. It's not the getting from A to B of the song, that counts, but the swagger, the way of walking. Unlike the singer-songwriter creed, attention is always drawn away from the song to the figure of the person working at it: there's a flagrant exhibitionism that forces us into the role of voyeur. Sometimes, with Prince, it's like watching someone else watching himself masturbate in a mirror.

The two criticisms commonly levelled at Prince are that a particular song is 'overdone' or that it's 'unrealized'. These privileged pejoratives show how firmly entrenched most rockcrit is within the tradition of Anglo-American literary criticism, with its values of proportion, symmetry, restraint, economy. What's all important is the narrative, the sequence of utterances, rather than the voluptuousness of utterance itself. For me, 'overdone' and 'unrealized' are just the opposite poles of a hyperactive musical intelligence. I like it when a Prince song is overwrought, has been worked at neurotically (Prince's music teeters on the brink of being addled by perfectionism, but never is stifled by attention, because every superfluous squiggle or quiver in the sound is a carnal appendage of the man's polyrhythmic perversity). And I like his doodles, follies and ideas toyed with and abandoned in impatience, the debris of a restless desire. It's all part of the generous gush of expenditure without return.

There's another set of poles around which Prince's music is organized, and these are tied to two figures of supreme influence. On the one hand, James Brown, whose shows made such a profound impression on the young Prince and after whose fashion Prince drills his musicians with dictatorial discipline. On the other, Hendrix, the noble savage in dandy's finery, the freeranging kaleidoscopic improviser. For all its Hendrix-derived elements of bravura free expression, dextrous embellishment and luxury, Prince's music rarely loses touch with James Brown's locked groove of desire, mesmerizing monotony and crude assertion of repetition. Discipline and dilettantism coexist. Another angle to this contradiction is the way Prince is torn between the urge to be naked and the desire to dress up, between porn explicitness and the veils of flamboyance. Both James Brown (sex machine with a bouffant hairdo) and Hendrix (the wild man swathed in foppish elegance) were prototypes for this collision of primitivism and decadence.

If *Lovesexy* is Prince's strongest record to date, it's because its strength lies in coherence. There's none of the dazzling leaps or appalling lapses that gave previous albums a dynamic range. There's nothing on *Lovesexy* as supersaturated as 'Adore', as out of kilter as 'Ballad of Dorothy Parker' or as vacant and cretinizingly compulsive as 'Hot Thing'. The songs on *Lovesexy* are fullbodied, throbbing, for sure, but the unnatural excitation of tissue, the swelling and the morbid flush that characterize Prince's peaks, are nowhere to be seen. The dominant tone is of jubilation, not the hysteria that makes me swoon in Prince.

Compared with anyone else in the world of the pop that sells, Prince's *Lovesexy* is choc-a-bloc with risk and dare. But by his own lights, the album has definitely been shaped by a measure of temperance. It seems likely that Prince, chastened by the relative fall-off in his popularity after the caprices and wilful erraticism that followed *Purple Rain* has opted for consolidation.

Nearly half the songs on *Lovesexy* explicitly expound Prince's nebulous ideas about salvation, and the rest of the album is limned with references to a 'new power', a positivism that is our answer to the problems of a world that's going to hell in a handbasket. In the glow of this new power, erotic love and spiritual love are somehow conflated (in a way that seems finally to overcome for Prince the apparent mutual antagonism between sensuality and righteousness that has hitherto perplexed him). But it's not really surprising that this accommodation should come to pass. Prince has always sacramentalized erotic love, and eroticized religion; made God raunchy, made raunch his God. The two were always interdependent for Prince anyway: pleasure only exists where there's a taboo, a limit to be crossed — as 'It' goes, 'feels so good/it *must* be a crime'.

I was thinking hard about why Prince pleasured me. It wasn't just the vertiginous span between his moments of exquisite taste and subtlety, and his lapses into the crassest vulgarity and corn. It wasn't just the sumptuous disproportion of form over content, or the ultra-vivid hypersexual bliss induced by his refinement and exaggeration of the mannerisms of passion. There was something else. Then I remembered what Ian Penman said, a long time ago, in reference to Prince and Michael Jackson: 'the greatest singers die into their music.'

There's something in Prince's voice, an itch that gets right into my pants, a dead centre, a Numan drone. It's there all of the time, but it comes out the clearest when all the 'dramatic inflections, subtle stresses and sympathetic accents' (Barthes), all the art of the singer, are abandoned, fall away, when Prince swoons, sounds like he's on the brink of insensibility. You can hear it on 'It', particularly in the final, protracted, delirious 'doin' it's'. Then there's nothing but the implacable, soul-less beat, and a subdued babble of shudders and metallic gasps. Prince sounds stricken, evacuated, annulled. Or 'Hot Thing', where his descending drone-chant of the title makes him sound like a machine, subjugated to the moronic sex-beat. Again the track trails off into languishing shivers and cadaverous moans.

If, as Bataille argued, eroticism is about destroying 'the self-contained character of the participants as they are in their normal lives', then this loss of separateness is a kind of momentary death. This violently-wrenched escape from 'me' shakes our 'ordered, parsimonious and shuttered reality' to the core. I think it's the loss of this sense of the singer (and listener) expiring, in the music, that disappoints me about mainstream pop today, but more particularly disappoints me about *Lovesexy*, for all its many splendours. This scream from a shattered soul is what really links Prince with Little Richard and James Brown, and why we link Prince to a lost golden era of pop when that pandemonium and hysteria was the norm, not a freak occurrence.

When Prince is the master of all he sees, when everything he touches turns to gold, when he's the supreme seducer — that's when my admiration knows no bounds, that cool is why he TOWERS in our imagination way, way above those meagre souls who statistically and fiscally dwarf him. But what sends me, ends me, is not when Prince is captivating, but when he's captured, enslaved by desire, a thing, even. That, paradoxically, is when Prince is truly God.

(1988)

THE POWERS OF HORROR

noise

Noise is the casual currency of eighties rock, practically all there's left to believe in. Such a satisfying idea — noise annoys — at once simple-to-grasp kernel and yet capable of inflation into the most grandiose theories of subversion. But. . . who is there to be annoyed, and in what ways? What is noise anyway?

NOISE/HORROR
If music is like a language, if it communicates some kind of emotional or spiritual message, then noise is best defined as interference, something which blocks transmission, jams the code, prevents sense being made. The subliminal message of most music is that the universe is essentially benign, that if there is sadness or tragedy, this is resolved at the level of some higher harmony. Noise troubles this worldview. This is why noise groups invariably deal with subject matter that is anti-humanist — extremes of abjection, obsession, trauma, atrocity, possession — all of which undermine humanism's confidence that through individual consciousness and will, we can become the subjects of our lives, and work together for the general progress of the commonwealth.

This dark, unmanageable matter of horror and sickness is a kind of cultural noise, causing a blockage and destabilization of the codes by which we make sense of the world, make life habitable.

Noise then, occurs when language breaks down. Noise is a wordless state in which the very constitution of our selves is in jeopardy. The pleasure of noise lies in the fact that the obliteration of meaning and identity is ecstasy (literally, being out-of-oneself).

Historically, what has happened is that the rock vanguard has shifted its focus from eroticism to the psychedelic powers of horror. When sex was a scarce, invisible, unattainable quantity, to sing about it was publicly transgressive and personally mindblowing (because unthinkable). But after the permission of the seventies, when sex was banalized by becoming available, it could no longer be the instigator of desperation (it's that state of mind that is indispensable to rock, not physical fun). The site, the cue, for jouissance, shifted to the unspeakable.

STOP MAKING SENSE

The problem is that, to speak of noise, to give it attributes, to claim things for it, is immediately to shackle it with meaning again, to make it part of culture. If noise is where language ceases, then to describe it is to imprison it again with adjectives. To confer the status of value upon excess and extremism is to bring these things back within the pale of decency. So the rhetoricians of noise actually destroy the power they strive to celebrate; they are the very start of the process by which subversion is turned into contribution, which is absorbed as a renewal for the system. As rhetoric enfolds a group or initiative, so fibres of meaning interpenetrate every strand of sound, ensuring that the experience reaches us already placed in a general scheme of significance, validated and rendered ripe for the ICA. We are constantly made conscious. However sick, vile and depraved the material may be, nothing can prevent an aura of moral and spiritual superiority from entwining the latest noise/horror collision, like a halo.

Here are some examples of noise overdetermined by meaning.

Noise as reality effect:

There is a widely held view that beauty and harmony are a lie, presenting a bourgeois vision of nature and society as fundamentally balanced and ordered. And that we have an obligation to listen to noise because it shows us the grim truth of reality. In this vein, Swans are astonishing, the ruthlessly dehumanized mechanism of their rock functioning as a perfect analogue of their argument — that social life is enslavement. Theirs is a sado-masochistic vision of the universe to rival Samuel Beckett's or Schoolly D's. But any vertiginous feelings are stabilized almost immediately by the rhetoric that enfolds the band (which they severely resent), which recruits their private obsessions into a grand scheme of subterranean resistance.

Noise as anti-pop gesture:

With the death of the parochial, the media now constitutes our new environment. Pop looms as the largest thing in our lives, but as something we've lost control of. Rock'n'roll was originally a revolt against straitlaced stuffy mores (encountered in the family, at school, in the small town), but now it's 'brainwashing media images and fantasies', the very institution of pop itself, that we define ourselves against, Indiepop is fast becoming nothing but commentary on pop — The Membranes' 'Death To Trad Rock', Sonic/Ciccone Youth's obsession with Madonna, Age of Chance's 'Kiss'. Oblivion is forestalled because we are constantly made conscious that this is a reaction *against*. Age of Chance are the most sophisticated development of this process. 'Kiss' is anti-anti-pop, a gesture against indie stasis. AOC's noise is practically inaudible beneath the din of intertextual meanings. Still, they have a good point. Anti-pop doesn't challenge its listeners, as it purports to, it flatters them.

THE SUBVERSIVE FALLACY

Both the above viewpoints represent noise as subversive. There seems to be a need to maintain the belief that 'straights', grown-ups would be shocked, damaged, altered, if they were around to hear the music. But the blindingly obvious fact is that no one is around to be disturbed. The fiction that 'the enemy' occupies the same space as our noisemaking seems integral to the pleasure people derive from noise, the significance they confer. Noise, in Britain, is always being *read*, furiously.

But the whole discourse of noise-as-threat is bankrupt, positively inimical to the remnants of power that still cling to noise. Forget subversion. The point is self-subversion, overthrowing the power structure in your own head. The enemy is the mind's tendency to systematize, sew up experience, place a distance between itself and immediacy. The American bands understand this, instinctively.

The goal is OBLIVION (a.k.a. jouissance, the sublime, the ineffable). What could be more UN-NOISE than the slickly-planned career moves and tailored manifestoes of the Age of Chance? For them I reserve my highest pejorative — journalist. They are the inbred offspring of ten years of music press ingestion. Theories do not make for liberating music. Give us poetry.

OUT-OF-YOUR-HEAD-IS-THE-PLACE-TO-BE

You can see a widespread hunger for oblivion, and a refusal to talk, throughout pop. The indie shamblers, the Goths, the B-boys, the noise bands, the new psychedelics, all are reluctant or unable to justify their thirst for noise. Opposed to this discrete tendency, steadily more redundant and isolated, we have two contingents — the soulboy soul-cialists and the decent singer-songwriters. Both are still committed to meaning, both want to promote pride and dignity, give us clear vision, a sense of sanity, encourage people to take control of their lives. The others want to lose control, lose their selves, in noise.

Noise is about fascination, the antithesis of meaning. If music is a language, communicating moods and feelings, then noise is like an eruption within the material out of which language is shaped. We are arrested, fascinated, by a convulsion of sound to which we are unable to assign a meaning. We are mesmerized by the materiality of music. This is why noise and horror go hand in hand — because madness and violence are senseless and arbitrary (violence is the refusal to argue), and the only response is wordless — to scream.

A DEAD END

The problem is that, as with any drug or intoxicant, tolerance builds up rapidly. The result is an exponential curve of increased dosages of noise/horror, an upward spiral that will one day, sooner than later, culminate in SEIZURE. As the barriers in the head get broken down, the noise buff becomes a kind of hip vegetable, by a process that paradoxically combines both brutalization and weakening. To be shocked (i.e. get your hit) requires that the individual be immersed to some degree in a culture or value system. But noise hipsters have uprooted themselves so successfully from their parent culture, they can cope with absurd levels of outrage/dissonance, and therefore require extreme after extreme in order to feel stimulated /mindblown. Burnout approaches.

The noise/horror aesthetic has driven itself into a dead(ening) end. A sublime, monumental dead end, that has produced some brilliant sado-masochist poetry from band and critic alike. But a dead end nonetheless. Here are some clues to THE WAY OUT.

INCONSISTENCY

Too often, noise has meant a level plane of abraded texture, which can merely add up to a different kind of blandness, a sense-dulling consistency. There needs to be more dips, swerves, lapses, use of space and architecture. Hip hop is something the noise bands can learn from. The current hip hop aesthetic, as displayed by the music of Salt-N-Pepa. Frick and Frapp, Beastie Boys, is based around the forcing-into-friction of antagonistic ambiences and idioms, sampled from random points in pop history. The effect is psychedelic, dispersing consciousness as effectively as any pure din.

TEXTURAL LUXURY

The guitar is still privileged as the source of noise. There needs to be renewed awareness of the capacity of the synthesizer and sampling to produce filthy, noxious tones. There needs to be a realization of how far rock noise trails behind the avant garde and new jazz. People have to attend to the possibilities for the human voice opened up by Diamanda Galas and Tim Buckley; listen again to Faust, Can, Hendrix, Sun Ra, Cabaret Voltaire, Suicide . . .

THE VOICE

All this depends still on the assumption that noise is a state with defined boundaries. But if noise is the point at which language buckles and culture fails, then you could argue that noise occurs in moments, tiny breakages and stresses dispersed all over the surface of music, all kinds of music. Maybe we should listen out for the noise in the voices of Kristin Hersh, Tim Buckley, Prince, Michael Jackson — the way they chew and twist language not for any decipherable, expressive reason, (that's to say, not to accentuate more deeply the conventional mannerisms of 'passion'), but for the gratuitous voluptuousness of utterance itself. In their voices, you can hear a surplus of form over content, of genotext over phenotext, semiotic over symbolic, Barthes's 'grain' (the resistance of the body to the voice) over technique. Of 'telling' over 'story'.

DIRTDISH V. UNEARTH

There seem to be two choices in noise right now, two routes to oblivion. One is the noise/horror interface, in which violent imagery and musical dissonance are applied concussively, inducing a shell-shocked state of catatonia. Big Black and Swans take this aesthetic about as far as is conceivable or desirable.

The alternative? The Blue Orchids' creed: 'the only way out is UP'. Here consciousness is not mangled but dissipated, the borders of the self expanded to the point of dissolution. Noise/horror undoes the self by confronting it with the other that dwells within it, the monstrous potential latent in us all, waiting to be catalysed by an extreme predicament; what I've called the new psychedelia undoes the self by letting it drift off and disappear into the otherwordly.

Noise/horror strikes me as a limited form of self-destruction, that can only yield diminishing returns. Compare its claustrophobic confines and concealed machismo with the open spaces and fragility of the new psychedelia, as signposted by A.R. Kane's 'When You're Sad', Husker Du's 'Up in the Air', Meat Puppets' 'Two Rivers', Saqqara Dogs' 'Greenwich Mean Time' . . .

FROST IN MUSIC

Both 'strategies' are alike in one thing — they demand from the listener an immobility — one stunned, the other spellbound. Unlike the soulboys or decent songwriters, resistance does not take the form of becoming a subject, but through becoming an object. Refusing (at least in the domain of leisure) to deploy power over the self; to escape, for a few blissful moments, the network of meaning and concern.

(1987)

wasted youth

As punk faded into distant memory, the grip of its vetoes and taboos began to weaken. By the late eighties, it was not just permissible but de rigueur for bands to grow their hair long, drop acid, use wah wah and other quaint effects, play solos . . . Led Zeppelin, Grateful Dead, Hendrix, Iron Butterfly, Blue Oyster Cult, Quicksilver Messenger Service etc etc, all became legitimate reference points for new bands. Above all, the goal was to GET WASTED. Sixties acid rock's quest for the mindblowing was given a ruinous, apocalyptic, eighties inflection: psychedelia's pristine bliss-out was polluted by hardcore punk nihilism.

Out of this strange interface between post-punk and post-hippy (what punk once aimed to bury), the key groups to emerge were Dinosaur Jr and Butthole Surfers, in the USA; Spacemen 3 and Loop, in the UK. Of these, Butthole Surfers were the most exemplary. This was a band inspired into existence by The Sex Pistols, but who had more in common with Sabbath, Hawkwind, Hendrix, Pink Floyd . . .

The Buttholes brought back to rock the expanded WAISTline, a conspicuously WASTEFUL attitude to sound. The Butthole Surfers burst the girdle of punk ideology, and let huge spare tyres of sound flop free. What they resurrected was the idea of orgiastic music, a feast of sound — something that contravened both punk's parsimonious and anorexic tenets of economy and tightness, and pop soul's belief that The Song is best served by understated, deferential 'backing'. Butthole Surfers led the way in erecting a new charter of values: overload, disproportion, over-emphasis, surfeit, gross out, turgidity . . .

1987's *Locust Abortion Technician* saw them dredging for the very dregs of sound. Using samplers, slowed-down tapes, echo-box, fuzz, wah wah, bullhorns, saws, car doors (from which they got slowed-down squeaking sounds), and tapes of cattle lowing, they plumbed new depths of the bass-spectrum, new limits in the degradation and deterioration of sound. *Locust Abortion Technician* was a glorious mire, a glistening palace of ordure, a cataract of dysentery.

Hardcore groups like Big Black and Butthole Surfers have two zones of impact. Total white-out in the HEAD — a rush of interference blanching the screen of consciousness. And seismic intervention in the ANUS. The importance of the rectum in pop is something rarely acknowledged, although it's been a constant; from George Clinton to the Beastie Boys (with their crapped-in-pants waddle-dance), a record's crucial when it has a lot of *bottom*. Butthole Surfers take their cue from Black Sabbath's dis-inhibitive combination of bowel-quaking 'low end' bass frequencies and booze'n' barbiturates.

But the scatomanic orgy of *Locust Abortion Technician* remains a work of real accomplishment. Guitarist Paul Leary Walthall is a virtuoso of abjection just as Hendrix was of free flight, his domain the sewer rather than the firmament which Jimi traversed like a comet. Where Hendrix transformed R&B into abstract, dragonfly arabesques, the Butthole Surfers reduce R&B to an invertebrate, proto-blues agony, an infantile squall.

After *Locust . . .* came 1988's *Hairway to Steven*. The Buttholes were hailed, by the farsighted, as the most masturbatory musicians around, and the opening track 'Jimmy' was a delirious frottage of surfaces and inflammation of tissue, a paradigm of ruination. But having got that out of their systems, on 'X-Ray of a Girl' and 'Johnny Smoke' they went into interstellar overdrive, in search of cosmic WASTELANDS. Going nowhere, vast . . .

For 1988 was a year in which the goal was to get TOTALLY WASTED. The Butthole Surfers and Sonic Youth's version of the acid experience is not a transcendental access to the benign spiritual principles that underlie and order the universe, but more like schizophrenia: succumbing to the chaos of both your own drives and of external reality. In particular the chaos of the media; where Front 242's use of TV images of terrorism and catastrophe was as a backdrop to their own survivalist strength, with Butthole Surfers it's more the case, as David Stubbs said, that they've fallen foul of the media overload, are carried by a momentum that is not their own.

What Butthole Surfers have done, what made and makes them so crucial, is that they've taken on the sonic possibilities bequeathed still unexplored and underdeveloped by acid rock but have jettisoned many of the disabling attitudes that originally trammelled that music — sophistication, expertise, the counter-cultural impulse to edify. They reclaim the access to VASTNESS those musics offer but redirect it towards primitive and puerile ends. They expand the consciousness to the point of bursting, but feel no obligation to raise the consciousness, elevate it to lofty concerns. Few bands sink so low, few soar this high. Nobody else can do both within the same song.

WASTE your life, lay WASTE to yourself. US hardcore has always been about self-squandering and auto-mutilation. There's a link here with hip hop's 'radical politics of the slob'. Both share a policy of ostentatious self-neglect, that's an unarticulated, instinctive reaction against contemporary yuppie culture's ideals of health and self-realization. There's a stubborn clinging to bad habits that benign social planners and therapists would like to 'liberate' us from, an obstinate refusal to 'move on up' and make something of oneself. Naff plebeian drugs, junk food, hoary sexism, a love of trash culture. . . hip hop and hardcore share all these, but where hip hop still has a guiding notion of cool (both music and style are minimal) neo-hardcore is prepared to LET IT ALL HANG OUT, horribly; the corset of cool has been ruptured and all manner of banished and forbidden rock memories have sprawled free. . . grotesquerie embraced as a defiant gesture against the sound track of yuppie culture — sleek, chic, designer pop-soul.

The conflict between yuppie designer pop-soul and hardcore is between two very different kinds of politics: the politics of self-realization versus the politics of dissipation, of debility. For those excluded from status and opportunity (blacks, women, gays etc) being strong, becoming the subject of your life, these are crucial goals. For white middleclass males, however, pride and dignity has little resonance, when all your life you've been trained to be aspirational and competitive. 'Pride and dignity' appears to be barely different from conventional ambition/self-presentation/self-nurture, ultimately amounting to little more than the uncritical desire to participate in society on its own terms. What does resonate is the fantasy of being unemployable, of being an unmotivated object rather than a purposeful subject.

Where designer pop-soul seeks to bolster narcissism ('learning to love yourself/is the greatest love of all,' as Whitney Houston puts it) and amplify one's sense of human capability to manage life, hardcore finds perverse pleasure in damaging narcissism, destabilizing one's sense of human mastery, by a morbid preoccupation with. . . psychic breakdown, arbitrary violence, random calamity, irrational impulses, the whole gamut of 'unemployable negativity' (Bataille).

What is the fascination of horror? Is it psychedelic, a fall of the self, crushed by a 'weight of meaninglessness'? Or is it that when the vile or appalling 'lies quite close, but cannot be assimilated... at the border of my condition as a living being' (Julia Kristeva), what is produced is a momentarily heightened sense of one's own aliveness, teetering on the brink of extinction? Or is it, as Leslie Dick suggests, that contemplating one's own self-destruction or mutilation is actually a way of perceiving and relishing one's wholeness — self-destructive fantasies as a kind of warped feast of narcissism? Or is it that the sudden perception of one's own constant vulnerability provides, in its black, clouded way, a dazzling, near-religious feeling of revelation — this is how things really are; that to be born is, by definition, to be a victim? To be prey . . .

Butthole Surfers are perhaps the ultimate expression of hardcore's predilections. They remind me a little of Georges Bataille's pre-war secret cult, Acephale, whose goal was to get rid of the head — starting with the moral guardian in one's own head, the super-ego, then moving on to all the other 'heads' (the father, the State, the Law, God). This was to be achieved through fascination with base material (excrement, big toes, freaks, anything that highminded principles and good taste decreed lowly); through an obsessional interest in ritual and religiosity, a pagan celebration of the moment rather than investment in a scheme of forward planning and providence, a pagan worship of the icon-in-all-its-materiality rather than of the Essence. (A worship of signifier rather than signified: the definition of fetishism?) Bataille's key notion was that of expenditure without return, an orgiastic squandering of time and self. Either in the profane — polymorphous perversity that threatens the law and order of the Phallus/Father/adult genital sex; a decentred sexuality without goals (neither reproductive nor relationship-bonding). Or in the sacred — ritual and sacrifice.

'Plunging in at the anus and tunnelling a giant point of exit at the sockets. . . one part giant surge of flesh, one part holy revelation.' David Stubbs's metaphor for the Butthole sound pleases me immensely, for he has unwittingly and uncannily arrived at the image that haunts Bataille's writing. From the fetid depths of his mind, Bataille dredged up a fantasy of human evolution one part pseudo-science, one part myth; as the apeman became homo erectus, all the erotic energy vested in the ape's exposed, provocative anus is sublimated and moves up to the head and mind. The point of this myth is that the base and the elevated, the profane and the sacred are intimately related, depend on excluding each other for their self-definition. For Bataille, the ultimate destination of rational thought is the revelation that we know and can know nothing, beyond the realization that all the towering projections of the human spirit are based on a primary denial of the abyss out of which we were formed. The realization that 'elevation is the fall; humanity is animality; insight is blindness; health is terminal pathology; God, when he knows, is a pig' (Allan Stoekl).

It's this fall, this unseating of our lofty conception of ourselves (as conscious, self-determining spirits) that Butthole Surfers love to induce: hence the fascination with surgery (exposing the meat and muck out of which we're made), with lapses into the unreason of psychosis or perversion. Against the US mainstream culture of rose-tinted kitsch (which Milan Kundera defines as 'the refusal to accept that shit exists'), bands like Big Black, Flipper and the Buttholes react by devising a near-catastrophic conception of 'authenticity'. It's as though only the worst in human beings is what's real, the hard core of reality. This is anti-kitsch — the idea that *only* shit exists.

Hardcore is obsessed with WASTE — both physiological and psychological. On *I Crush Bozo* and *My Skin Covers My Body*, Happy Flowers take hardcore back to its primal matrix of unrequited desire and disproportionate rage: infancy's uncontrolled appetites for oral and anal gratification, its delusions of omnipotence, its terror of the breakdown of the borderline between identity and the primal abjection out of which it's formed. The Buttholes are driven by an almost mystical nihilism. They're obsessed by the shit out of which we're shaped (surgery), the shit that could befall us (horrible accidents), the shit in our souls (the drives and impulses we suppress and expel in order to constitute ourselves as normal, but which sometimes break free in perversion or psychosis). 'X-Ray Of A Girl (Passing Gas)', is a love song of sorts, an excremental vision worthy of Swift (recalling his 'O ! Caelia, Caelia, Caelia . . . *shits*' ode).

The strength of Butthole Surfers is their heterogeneity; they don't turn 'filth', 'the dark side' into a religion-in-negative like so much hardcore, heavy metal etc. Their nihilism is jumbled up with a mystical affirmation of experience (horror for the Buttholes is awe-full) but also with humour (they've advanced through parodying successive rock idioms, exaggeration improving each one by making it more extreme). As their fascination for the appalling, arbitrary and marred has got more religious, so their sound has begun its ascent into the cosmos.

1987/88, then: the reign of WASTED YOUTH — of devastated vastness, sublime vacancy, vertigo, virulence and 'the gift of the void'.

(1988)

nick cave

Discipline and punish

Nick Cave looks the part. Deep gashes of black under the eyes, skin the colour of ashes, a slight wobbliness to his movements. His speech is fastidious, precise in a way that would seem pompous if he were at all ebullient; but with his small, grave voice — sometimes withering, always withered — the impression is of a wary distrust of words and the ways they can be misconstrued. But he's much more forthcoming than in an earlier, abortive encounter. Almost affable.

Pardon the ignorance, but what exactly is 'The Mercy Seat'?

'It's the throne of God, in the Bible, where he sits and throws his lightning bolts and so forth. But it's also about this guy sitting on Death Row, waiting to be electrocuted or whatever. It's juxtaposing those two things. A person in his final days, thinking about good and evil and all the usual fare.'

So the fallibility and the arrogance of human justice is something that obsesses you?

'It's something that interests me a lot. My social conscience is fairly limited in a lot of ways, there's not much I'm angry about that doesn't affect me quite directly. But the prison system — not particularly capital punishment — but the penal system as it is, and the whole apparatus of judgement, people deciding on other people's fates... that does irritate, and upset me quite a lot.'

Is that why you got involved in the film about prison life, *Ghosts of the Civil Dead?*

'It's a two-way thing: I had those feelings long before I wrote drafts for the script, but the process of writing and research inflamed them. It should be clear to anybody that the basic idea behind the prison system is corrupt and unjust, but the more I worked on the film, the more I understood how extreme the injustice was. This particular film has quite a strong political statement to make, which is something that I'm not really known for. I was involved in writing the first two drafts of the film, but by the sixth draft there weren't that many of my ideas left. I also have a small part: I play a kind of known provocateur, who is brought into the prison — one of the new hi-tech ones — in order to disrupt the equilibrium. He's a psychotic with some kind of death wish . . . spends his entire time screaming abuse.

'What angers me about the system goes beyond the unreliability of "proof". . . it's that the way criminals are dealt with has nothing to do with rehabilitation and readjusting people who've stepped outside society's norms. The same goes for mental institutions and so forth. But it's also the very idea of someone being judged "criminal" or "insane" because they're unable to fit into what a basically corrupt society considers "social" or "sociable".'

So you take issue both with the very idea of 'the normal' and 'normalization', and with the fact that the authorities don't even bother to fulfil their professed project of 'rehabilitation'?

'Yeah, something like that. I did a lot of homework when I started working on the script. The initial plan was to use the prison world to create a certain kind of readymade atmosphere. But over the eight drafts, what emerged was a particular vision of the whole penal system as almost a plot by the higher powers to perpetuate the whole system of crime, keep it rolling, keep criminals on the streets. . .'

In order to terrify the population into accepting the existence of the police. All this reminds me of the ideas of Michel Foucault. He looked back to the era (pre-industrialism) before the things we consider 'natural' — prisons, asylums, hospitals — had been devised, in order to trace the 'genealogy' of pseudo-sciences like penology, criminology, psychiatry and sexology. What he discovered is that these 'disciplines' were not really about uncovering truth for its own sake; the 'knowledge' they generated was inseparable from and instru-mental in 'techniques of domination'. Later, he shifted his focus from social hygiene (segregation/surveillance/normalization) to study mental hygiene: the ways in which each individual is involved in self-policing. We define ourselves as 'normal' by repressing our own capacity for violence or the visionary — just as we suppress and marginalize those people in the body politic who've gone over limits. Looking back, it's clear that Cave has always been obsessed with this latent other within each individual, that can be catalysed by an extreme predicament. See how he describes his novel *And the Ass Saw the Angel* :

'It's set in a small valley in a remote region somewhere in the world. A sugarcane-growing valley. It's the story of the people who live there. The fascination of these closed communities and hemmed-in lives, that recur in my work, is that they breed a certain ignorance, can be the breeding ground for very extreme, absurd emotional releases.'

In Cave's work, most of the characters are in a sense prisoners — of an obsession, or a claustrophobic environment. But maybe this sounds glib when set against the specific and extreme misery of imprisonment.

'I've been writing songs about prison ever since I started writing songs. But I have a less romantic conception than when I started. The film is in two sections — the population section and the maximum security section. When the film-makers were in America, going from penitentiary to penitentiary, looking in libraries, interviewing people, they stumbled on this amazing story about Marin. Over six months, the inmates were subjected to these totally unfair changes of routine, from small things like not getting coffee one day, to next day having their cells raided and all their possessions confiscated. The whole balance between guards and inmates was totally disrupted. The convicts became more and more upset, the guards were afraid, but they kept getting orders from above telling them to maintain these random violations of the equilibrium. Until eventually it broke — and a prisoner stabbed two guards to death. This was leaked to the media, who began to clamour for stricter control. Marin was put onto immediate lockdown — which is where no one is allowed out of his cell and all privileges are removed. Twenty-one months later it was still in lockdown. The point is that two guards were sacrificed by the authorities in order to achieve this control situation. That's the kind of system you're dealing with.

'*The Mercy Seat* is about this person in solitary confinement, becoming more sensitive to inanimate objects, and as he sits thinking about human and Divine Justice, finding himself judging these things as Good or Evil.'

Some say that *The Mercy Seat* is the best thing Cave has done for five years, since *Mutiny in Heaven.* I wouldn't go so far (that would be to devalue all the peaks in the interim) — but the single is stupendous. It's a gigantic, near-illegible swirl-surge, a horizontal, disciplined avalanche. With its maddened strings, echo-chamber vocal and the odd filigree of lonesome country whistling, it is vaguely suggestive of the sixties pop-melodrama of 'Wichita Lineman' or 'Something's

THE POWERS OF HORROR • 71

Gotten Hold of My Heart'. But a sense of the epic driven to such histrionic pitch
that it verges on Velvet's white noise and viola hysteria.

'Dignity' is not a word that figures in my lexicon of praise (too redolent of the
prattle of soulboys) but with Cave's work since *Kicking Against the Pricks*, it's
appropriate and unavoidable. A ruined dignity, the courage of someone staring
into the abyss with 'nothing left to lose'. Here it's the condemned man waiting to
'go shuffling out of life/just to hide in death a while'. Eventually, the song
becomes a real-time simulation of a locked groove, an out-of-control rollercoaster of dread but also of resilience: 'And the Mercy Seat is waiting/And I think
my head is burning/And in a way I'm yearning/To be done with all this
measuring of proof/An eye for an eye/And a tooth for a tooth/And anyway I told
the truth/And I'm not afraid to die.' Over and over and over, 'til you think your
cranium is set to bust.

MADNESS AND CIVILIZATION

Nick Cave is afflicted and empowered by a certain, crucial deficiency of humanity.
Or rather, more accurately, he's estranged, wilfully, from the confining notion of
'full' humanity that's been installed by the post-Live Aid popular culture —
extroversion, civic engagement, the benign totalitarianism of caring/sharing/
opening up, the cult of health and efficiency. Morbidly inward, unforgiving, Cave
goes against the grain of the times by being sick but refusing to be healed and
integrated. His obsessions are wounds he deliberately keeps open. Looking back
over his oeuvre, you see not development, but fixation. 'Lyrically, thematically,
my work is still changed to the same bowl of vomit.' In fact, Cave and his ilk
(Michael Gira of the Swans, Blixa Bargeld of Binsturzende Neubauten) are
'agitating' for a broader definition of 'the human', one that incorporates lapses
into the inhuman, incompleteness, a dilapidation and destitution of the soul.
They hark back to an older, more religious notion, where it's not a question of
wholeness of being, but of holes.

Would you agree that your sense of the world isn't secular and humanist, but
religious?

'I have no cut and dry philosophy, but I can't believe that we just die and
become dust. It just doesn't seem particularly logical or rational to me, that you
live and strive for a while, then die. Without sounding too clichéd about it, there
should be more to it than that. But what, I don't know.'

Do you think these vague presentiments of a beyond or after could ever draw
you into organized religion?

'That has a lot to do with my state of mind at the time. I almost became a born-again Christian on the flight over from Australia. Two days sitting in the plane and fifty bourbons later I had this young born-again advocate holding my hand and praying for me at the top of his voice. He was actually asking God to show me some sign. In fact later on during the flight, when I'd unravelled myself from this guy and was playing poker with some French people, I asked God to give me the sign then, in the hand I was about to get. And I had three kings and two queens, which sobered me a little bit. But I guess it was just a lucky hand.'

Was this Christian especially voracious or were you just unusually vulnerable?

'Well, whereas the rest of the passengers were basically gearing up to tear my girlfriend and me to bits if we continued to go the way we were going — you get a kind of cabin fever on these flights between Australia and England — this Christian and his wife decided to adopt us, I guess as a kind of test for themselves. There's something about that flight. . . every time you do it, you just get off the plane shaking your head and thinking how incredibly tolerant the staff are. They must be trained in channelling animal behaviour.'

Were you brought up religiously? Did this missionary have anything to work on?

'As it turned out, I knew the Bible better than he did. He started quoting things from his Modern translation, which I find really irritating. I find the King James version in its original translation to be incredibly inspiring. To find it so utterly demystified by these modern religions keen to allow people of today to understand. . . it really appals me. And the translations are so incredibly liberal, there may as well be no original text at all.

'It was basically the novel that made it necessary for me to look into the Bible. I started by looking up quotes for characters to say, and found myself reading four or five pages, until I found myself reading the Bible and only the Bible for quite a long time. And then the Bible and Christianity became more and more central to the novel.'

Another sense in which you're anti-humanist is that you have no truck with ideas of personal (or social) progress — people achieving self-sufficiency and fullness of being by becoming more 'conscious'.

'No, I don't have that view of the world. I see everyone as very much alone. To see yourself as part of some greater humanist scheme. . . I can't really abide by that myself. I'm someone who has very little concern with any kind of social problems, someone who's very much concerned with their own particular plight. . . I don't know what this is founded in, but I believe that there must be some kind of basic system of balance, where everything's weighed up and when all the pain we've created in the world gets salved because we live again. I have some kind of feelings towards that idea.'

FROM HER TO ETERNITY

Nick Cave surfaced at a time when post-punk's handle on the workings of desire was diagrammatic and programmatic. Punk had bequeathed the idea that demystification was the route to enlightenment. 'Personal politics' was the buzzword: the acknowledgment of the 'dark side' was always grounded in progressive humanism, the belief that what was twisted could be straightened out, that the shadows could be banished by the spotlight of analysis. The idea was that through deconditioning, unblocking, a ventilation of the soul ('airing your problems'), it was possible to achieve some kind of frank and freeflowing exchange. Against this view of love as contract, Cave, in The Birthday Party, was almost alone in reinvoking love as malady, monologue, abject dependence, whose ultimate expression could only be violence: the recurrent theme of girl-murder, or at the opposite pole the paroxysm of desire in 'Zoo Music Girl', 'Oh! God! please let me die beneath her fists!' Cave was the first writer, in a post-punk climate of positivism, to start using Biblical imagery (sin, retribution, curses, bad seed, revenge) . . .

'Perhaps I'm kind of emotionally retarded. . . but basically I've just written about things how I've felt about them, myself, emotionally. Things like revenge, which you talk about as almost an Old Testament feeling, I see as completely now. It's just one of those things this society has suppressed, along with any other strong or extreme outburst of emotion. I think there's a certain numbness in the world today. . . that accepts certain kinds of violence, but is against other kinds of violence.'

So you have a kind of ethics of violence? Certain kinds of violence — the crime of passion — have a kind of aesthetic integrity?

'That's one way of putting it. . . There's something more noble in revenge, than in. . . sadism, or violence through greed. Maybe there's something more aesthetically pleasing about it, I don't know. . . I just find those subjects the easiest to deal with: on the one hand, they're the most tangible feelings I have to pull out of myself; on the other, they make me want to make a stronger statement when I ultimately do that. I don't deny feelings of happiness just because I don't write about them. For me, there's just something more powerful in Man's ultimate punishments — whether they're on a humanist level or a more mystical level —

than in his ultimate rewards. The rewards of happiness and contentment and security, I see as mostly drawn out of a routine of things. And they have no aesthetic interest for me, or much lasting value.

'But then again, my favourite song in the world is "Wonderful World" by Louis Armstrong. If any song really chokes me up, it's that one. If there's any song that I would like to do, but would never attempt because I wouldn't know how to begin, that's the one. If I could produce the same effect on other people as Louis Armstrong does with that song, then I'd be really happy. But there's something so unintentionally tragic about that song. Although I'm sure that has a lot to do with the way I listen, Louis Armstrong being this all-time winner and happy guy.'

Do you resent the arbitrary power that beautiful people have? Something shallow, unearned, but capable of putting you in thrall. Revenge would seem to originate in this feeling of powerlessness.

'You're asking me if I'm some sort of embittered, wounded animal, who only wants to reach out and break things because he can't be happy or possess them?'

No, more generally than that: the idea of beauty as terrorism. Of possession as the delusion we all run aground on. It seems like there's a negativity at the heart of romantic love, because love is nothing if not the always already doomed fantasy of possession. Doomed because of the flux (growth or decay) that is the loved one. You were talking about life's punishments just now, and maybe the fact that love is doomed from the off is one of them.

'There's lots of different angles you can look at things from. I accept all that. Although I don't think it's impossible that it can't be the other way, that two people can't grow toward each other. I don't particularly believe all love is doomed. But I guess, one is usually kinda suffering from some aborted love affair or association, rather than being at the peak of one. I think it's fairly obvious that a lot more suffering goes on in the name of love than the little happiness you can squeeze out of it. But I wouldn't like to dwell on it. Perhaps you could lighten up a little bit.' Condescendingly, like an agony aunt or something, he adds: 'There are plenty more fish in the sea.'

THE SINGER

Since the death of the Birthday Party, Nick Cave has steadily made a transition from exhibitionist, incendiary live performer to something more stately and, yes, dignified. The fireball has become an ember. *Kicking Against the Pricks*, an album of cover versions, marked the key shift from poet visionary of sex-and-death to interpretive balladeer, from torched singer to a croon the colour of cinders, from Dionysiac excess to a ruined classicism. And on *Your Funeral . . . My Trial,* Cave and the Bad Seeds were staging their own dilapidated equivalents to 'By the Time I Get to Phoenix' and 'Something's Gotten Hold of My Heart', in the gently obliterating, slowly gathering, morose grandeur of 'Sad Waters' and 'Stranger Than Kindness'. Cave has influenced other kindred spirits to leave behind self-immolation in favour of The Song. When did he start getting into what he calls 'entertainment music, although some might call it corn'?

'I've just found myself usually more affected by the clichés in pop, in art, in life, than I have by the. . .'

Wilful difference?

'Yeah. I find that wilfulness in itself is enough to make me turn away from something. When people are attempting to be different for the sake of it, I find it incredibly irritating.'

Do you have different influences now than when you started?

'I think I've been through being influenced by people. I don't think that could happen to me now, in the way that it did in my formative years. My ideas are self-generating now, they spring from what I've done before. It's all very inward-looking, and a lot of the time I find myself — it may sound unforgivable — ignorant of what's going on outside me and the influences that are going around. I don't think I'm fully formed or ever will be, but my basic creative journey is now self-perpetuating.'

But musically at least, you've moved from Stooges-meets-Beefheart conflagration to something more classically structured: the songs are like the charred and gutted husks of magnificent pop architecture. And figures like Dylan and Leonard Cohen and Tim Rose have become important to you . . .

'But not as a matter of influence as such. I only look towards someone like Dylan because I see the things that have happened in his career and the conclusions he's come to and the way he's responded to outside forces, the audience, the press. . . and I recognize a similarity to how I feel in my career. I have a vague inkling of why Dylan has progressed the way he has, which I don't have about other people. The particular songs of his which affect me have helped me to understand what I ultimately want to make of my music, and what I'm failing to make of my music. What I've found to be the most inspiring of his work have been the songs which are ultimately almost meaningless in their simplicity.

'Take *Nashville Skyline.* I found the fact that he made that record much more affecting than, say, *Highway 61 Revisited. Nashville Skyline* was one of the albums he put out after his motorcycle accident, from which the critics concluded that he must have somehow injured his brain . . . All the complexities of his lyrics were ironed out. . . He made some very basic country records. It's these songs, or albums like *Slow Train Coming*, which affect me more than *Blonde On Blonde*. The simplicity of the statement, and the bravery . . . in a way, it requires more courage than making something more "experimental".'

So you feel the same enlightenment that happened to Dylan has also befallen you? You no longer want to be marginal or difficult?

'I am still waiting for what happened to Dylan to happen to me. I'd be a lot happier if I could disentangle myself from what I've already done and create songs from a completely fresh perspective.'

THE BAD SEED
When did you first feel different or destined? At school? Later?

'I assumed everybody felt they were different from everybody else. . . it would be a pretty sad individual who didn't feel that they were unique.'

But such an individual usually defines him or herself against a body of people who are meant to be homogeneous and standard-issue.

'I didn't have any great coming out. Perhaps my basic thoughts were externalized by reading *Crime and Punishment* by Dostoievsky, and realizing that I had a basic Napoleonic complex. That was quite a revelation in those years of juvenilia. That book is all about the idea that the world is divided into the ordinary and the extraordinary, and that the extraordinary shouldn't have to live by the dictates of the mediocre majority. As an adolescent, this made sense to me.'

Do you think everybody has the potential to be extraordinary, if pushed over a limit?

'No, I don't, actually. I think everybody probably does feel they do. But I think they're probably deluded. I don't believe that we're all born equal, as lumps of dough that are later shaped by our peers and parents and so forth. . . I believe in innate inequality.'

Did you have an unusual childhood? Was there something to colour your worldview with its tragic perspective?

'I'm sure there was. . . but I'm not about to start psychoanalysing myself. . .'

You see it as a bogus science?

'Yeah. Anyway, rather than attributing it to my childhood, I prefer to believe that I was born into the world with greater or lesser faculties than other people and that I can take full responsibility for them. I wouldn't put it down to the way I was manipulated as a child.'

Doesn't that mean you have even less responsibility? Wouldn't that make you even angrier with the world?

'I think people get even angrier if they think about this precise thing that was done in their so-called formative years that made them the way they are. I just feel that I can take credit, or blame, for what I do and have done. That it came from within me, not from without. I'd rather see what makes me different as something almost congenital. And I have these inklings that what you commit or endure in this world, relates to some kind of system of justice or balance. Maybe if you get a bad deal in this world, it is because of something you did, or were, in a previous life. Which is why I don't feel sorry for the poor.'

Cave's departure from progressive humanism, with its belief in individual and social transformation, is so extreme that his worldview verges on the Mediaeval: the language of curses, bad seed, the worm in the bud. The world is a vale of tears, a giant ball of dung. Even more than Morrissey and his bad memories, Cave's vision is the antithesis of the idea of pop as a remaking of yourself. For Cave, the sole possibility for heroism is in fatalism, a stoic dignity in the face of your plight, the blight that is your negative birthright.

(1988)

THE DEATH OF SOUL

all souled out
(written with David Stubbs)

THE QUEEN IS DEAD AND HER NAME WAS ARETHA FRANKLIN
What is strangling pop? What has turned its face that grey colour? Passion. Passion
is blushing furiously across pop, rapidly turning it to ashes in its shame. The
blight of '87 is not media cowardice, record companies asleep at the wheel,
callous insipidness, the return of rock, incoherence, a lack of great songs, but
rather, a surfeit of PASSION.

In 1987, the consensus is that everything must be stamped with soul and
franked with passion. We're thinking Terence Trent d'Arby, but also U2; Tina
Turner, but also Chuck Brown; Mick Hucknall, and all soul music.

But Passion is spent! Soul is dead, like God is dead. The battles are over. The
hour is late, but the likes of View From a Hill and Hothouse Flowers won't admit
it. In the age of sampling, they're still using a Hammond organ. What is the
thinking behind this small insistence? Our culture is clearly a riotous heap of
fragments and Erasure are asking us why we can't live together. Who are they
trying to kid?

We could tolerate these sentimental Luddites but then hot-foot comes the final
straw on the broken back of a donkey: a ferry sinks, claims the lives of dozens,
questions are raised about profits gained at the expense of passenger safety, and a
bunch of pop stars gather together, whimper, implore, shed buckets for us to
throw money in, unite in the passionate cry 'LET IT BE!' Sorry, we believe that
should read: 'Pursue the Matter to the Highest Court'!

Is this what Womack has come to? A stick to beat us with? Cajole, shame, bully,
push away? For too long, we have stared from the moon in reproachful silence at
this spectacle. Better that Aretha Franklin had not been born than that we should

endure a drop more of this acid rain of spittle! Soul? My arse — the Queen is dead and her name was Aretha Franklin!

VINTAGE STUFF

In 1987, soul is no more than a packed vehicle beating a hasty retreat from what are perceived as the excesses of white modernism. This reaction owes its first impulse to the early days of punk, when groups like Marine, The Pop Group and A Certain Ratio first dabbled, intrigued, in funk. What began as an exotic flirtation with the Other, a pop foray into a perceived Heart of Darkness, soon turned into a full-blown dance initiative in those irony-clad years of 1980–81, with everyone from Japan to ABC to Cabaret Voltaire to Spandau Ballet to Heaven 17 conspiring to venture a white funk whose snappiness was a jeer at the indies, a white funk that would saunter easily into the charts and every other public place and, with their manifestoes, make them better places to be.

While that particular strain of thinking was busy degenerating into New Pop, scholars, as they will, peeled back this pop cartoon to find the real thing feeding it from beneath . . . torch singers. Lost Soul. Billie Holiday. Aretha. There swiftly followed a post-modern embarrassment of Charly re-issues, soulboy standards, and a wave of remorse swept over *Face* readers the world over (well, London over). 'My God. We can never be this good again.'

Thousands took the pledge and joined the anti-rock wagon. There are people now in the Wag Club whose musical digestive systems would probably collapse if they were to be inadvertently fed a powerchord.

New pop was born, concurrently, with Yazoo. Alison Moyet's voice was a wholesome barrage of body, a humanist apology for the perceived thin-ness of Depeche Mode (her partner Vince Clarke's first group), a fiery torch brought to bear on a cold, metallic sound (synthpop, modernism at its coolest). The upshot, you know — death, as it were, warmed up.

Today's pop, be it Moyet, Curiosity, even Phil Collins or Tina Turner, reads as a continued act of contrition for past pop mischief — how could Clare Grogan eat ice cream when, as we all know, Billie Holiday spent nine months in a state asylum?

It's a music that boasts some kind of spiritual superiority to the allegedly ubiquitous 'synthetic rubbish' that is elsewhere smothering our lives like nylon. But where is this 'white trash'? It's been marginalized, become a myth.

The truth is that today's pop — Whitney, Simply Red, Tina Turner, George Michael, Anita Baker, Fine Young Cannibals, Percy Sledge, Ben E. King, The

Communards, Gabriel, Erasure, The Christians — are about shame about pop. They're right to be ashamed, but of themselves, not of pop. There is a tedious pounding at the heart of this music, a sincerity that allows for only one angle of delivery, a passion that has created a pop atmosphere in which it's impossible to be clever, cool or cynical, a soul whose impulse is NOT to embrace the avant-garde, like Faustus, and be cut into a thousand pieces by a sampling machine.

This pop will never trivialize itself, and so can never be lauded as cheap tack. Nor, conversely, does it aspire to art-pop status, because its aim is to be truthful to its mediocre soul.

It is therefore neither fascinating, nor 'literate' — just warm.

If you want to know why the charts are no good these days, therefore, don't blame Radio One: blame Billie Holiday, Stax, Sam Cooke, Blind Lemon Jefferson even. Or rather, the people who decided that they were 'relevant'.

THAT PUTRID EMOTION

In what ways are 'passion' or 'soul' appropriate signifiers for these times? Is Mick Hucknall really how emotion sounds? A regular, freeflowing effusion of passion? This soulful thrust, this loud inundation? What information does it really carry, apart from telling you about the therapeutic inclinations of the caterwauler himself?

For us, there is more emotion in the undemonstrative numbness, the ironically incomplete account given of self by New Order or the Mekons, than in the silky signals emanating from your Anita Bakers. Can you find dejection, prostration, the sticking in the craw of the intolerable, in the passionate grit of a Terence Trent D'Arby?

Sometimes, the dis-passionate vocal can express more grief — the wounded, bloodlet voice of a Kristin Hersh, or the muezzin prayer wail of a John Lydon or a David Thomas — an upwardly spiralling peal that emanates from exile, a gaping chasm where SOUL once plumply resided. In the drowsy drawl of Arthur Russell or A.R. Kane, the emotional content hangs as beautifully as bromide, approaches oblivion, unconsciousness or drifting consciousness, as opposed to the rigid wide-awake club that comprises the Totalitarians of Passion.

THE EXAMPLE THAT HOWLINGLY TOPS THEM ALL: The Fine Young Cannibals' cover of The Buzzcocks' 'Ever Fallen In Love'. THE ORIGINAL: a sullen, inexpressive wail, a fallible voice as small and sorely limited as a back bedroom, a fey, frustrated frailty. THE COVER: Roland Gift's overdressed, over-stressed surfeit of overtures glows with an odious, and utterly irrelevant magnificence! Gift's bombast is quite at odds with the gnawing sense of LACK at the heart of the lyric.

The problem here is, of course, one of stylization. The Totalitarians of Passion have reduced their technique to the state of James Brown's knees — a splintered mess, tattered through over-use. Although the passion-merchant, the soul man, is in pursuit of some sort of authenticity, a confirmation of his depth of feeling, his is not his own voice, is rather the convention, a tear-jerk reaction. When someone uses the conventional cues and triggers of emotion in this way, all they end up communicating is the desire to cue an acquired reflex.

Insofar as soul is about sex, one result can be a musical hypersexuality, where the signs of passion are learnt, exaggerated, inflated and unmoored from the 'real thing'. With Prince or Zapp, this is most fine, as they achieve the other, an ultra-vivid (Prince), more super-human sound (Zapp's vocoder). Prince is the Hendrix, in terms of achieving this emotional swell: Mick Hucknall the Gary Moore.

THE FETID BLIGHT OF HUMANISM

SOUL was once — a very long time ago — the sound of a psyche breaking up, shattered by desire or loss — a wracked catharsis, an ailing, dejected, broken sound, essentially tragic. Today, soul has become a token of strength of feeling, strength of being. Beige popsters take a vicarious pride in the slow baptism of fire that their chosen genre and its protagonists underwent. They imagine that they can bask in the reflected glory of their martyr, Sam Cooke, of legions of underpaid, socially alienated, forgotten black vocalists. Beige vocalists admire and envy the 'blacks' for being more in touch with their emotions, their bodies, the unfettered ignorance of their self-expression.

Faintly irked by the 'crisis' of white music — that its body has been 'forgotten', its attention allowed to meander across the debris of a vast information explosion, away from the folk fire, to be easily bored, jaded, distracted — beige vocalists attempt to construct an ersatz black body to signify . . . what?

Health! The vocal dexterity, vigour and power of the soul man amount to. . . passion as workout! In our culture, which sets such a high premium on self-enrichment (in every sense), the robust, emotive and expressive aspects of soul act as a sort of therapy, helping us to 'liberate' ourselves by getting back in touch with ourselves, opening up, unblocking, becoming more functional and there-fore (it runs) more 'free'. The musclebound exhibition of soul works as a boast — see the depth of my feeling, hear the wealth of my emotion! see how I am moved!

Yes, it is quite as sinister as it seems. 'Totalitarianism' is not too strong a word. This humanistic vision of vigour and common purpose quite simply writes out deviancy, strange pain, breakdown of communication, the incapacity to be 'moved'. Even when the soul man is 'hurt', it is only a celebration of his ability to be 'touched'.

Today, every voice in pop must be a Voice, must measure up, because today, anything less than a raucous tear-blob sounds simply feeble on Planet Pop, must die like the runt. We all heard about the Consensus Terrorism at work in Band/Live/Ferry Aid. It could not have found a more appropriate, more common voice than the soulful. The sub-text of 'Feed the World' was anxious self-congratulation, an insidious demonstration of feeling. 'Look at the strength of our concern!' The bluster of the tear-stained pop stars simply buffeted, pushed away the possibility that the lyric ought to have contained certain small truths such as 'WE ARE THE SICK ONES, WE IN THE WEST'. The all-prevailing, extended blubber of Passion has become incapable of expressing sickness. What we got was the jelly-like wobbling of Western pop's fulsome, milky tit in the face of the starving.

More recent, more passionate, more obscene still: The Ferry Aid single. To say nothing of the fact that 'charity' should not have been invoked in this issue, the fact was that the excruciating passion levels broke all records on this outing, bust all guts. And, once again, the incontinent hysteria of the massed popsters was an utterly inappropriate treatment for the hushed resignation of 'Let It Be' (itself an inappropriate song!!).

It's quite clear that the influence of soul music in pop has become poisonous, repressive, grey and total. It's time to haul away from the centre of pop, the humanist body (Terence Trent, U2, Simply Red) and leave in its place a ghostly un-body (Public Enemy, Throwing Muses, A.R. Kane). To move from the FULFILMENT, SELF-ASSURANCE, STRENGTH, and SELF-POSSESSION implied in passion to a pale sense of LACK, VULNERABILITY, of being POSSESSED. To snuff out the FIRE OF PASSION and shiver again to the CHILL OF AWE, of magic, trance, falling, yearning. It's time to put a bullet through the head of SOUL HUMANISM and find liberation in the inhumanity of the mechanical, bestial, angelic, demonic, ghostly. To leave the crowded, tear-stained, blackened spaces of Planet Pop and drift to the MOON. To share there the cold, quietly admonishing gaze of He Said, The Stars of Heaven, Happy Mondays, Meat Puppets. To go UNDERWATER and swim with Arthur Russell and A.R. Kane. Or UNDERGROUND, to join Big Black, Butthole Surfers, World Domination, Skinny Puppy . . . Blast Passion, which has blasted all doubt, mischief and intrigue onto the peripheries, drowned pop in shame.

A CONCERNED SOULBOY DOUBTS OUR WORD

CONCERNED SOULBOY: 'Very provocative, I'm sure, but none of this seems all that radical to me. When it comes down to it, all you're saying is that the likes of Tina Turner and Mick Hucknall have created a bloated travesty of soul. Well, I'd go along with that — but you seem to forget that Tina Turner is fake soul, not real soul at all.'

Ah, but it's this very desire for a 'real soul' that is the malaise. A yearning for a 'new Marvin Gaye' to throb miraculously at the centre of pop to resolve its own, fabulous identity crisis. Do you imagine that any single figure in pop can tell us precisely What's Goin' On? And would such a figure — an auteur with a carrying voice to bring us all within earshot — be helpful, or even possible? (Terence Trent D'Arby, ha ha ha!) Why do we need more and better soul — why should it not swiftly become a fat, sweaty, obscenity, like the last lot did? Ultimately, the Campaign for Real Soul amounts only to an ostrich-head-in-sand retreat from the future: a future pop based in soul-less, ground-less dis-corporation.

CS: 'You can say all you like, but it's clear that soul music is more popular than it has ever been, worldwide.'

You do not seem to appreciate that the point at which Soul is stretched the furthest, globally, is the point at which it is weakest. Spread thin, ubiquitous, where once it was rare, exotic, precious, a sob in private. A little too much of anything suffocates pop.

CS: 'And I suppose you think there's been a bit too much soul. So, after all this, what do you foresee as the consequences for hip hop, Chuck Brown, Tashan, Alexander O'Neal? I know you like them all.'

Black people are quite as capable of evading the totalitarianism of passion as whites are of perpetrating it. This is not an issue of race, but of creed. Take hip hop and house. Twelve-inch culture kills soul! Hip hop is anti-soul, disperses consciousness, quite literally CUTS UP THE BODY.

From here on, the likes of Tashan must be discussed not in terms of 'spirit', passion, emotional commitment, but ether, wire, the ocean, the paintings of Chirico, peculiar grace.

We have no quarrel with the delicious plastic that Tony Blackburn plays on his daytime show.

CS: 'You bastards! There's more of worth, more that uplifts in a single chorus of "We Need Money" than in a dozen of your picky, pedantic articles!'

A dozen or more examples of the soulboy's discourse have made it impossible for us to listen to virtually any 'black' record with any real pleasure, without ghastly phrases like 'pride and dignity' popping into our heads. This is nothing personal, you understand — your voice is not your own, you are the product of a discourse.

CS: 'You bandy about the word "totalitarian" — you're scarcely immune from that yourself! No soulboy would propose a five-year boycott of Velvet Underground LPs — yet that is precisely what you propose for Marvin Gaye, Aretha and Billie Holiday!'

We realize that it is hard. To you, it doubtless seems as 'unnatural' as ripping out your own heart with a mechanical claw. But there is no longer a 'natural' role for soul. With the death of God and the death of the Ground, all that is left is — the Air. Try to understand that Pop should be up in the air, supernatural, alive to all angles and shades of emotion, plastic and twice-cooked. Bless Marvin Gaye — but we don't need him at the moment! This is the age of the Aerial!

(1987)

from 'young soul rebels' to designer soul-cialism

Dexy's Midnight Runners were perhaps the prototype for the new soul militancy of the eighties. Soul for them was a form of exertion; performance that Barney Hoskyns called (in reference to The Jam, as it happens) 'a gymnasium of exhortation'. Tenderness and languor did not fit into the 'Young Soul Rebels' scheme. Dexy's songs were a series of manifestoes and clarion calls for a new, pure music, always *about* to be born. This was meta-music, its subject an alleged degeneration of pop culture, its mission to bring back a sense of a mission to music. All Kevin Rowland seemed to be saying was that he had something to say. He was a zealot for zeal in itself. Dexy's used to workout together, they abstained from alcohol and drugs. Developing your body and your soul, exercise and suffering, were both facets of a supremely masculine fortification of the spirit. (*Jamming* on Dexy's-clones Big Sound Authority: 'wait till you see this man sweat' — sweat as the tangible proof of authenticity, commitment.) Kevin Rowland's first group — a punk band — were called The Killjoys. Rowland — with his paranoiac hatred of the music press, his fervent work ethic, his privileging of 'projected passion' over intellect — turned soul into a kind of micro-fascism. All that was needed was for someone to take Rowland's ascetic vision/version of soul fanaticism and commandeer it for political ends.

SOCIALIST REALIST POP

The Redskins are 'Young Soul Rebels' *with* a cause. An ultimate agit pop group, sat painfully pat at the confluence of three socialist realist orthodoxies: that there is a necessary and simple fit between pop culture and radical politics: that youth culture is a working-class phenomenon; that black music alone is the only unembarrassing and legitimate basis for protest. They take the intensity of soul and clench it into a fist rather than using it as a form of release. The euphoria of R&B is made the vehicle for constructive ends. Scrape past the Soul Man postures and you find . . . The Clash, or worse, The Tom Robinson Band. The Redskins' link-up with the Socialist Workers' Party is the most stringent and emphatic attempt to thrust pop into some sort of relation to the 'real' world. This is the most deluded fantasy of all — the idea that, by buying certain pieces of vinyl and by going to certain gigs, instead of consuming a commodity, you are participating and making a contribution to 'the struggle'. In the agit-pop scheme of things, pleasure-in-itself has no value. Expenditure without return, the sheer waste of energy, is forbidden. The guilt of consumption, of being consumed, has to be expunged, validated by a second, ulterior use (drinking Nicaraguan coffee annoys Reagan, going to a rock benefit is fun with a purpose). Agit-poppers constantly castigate pop for its dereliction of duty and its straying from being aligned. For instance, witness Steven Wells fulminating in the *NME*: 'Pop can be treated as the vile pus that drips from sores of a cancerous body politic.' Its only value is as 'a platform for propaganda'. Of course, the left has traditionally had a purely instrumental attitude to culture, leisure, fun. Art for art's sake has been dismissed as 'apolitical', 'solipsistic', 'bourgeois'. (But isn't the terror of expenditure without return the very epitome of bourgeois economic continence?) In the fifties, socialists railed against the decadence of youth consumption, youth's hankering for Americana, like zoot suits, comic books, quiffs and the 'meaningless gibberish' of rock'n'roll. What was detested was an excess of form over content, the gratuitous flamboyance of tail-fins on cars, extravagant use of cloth in clothing. Paul Weller's Style Council and Red Wedge are the latest incarnations of this tendency. Weller is trying to make political idealism glamorous by linking it with being a stylist, and validate being a stylist by aligning it with political ideals. There's an idea here of consumption with integrity, the notion that certain consumer choices have a natural fit with certain political choices — hence the cover of *Our Favourite Shop*. What is fantasized here is a perfect life — a smoothly running, perfectly functional, utilitarian consumer aesthetic that has a natural congruence with socialist politics. Weller's shopping list of socialist good taste includes Bass Weejuns, Burberry raincoats, Motown and Stax 45s, Italian design, Blue Note LPs, etc. But what is included is less revealing than what is excluded: all the excessive elements of working-class consumption that refuse to fit neatly into this socialist continence — Stanley knives, lurid cocktails, *Blind Date*, trash videos, tabloids, bingo, heavy metal, Club 18–30 . . .

DESIGNER SOUL-CIALISM

You can find a similar idea of consumption with integrity in *The Face*, where the Disinformation column snuggles next to photographs of exorbitant clothes and furniture, the implication being that avant-garde design is part of some grand progressive thrust that also includes socialism. This is designer socialism: the belief that buying tassled loafers rather than winklepickers, is somehow as much a part of the struggle as being on the picket line at Wapping. The semiotic approach to subcultural style pioneered by Dick Hebdige and his cohorts at Birmingham's Centre for Contemporary Cultural Studies — reading into working-class consumption for evidence of myriad micro-resistances to the status quo — has been turned arse about tit. 'Pride and dignity' is the soulboy soul-cialist's supreme tenet. This too has its origins in subcultural theory: Hebdige's hypothesis that the 'classy' look of Mod style was a challenge to the class structure in sixties Britain, an expression of resilient self-belief. But this begs the question: does 'pride and dignity' amount to anything more than the aspiration to participate in society on its own terms? What use is the Staples Singers' exhortation 'respect yourself', if the notion of self-respect is still bound to conventional notions of respectability?

ROOTS RHYTHM RADICALISM

In the early eighties there was a massive defection of Social Realist Pop to the cause of black music. Weller led the way, dropping The Who as his model for political protest in favour of funk and early seventies disco. Agit-poppers convinced themselves that rock was archaic and debased, no longer capable of functioning as a medium for radical comment. The energy of punk, of the whole Rock Against Racism initiative, had faded. At similar moments of entropy, black music has functioned as an alluring outside for white youth — the old notion of the Black as other, incarnation of sexuality and the forbidden. But whereas previously identification with geographically-proximate black subcultures was the influence (punk felt an affinity with Rastafarian dub, for instance), this time round there was a dissemination of certain ideas of blackness through the media, a borrowing from the files of history. ROOTS RHYTHM RADICALISM — this cluster's perceived identity was what lay behind the drive for an infusion of blackness. The assumption behind this shift was that an ideal black music would naturally link up with socialist politics. And so a sanitized canon of soul and funk was drawn up: James Brown's 'Say it Loud, I'm Black and I'm Proud', Curtis Mayfield's 'Move On Up' and 'We've got to Have Peace', Timmy Thomas's 'Why Can't We Live

Together', Gil Scott Heron's 'The Bottle', Grandmaster Flash's 'The Message', Brother D and the Collective Effort's 'How We Gonna Make the Black Nation Rise', James Brown and Afrika Bambatta's 'Unity'. What's brought to the fore is the political content of the music, but what's written out is the 'unsoundness' — the anti-social, anti-egalitarian narcissism of black pop, the brutality of hip hop, the show excess and upward aspirations of mainstream soul. In its insistence on the Message and on street-cred, the new soul is very much cramped and shadowed by the dowdy spirit of new wave, with its emphasis on lyrical 'relevance'. New soul carries on the side of punk that was least interesting (slogans, youth rhetoric, documentary realism) rather than the more artistically provocative element (punk's theatre of rage and disgust). If The Redskins are the Clash of the new soul, what we need is soul's Sex Pistols, a group that can work from soul's *un*realism, its dangerous ecstasy, to make unreasonable demands. All that's happened is that, in switching from rock to soul, agit-pop has shifted emphasis from denunciation to affirmation, or what has been called offensive optimism. 'Shout it to the Top', as The Style Council have it.

THE COST OF LOVING

It's a strange journey Paul Weller's made, but stranger still is that he's managed to take the greater part of his audience along with him. Somehow he's managed to lead one of the most entrenched examples of playsafe rock consensus 'forward' into apparently digging music that sounds just like Con Funk Shun, Rah Band, Loose Ends. The problem is that Weller, ever earnest, has internalized too thoroughly the edict Rock is Dead. For every past powerchord and epic gesture he now endeavours to atone, publicly, by the slavish imitation of the most slick and redundant aspects of contemporary black music. Once he believed The Jam was the true sound of 'when you're young'; now he's wised up, got hip to the fact that where the 'real kids' are at is. . . Robbie Vincent, LWR, all the loathsome details of fake sophistication ('light those candles. . . open the freezer door'). Embarrassed by the rash declamatory urgency of his past with The Jam, Weller wants to leave behind adolescence, and 'progress' from gauche to smooth. The Style Council sound is a condensation of the whole gamut of naff provincial fantasies of sophistication — vibes, Hammond organ, strings, jazzfunk, drummers who use a brush; easy listening that appeals to spivs of either political denomination. No longer a rock band, where a certain stiffness in the limbs is a virtue, but not yet virtuoso jazzers, The Style Council are stuck at that most useless of levels — semi-fluency. Who needs spineless pastiche of 'My Guy' perkiness and Modern Jazz Quartet cool jazz? Five years on, anti-rockism is the new hippiedom. Weller has simply transposed one 'reality' of English suburbia for another, the smalltown smallness of 'English Rose', 'That's Entertainment', 'Smithers-Jones' (derived from mod) updated to a world of winebars and nightclubs. But is deference to 'reality' such a good thing anyway? What exactly is of value in this nouveau-riche southern heartland of Thatcherism? *The Cost of Loving* sees Weller severing, finally, from the sixties. The music is a surprisingly accurate imitation of that most toothless, spineless idiom, Britfunk. . . Philly pastiches, jazz-funk ballads, *Streetsounds* stuff . . . none of which approaches the real mind-lessening ecstasy of disco. It's irretrievable naffness can be conveyed in only two words — Junior Giscombe. Songcraft, good intentions, an anxiety to avoid love clichés — all these are the very death of disco.

Worse still is when Weller attempts to remotivate the sound of Saturday Nite, make it bear the burden of his meaning well. I liked them more when The Style Council played with pop history, assembled their own fantasy of 'perfect pop' out of Philly, Blue Note, Left Bank, Holland-Dozier-Holland.

Dear old Paul Weller. We're all on the same side. No doubt I'll be voting Labour with exactly the same mixture of dutiful resignation and frustration there's no more incandescent alternative, as he will. I even have a sneaking affection for the man. But the sad fact is that even if it is possible to achieve a co-incidence between desire and responsibility, ecstasy and concern, Weller is incapable of such a balance. The problem is the fundamental modesty of his aspiration, of his person — those unvoluptuous good looks. Within The Redskins' drastically curtailed emotional range, they worked, because there's a potential for romance in streetfighting and revolution. But . . . how can you make the Labour Party seem exciting? That's the flaw in Red Wedge — their chiding logic of pragmatism ('as good as we'll get . . . let's face facts') is in fundamental antagonism to pop's intolerant utopianism. On *The Cost of Loving* there's a track called 'Right To Go', recorded with 'homegrown' rappers The Dynamic Three. It's dated, flailing and useless, hardly crucial or fresh, but the real problem is: how can you conceivably make trudging through the wet leaves and puddles to your local primary school, in order to tick a piece of paper in a polling booth, seem like a glamorous and dynamic act of self-realization, or even solidarity?

THE CHRISTIANS

Nothing makes me more downcast than the 'uplifting', nothing elevates me more than the de-jected. Only music that stems from spiritual impoverishment enriches my life. Oh, like everybody else I had my summer of soul, like a lot of white boys, thought I'd found my truest voice. But what was once a breakthrough, a crucial realignment of taste among white rock fans, has subsequently congealed into orthodoxy. In the process, soul has been installed as something that bolsters your life, rather than knocks the ground from under your feet. The extremism I once heard in soul has been evened out. Britpop always lags far behind black American pop. In the sixties and seventies the blues boom and heavy metal were vulgarizing the blues years after the fact. Now it's early seventies black pop that's being bastardized, the exquisite anguish of your Timmy Thomases reduced to a blunt compassion. What groups like The Christians do to soul is both coarsen and mute it, at the same time. But that's as maybe — even if The Christians were this decade's Temptations, Mayfield or Gaye, they still wouldn't be needed. Speaking purely politically, in the current climate, cultural representations of failure have more resonance than fortitude-in-adversity. Pop's prime mover is narcissism, always will be, and so self-pity is more crucial a pop response than altruism. Pop was never meant to be this vicarish. 'How Long Can This Go On', 'Save A Soul In Every Town', 'Ideal World', — even the CRASSest agit-pop militancy is preferable to this cooing and billowing Radox bath of sententious platitudes. Give me rage and hate anyday. Sure the world needs more love in it; sure, the brutal and uncaring hold the reins; sure, some people have no choice about having their lives wasted — but I celebrate the brutal and wasteful in music because I know what fascinates me, and it's not this ghastly New Wave soul with-the-one-saxophone-tacked-on. I also know that nothing 'political' happens at Christians gigs, not with words this literal, emotions this plain and simplistic. People may be moved, but no one is *moving*.

(1985–7)

smooth operators

What is it with today's teenyboppers? Why is it that they bestow their ardour upon the well-adjusted, wholesome architects of pop's fatal new maturity? In the old days, there used to be crazes, Adam and the Ants, Gary Numan, absurd figures who nonetheless possessed a certain mesmeric force, managed to induct us into ludicrousness, like the Pied Piper. Maladjusted, inadequate characters with a grudge against the world and a lot to prove (both Adam and Numan had mammoth chips on the shoulder about the music press). These fanatics used fame as a chance to impose their own loopy private fantasy world on pop kids' imagination.

Today, the level-headed hold sway, pop planners with sufficient self-confidence to want to use pop to do more than celebrate themselves. Unlike the damaged narcissists, with their compensations of spurious glory or morbidly melodramatized misery, the new pop workers want attention not for themselves, not for their make-believe world, but for what they have to say about the outside world. I allude, of course, to the wave of middlebrow mature pop for whom the Song is more important than the Star — Wet Wet Wet, Deacon Blue, Hue and Cry, Blow Monkeys, Danny Wilson, Microdisney, etc. Fame is not the spur, it's a liability, or a 'necessary part of the process, y'know' . . .

This decade has seen the old bogey of progressive rock gradually replaced by progressive pop: the site for left-liberal well-meaning and pensiveness has shifted from concept albums and pomp rock, to the three-minute song and pop soul.

Prog pop (like prog rock before it) is an embarrassed attempt to leave behind adolescence — that unsettled interim state so fruitfully prey to traumas, visionary states, loosemindedness, impossible aspirations. To move 'forward' from self-absorbed narcissism/doubt to adult altruism/commitment. And so the sound of pop is no longer adolescent — urgent, frustrated, awkward, rampant — it's 'assured' and 'classy'. Ricky Ross from Deacon Blue talks about not wanting to seduce the audience: 'I don't like the idea of people throwing themselves over to our music. . . abandonment is a great idea but it worries me because it's all so power-orientated.' All that's left is 'communication', pop as vehicle.

The desire to ingratiate a way into the listener's consciousness and thus inveigle an all-important content is the reason all these groups draw inspiration from Sinatra, Bacharach and David, Sondheim, Steely Dan, early seventies' soul, to produce slick, crafted, sophisticated pop. Unfortunately, the decision to opt for smoothness rather than scruffiness, composure rather than gaucheness, is not an innocent choice. Sounds have political resonance. The lyrics may be concerned and caring, but the music sounds nouveau riche, ostentatiously flashy, costly. The invariably suave vocals bring to mind the phrase 'smooth operator', and the only people who want to be smoothies are Thatcherite southern spivs. To aggravate all this further, the records all sound as though they were designed to be played on compact disc.

For these groups, 'classy' and 'classic' have become elided, identical. They've scoured their record collections for their favourite chic embellishments so as to enhance the luxury commodity aura of their product. Danny Wilson use Lester Bowie's Brass Fantasia. Hue and Cry jet off to Sigma Sound, NYC, to work with Jimmy Biondolillo (Sinatra's strings arranger) and the horn section James Brown used for *Living in America*. Wet Wet Wet mosey down to Memphis to work with Willie Mitchell in the studio he used to record Al Green; Dr Robert duets with Curtis Mayfield. With the entire wealth of pop history on hand, the temptation is to indulge in the kind of free-for-all pick'n'mix that has been called retro-nuevo. The result is that any notion of musical futurism has fallen into abeyance.

The idea of the New has always been a crucial part of pop's rhetoric: the idea that the future is going to be an improvement on the past (that sixties' feeling of being on the brink of a whole new order, the beginning of an endless breaking down of barriers and limits). In the eighties, though, everything from pop to advertising is telling us that all the golden ages are located in the past. And on the other side of the Atlantic too.

All the mature pop groups come from Scotland or the northernmost parts of England, but all their musical reference points seem bound up with American ideas of sophistication and glamour. It's curious how someone like Pat Kane mixes being staunch SNP and singing in an American croon. It's also curious how most of these groups have written at least one song about the meretricious lure of the capital. Wet Wet Wet's 'Wishing I Was Lucky' is about going to London, then returning disillusioned to Clydebank; Danny Wilson's 'Davey' is another anti-metropolis warning; Hue and Cry's 'Goodbye to Me' is about the disorientation and displacement of the jetset life, while Deacon Blue's 'Town to Blame' and 'Dignity' and Kane Gang's 'Looking for Gold' are about escaping smalltown constraints.

There seems to be a common thread here — a desire to rise above northern grim limits into a world of sleek, cosmopolitan opportunity, and at the same time an anxiety to retain one's roots. The result — a strange (but not particularly compelling) mismatch between form and content — American finery meets northern realism.

These groups have made strenuous efforts to get it right — to get the sound they always wanted, with none of the cheapskate shoddiness that British soul/jazz groups often settle for: to counterbalance that lush, affluent sound with concerned lyrics, nods to their roots and tons of soul-blaring compassion. And they're dead keen to suppress any burgeoning, ego-trip tendencies. You can almost hear them thinking, 'Who could hold anything against us? What have we done wrong?' But I can think of several reasons to resent their existence. Because they strive, but can never counterfeit the ease or inevitability of great soul; are smart but never opulent, well-turned but never flamboyant. Because they choose their words too carefully, jealously control their meanings, and if they're sussed enough to believe in ambiguities and contradictions you can be sure each one is carefully mounted in position for you, the listener. Because they're *almost there* — unlike previous white soul or funk aspirants like Kevin Rowland or A Certain Ratio who fell so far short of their ambitions they inadvertently created something different, these groups have, through graft and expense, come close, and so clog the second division of pop-soul. In the process, they participate in the global installation of a kind of universal grade of emotive competence, a standardization of the voice which is marginalizing deficient or regional voices. Because they denigrate the guitar. And — despite the cosmopolitan sheen of the music — precisely because their feet *are* still firmly on the ground.

SEDUCED BUT NOT ABANDONED?

Hue and Cry are the most interesting of the new pop sophisticates, not so much because of the music, but because singer and lyricist Patrick Kane is an intellectual firebrand who's more sussed than most about the contradictions and complexities of trying to infiltrate intelligence into the world of teenpop. Recently he penned probably the most abrasively intelligent letter ever to appear in *Melody Maker*, in which he laid out with admirable succinctness the differences between his pop aesthetic (making sense of the world, pop as motivator) and what he identified as the *MM* aesthetic of pop as dissipation.

Why the obsession with American culture?

'I don't think I need to tell us how saturated we as a people are by American culture. You cannot evade the fact that we are cultural Americans, dreaming American dreams.'

But there are so many different Americas that fascinate and shape us. In Scotland there are two in particular — there's the pop scene that draws its inspiration from American bohemians like Lou Reed, Arthur Lee, Tom Verlaine, and there's your scene, which takes its cue from Bowie's *Young Americans*, Average White Band, Steely Dan, Chic . . .

'People have attributed that vision of America to an upwardly mobile Glasgow scene of bands addicted to dancefloor culture. Glasgow 1982–83 was a lot like New Romantic era London. A lot of the pop soul, nouveau muso thing came about as a reaction to Postcard, or the post-Postcard janglepop. The wilful amateurism and naïveté started to grate on everybody's nerves. The Postcard vision of America is a late sixties' America . . .'

A kind of anti-American America. . .

'It's an anti-lush America. Which is the America I love — the America of classic showbiz, a wee utopia of lovely surfaces and lush expensiveness. . .'

But I thought you were political. . .

'Political in the sense that if I threw this glass of water over you in an interview, that would be a political act. C'mon, life is political. Rick Astley is political. . .'

But whereas Astley, like anything else in the world, is full of inadvertent political resonance, Hue and Cry are trying to control their political meanings. Smuggle 'improper' ones in. Isn't the danger with using an expensive sound the probability that people will take it straight, as un-ironic luxury?

'Yeah, but a song like "Strength to Strength" is a joke we're playing on the English working class after the election. If they want a kitsch little anthem they can sing while aspiring to the next set of double glazing or automated garden gnomes, that's okay by me, because that song is a BOMB delivered from Scotland.'

It occurs to me that Kane is overly optimistic here on three counts. He over-estimates the importance of the text in pop. He assumes that 'ordinary' pop fans are attuned to reading off 'subversion' or 'importance' in the same way music press readers are — it's an approach in which you have to be initiated. Most people may not be primed to be 'subverted' because they think of pop as light entertainment. Finally, he underestimates the ability of pop fans to live with hidden or even overt meanings in pop that ought to affront them. I've encountered *Arena*-reading Young Conservatives who get off on The Smiths and Sex Pistols: I knew a girl whose favourite group is The Jam but who claims to be apolitical and whose one great desire in life is a Mercedes. There's no accounting for how people (mis)use pop.

Being aware of the mechanics of fan idolatory, do you feel a responsibility?

'Aye, but you respond in a funny way. I'd rather be seen as a big brother than a juicy sex symbol. Someone who gives you advice that you don't want to hear, but it sinks in anyway. A sententious older brother. But a lot of people are looking for pseudo-satisfaction through lusting after this complete stranger, and you have to accept that, fight on that terrain.'

So you're confident that intelligence can withstand the spotlights unwithered, untrivialized?

'Course it can. Everybody's intelligent, everyone's trying to make sense of the world, even if they're not plugged into larger systems of thought like some of us. Everyone's making choices everyday.'

Having taken on all these images and elements of pop mythology, do you want people to be aware there's an element of irony involved?

'It's got to be a sugared pill, always. On the subject of using the past, making references, it's just that it's impossible to evade the past, it's here, it's being thrown at you, and you have to deal with it. Sure, it gets to be like a supermarket of history, pick'n'mix, and yeah, I don't know what happened to labour history, working class dignity . . .'

'Springsteen bought it all,' pipes up Greg, Pat's engagingly sullen brother.

Pat: 'Well, there you are — Springsteen's authenticity is as much constructed out of signs as anyone.'

Discussing how Hue and Cry have left behind notions like 'modernism', 'rock' and 'youth', we somehow get round to what is the point of pop. Pat — an avid reader of the music press and an ex-*NME* crit himself — explains my approach . . .

'His theory, Greg, is . . . how long you got? . . . his theory is that the best music is the stuff which makes you go doolally, lose yourself. I love the consistency of the theory, but I hate the actual theory.'

Because it doesn't equip people to do anything with their lives?

'Because it doesn't look at the object of music. If everybody was just gonna get off on weird sounds, there'd be no words. And there *are* lyrics and it makes sense, and that's what pop music is — popular poetry. Even the most banal song makes sense. People like thinking, like making sense of things.'

But there's no single, proper use of music, no correct hit that we should all be getting. I certainly wouldn't claim that the loss-of-self aesthetic was valid outside of a probably quite limited, class- and gender-specific group of people who need their over-orderly thought patterns disrupted good'n'proper. But Kane was right when he identified in his letter a broad-and-loose *Melody Maker* aesthetic that prefers transports to truths, rapture to appreciation, magic to meaning, the letting loose of ecstasy to the clench of commitment.

So if you hate the theory so much, how come you're so boned up on it? What's this huge stack of post-modern journals you've got here? (One of them, *Seduced and Abandoned*, a collection of Baudrillard-influenced essays, supplies the title of the Hue and Cry debut LP).

'Because it's the only thing that's happening, intellectually. I read it to know the enemy. I think all that stuff is just lying down in the face of the mass media. Certainly, people are seduced and abandoned by the media, by its lush images — but you have to deal with that, infiltrate ideas in, give people back their vertebrae.'

Baudrillard would argue that radical initiatives only end in re-energizing the pop machine, are more grist to commerce's mill.

'But that guy's a pessimist, a fuckin' nihilist.'

THE COLLABORATORS

What Kane proposes is the strategy of ENTRYISM — which in its original connotation was a strategy of entering mainstream political parties undertaken by revolutionary groups so as to subvert from within. The idea (rather than the term) first had rock currency in the punk aftermath. After the initial flight to the margins, there was speculation on how to build on the energy of punk. It was around then the following formulation took hold: radical meanings required radical forms of musical expression. After some time, when people began to chafe against the impotence, isolationism and élitism of the post-punk avant-garde, this notion, indeed the very idea of the 'alternative,' was gradually dismantled.

Entryism — the idea of concealing radical meanings within a conventional pop format — was born. A syndrome — which was to recur again and again, from ABC to Age of Chance — of indie bands lashing other indie bands for their defeatism in not taking on the mainstream, was inaugurated. ABC extolled irony, detachment, and doffed tuxedos as a gesture against post-punk stasis. As Martin Fry said later: 'I am a punk. I always will be,' claiming that taking on the pop funk sound of the moment was a perfect fulfilment of punk's evangelist logic. Scritti Politti also moved out of the shadowy margins and proposed a schizoid project — the making of perfect pop that contains its own internal deconstruction. Pop that seduces as it unravels the very iconography/mythology (absolute love, the perfect girl) which drives it. Between the two of them, ABC and Scritti, with their widely disseminated interviews and much-parroted rhetoric, made rock an embarrassing relic, pensioned off the guitar, discredited the indie ethos, and made soul and funk de rigueur.

1987 and the influence of ABC and Scritti is everywhere, still, albeit filtered and degraded by intermediaries like the Kitchenware stable (Kane Gang, Friends Again, Prefab Sprout, Bourgie Bourgie) and The Style Council. ABC are everywhere suits and irony hold sway (Pet Shop Boys) while Wet Wet Wet took their name from a lyric in Scritti's 'Gettin', Havin' and Holdin'. Generally ABC and Scritti's ideas — that rock music is finished, and only black music is a viable vehicle for intelligence; that if you believe in what you do you owe it to yourself to dive headfirst into the mainstream — still exert something verging on hegemony.

Me, I find myself steadily drifting back to the unfashionable conviction that radical meanings are betrayed by conventional forms; that if melodies, key changes, and vocal cadences follow expected paths they can only reinforce commonsense perceptions. I am drawn more and more to a resurrected belief in the marginal and its value-in-itself, beyond any consideration of its power to infect pop's arterial thoroughfares. A belief in the 'alternative' — not so much in terms of an independent business infrastructure — but in the sense of otherness: music that explores the otherwordly, or the other within yourself. Instead of 'subversion', the cunning interpolation of irregular meanings into pop's circuitry, I'm interested in a more literal up-turning — topsy-turviness, the vaporization of meaning itself. It's the difference between putting across a point of view, and sharing a vision. Between Hue and Cry and The Sugarcubes.

Groups like Microdisney and Danny Wilson, who try to use MOR in order to get their messages over to as many people as possible, are doubly misguided. How can words stir anyone to action or even reflection if the accompanying music fails to quicken the pulse? And isn't it the case that real MOR — the stuff that sells, boys — has words that are anodyne too, that reinforce commonsense views of normality and (human) nature?

More than any other group I can think of, Microdisney are victims of rock's over-privileging of the text. The words, and the need to get those words within earshot of the maximum number of people, have subordinated the music to the level of glossy paper — designed to interfere with clear transmission and reception of the message as little as possible. Maybe they genuinely like their kind of aural semolina. Give me un-easy listening.

All that wasted intellect. Four years ago, we would have said of blokes like Cathal Coughlan and Patrick Kane: pop needs more figures like them, spiky, striving, sussed. Now I just think their struggles sustain the fiction that intelligence can work within pop, can avoid being misread, misappropriated, or plain ignored. The only hope we have for intervention in pop is as a visitation, a bolt of strangeness, something whose *point* is to be undecodable. Like M.A.R.R.S. or The Sugarcubes. Music that could never be taken as light entertainment. But why bother anyway? Let pop die. And let those who contribute to extending its life's breath be called — COLLABORATOR.

(1987)

schemers versus dreamers
(written with David Stubbs)

ROCK HEAVEN, POP HELL

In 'Smooth Operators' I took to task the brace of pop collaborators — Hue and Cry, Wet Wet Wet and so forth — whose reading of white funk has implicated them as collaborators in pop's current fixation with sincerity, soulfulness, positivism. Groups who have drifted from our ranks in a misguided attempt to make decent pop's terrain, render it a worthy environment for Ben E. King. These bands are juniors in a hegemony established by Live Aid, that unprecedented feat of anxiety, in which the likes of Quo, Dire Straits, U2, Phil Collins, even Boy George, closed ranks, created, as well as a spectacle of pop unity, an unbeatable mediocracy.

Since the failure of ZTT and Sputnik particularly, it has never really seemed likely that our own spiky tarts could share the limelight with the outright MOR. Today, pop is a closed circuit, a self-sufficiency. A chasm has reopened between a galvanized, airborne rock, the rock celebrated in the pages of *Melody Maker*, and the sealed, well-rounded, well-grounded entity that is pop. Once more, it's Us and Them. So what happened to the infiltrators, the double agents, the strategists?

POP STRATEGISTS

Pop strategy began and ended with ABC, Heaven 17, Scritti Politti and Malcolm McLaren. These were the days when rock was being shooed out in disgrace, a lumpen confusion of scratched armpits and muddled motives. New pop was a shiny parody of efficiency, of 'wanting in'. Heaven 17 appropriated the jargon and paraphernalia of industry, presented themselves as a well-heeled corporation, offering 'Music Of Quality and Distinction' which suavely played pop at its own game. Scritti Politti appropriated the labels of luxury commodities on their record sleeves, a gesture against their early DIY sleeves (photos of squats, photocopies of litter). Both were provoking a spectacular confusion of signs — 'quality', the 'finer things in life' restored to the avant-garde hipsters who, like ABC, 'know what trash is'. Malcolm McLaren disseminated Situationist ideas through Bow Wow Wow, naked and primal jumbles of desire — 'I Want Candy'.

Later came Sputnik, with their third-generation pastiche of ambition, masterplan, world domination; their relentless colourquest for the ultimate pleasure product, for hyperstimulus. There was ZTT's Frankie Goes To Hollywood, and Propaganda; Paul Morley promoted them on the assumption that pop was run by flabby-faced cowards who didn't even know how to do their own job — in other words, it took an aesthete to know and score a hit. But he fell victim of the dawning disenchantment when he declared in an interview: ' "Two Tribes" can be number one for nine weeks and then it's toppled by George Michael's "Careless Whisper". You see, nothing happens.'

Of course, 'something happened'. It's possible to trace George Michael back to the colourmotion, the white funk irony that more or less began with ABC and spawned a straight, bleached-out generation of Howard Jones and (eventually) the Hues, Wets, Styles and Curiositys ad nauseam. Nothing else though. Yet there are still a smattering of pop ironists trickling sporadically, lip-first into the fray.

There's Win, still carrying the cheeky pennants and slogans of '81, boasting of chewing gum for the ears, expressing admiration for advertising jingles. Or Age of Chance, grunting urgently about 'go for it' assertiveness training, positive power, hi-impact multi-sensory overload, cartoon Ballard litanies of 'crush collision'.

And there's Transvision Vamp, a chink in that chimera 'the new glam', who offer us the usual tenth-hand situationism, trash reappropriation of spectacular signs (guns, stars and stripes, peroxide, Warhol), proposing 'cinepop' (that old '81 line about multi-media infiltration) and posturing as corporate buccaneers. And there's Act with their amoral fascination for the artifice and decadence of showbiz.

All of these bands explicitly lambast indie parochialism and neurotic fear of major label compromise; all peddle an obsolete notion that the brash and the colourful represent a victory over the hegemony of a vague grey, with the naïve optimism of nineteenth-century dandies. But modern bourgeois suburbia *is* colourful, tacky, vulgar, and these groups only mimic this different kind of banality. All talk of plunder, piracy and plagiarism in a shopworn discourse of 'irreverence' and boisterousness, as if Westworld kick up some kind of a rumpus on pop's trash-heap of efflorescences, as if there are still grandmothers to be shocked and purists to be cheeked.

What these bands have most in common, however, is that they FAIL ABJECTLY. Win lost! The Age of Chance's number never came up. As for Transvision Vamp — well, what about them? You'll find them next year all commingling ignominiously in the bargain bins with the indie 'underachievers', the Motorcycle Boys and Shrubs, all malingering in the same space. The Pop Tarts are the apotheosis of this disparity between rhetoric and achievement. They talked a good interview. They had 'attitude' — boy, they had attitude. With a cleverly effete waft they dismissed 'anti-pop' (The Smiths, REM), were 'pro-product, anti-celebrity', namechecked Hermes, Giorgia, Ralph Lauren, wanted to proliferate in every medium from cinema to truffles. They didn't even get a record deal. Even Stockport indie gerbils A Witness could boast more than that.

Even when the music's good, (Act's first single was superb, the Age of Chance LP was surprisingly listenable) the problem is that the pop schemers have made MASSIVE POPULAR SUCCESS such an integral part of the product. As with Frankie, so much of the pleasure is bound up with the sense of something breaking out all over the surfaces of everyday life, and you being in on it from the start. Without that sense of reverberation or sensation, the brash colours and sharp slogans flail in ignominious and redundant isolation. Exhibitionism ignored is a pitiful sight.

So why is pop impervious to these bright entryists, these studied simulators? You'd have thought anybody with two brain cells to rub together and a spark of wit could find a way past Mike Read and Phil Collins.

There are several reasons:

1) 'Simulation pop' is generally couched in brazen, nakedly aggressive terms, conceives of pop as openly cut-throat, ruthless, plastic, self-adoring, cynical (as Age of Chance put it, 'Don't Get Mad, Get Even'). In fact this vision of pop is as fictional and irrelevant today as the indie notion of 'perfect pop' (an airy idyll of sixties' byrdsong). Today's pop is soulful, concerned with banishing inhuman traces, yearning for a lost passion and integrity. Which is why a 'real' popster like Mark Knopfler would shake his head in genuine dismay at Jamie Reid's manifesto for Transvision Vamp, why your Climie Fishers make it and your Sputniks burn up in orbit.

2) Pop as Pure Pleasure Product, pop as blipvert, does actually enjoy a routine, marginal existence — house, Hi-NRG, Stock Aitken Waterman — functioning

blankly, without recourse to discourse, with no need of a statement of intent, unMEDIAted.

3) Everything is sewn up. The biz is no longer in the state of confusion of seven years ago, when Altered Images could giggle and tumble their way onto TOTP. Today, the industry has no need to feed off the margins, needs no lessons from Sigue Sigue Sputnik about the Global Leisure Industry, movie tie-ins or the killings to be made in the future collusion of pop and advertising to create new needs. With pie diagrams indicating that the major pop consumers are the staid, over-25s, the development in the ad industry of 'psychogeographics' (the science of using pop to home in on specific taste publics — i.e. Springsteen fans are likely to desire different products from Whitney Houston fans), and the construction of bands in the studio, pop has never required less urgently a rush of theory from the 'left'.

4) By exposing the workings of pop (the way myth is stagemanaged, the way glamour is constructed) the new pop entryists actually deny the listener the chance to lose themselves in the 'commodity fetishism' they purport to celebrate. They force the listener to be aware it's not for real. Their foregrounding of this unreality, their knowing winks, are actually an abstention from immersing themselves fully in the 'pop process' in all its madness, carnality and glamour. A cowardly vacillation, this hesitation to commit themselves to being myth.

In fact, at this point it's worth taking a pitchfork to that grossly over-rated entity — CAMP. It's a terrible mistake to believe that you can consciously create camp, at this late hour. Camp is an aesthetic of consumption, not production. Camp is a response to pop performances that are artificial, ludicrously stylized (Liberace, Tom Jones, Shirley Bassey), but whose stars enter into it all with a seriousness, a passion that affects with its holy, innocent imbecility. (Precisely the immersion-in-myth, the plunge, that our knowing pop double agents refuse to make.) Camp is a schizoid pleasure; you're amused by the absurdity and touched by the sincerity, at the same time. Manifest inauthenticity on the surface, inner authenticity soul-deep.

All this means we can forget about The Communards' cover version of 'Never Can Say Goodbye', and we can forget about the wretched Pet Shop Boys, the only successful contemporary pop ironists. This group's only sin is their wry self-consciousness which falls smugly short of arrant narcissism; the fey, running commentary implicit in their song-titles ('Rent', 'Shopping', 'Suburbia', 'Opportunities [Let's Make Lots of Money]') signifies detachment, and finally alienation from the allure, the lush materiality of pop. This isn't even pop about pop, this is fop about pop. It shows that camp is a defensive attitude, a flight from real involvement. Rather than simply consuming pop (which makes clever little references to its commodity status) we should look to music that consumes US. That exceeds the commodity relation and its in-built alienation, and allows us to worship.

DEMYSTIFICATION

The 'Simulation Pop' of the Pet Shop Boys, Pop Tarts, et al, is the end product of a discourse of demystification that began with punk, its DIY ethos, its 'anyone can do it' clarion call. The original notion was to demystify the means of production, in order to liberate creativity, marginal voices. But the logic of punk's evangelistic drive to change things led to an attempt to take demystification to the people: the pop deconstruction of ABC (exposing pop's stage managing, as on the sleeve of *The Lexicon of Love*) and Scritti Politti (affirming and unravelling, simultaneously, the lover's non-sensical discourse).

DIY's original idea was that anyone could find something brilliant to create within the limits of their (in)competence. But the false legacy of demystification is the belief that anyone can be pop stars — a flagrant falsehood! Aided by cheap drum machines and synthesizers, these canny aspirants endeavour to construct a spectacular pop by distilling the pop essence from all past efflorescences, using the hindsight sophistication of the present day.

But all the ambition, striving, graft, pop-learning in the world can't earn you pop divinity. Attitude is never going to count for as much as the Gift — the untranscribable charisma, the arbitrary aura, the unequally-bestowed vocal magic that no amount of homework or calculation can procure. It makes sense that the ineffable languor of Prince is infinitely more fruitious than a thousand sinewy Age of Chance slogans. Pop should be a scarce resource, rather than something 'deserved' (like free milk).

The pop entryists — whose creed is that anyone with attitude, a masterplan, a nice line in self-salesmanship, can break on through — disqualify themselves from becoming objects of worship. Pop that unravels its own workings, undoes itself. Pop, by definition, must mystify. Marc Bolan, who knew about these things, said it best: 'pop should be a spell.'

Now of course it hasn't needed a lambast from the likes of us to prompt the breakdown of pop entry. It has pretty much happened, we're chasing its last desperate apologists down a hole of their own making. A chasm has undoubtedly developed, but the sporadic re-emergency of the blasted simulators — they keep crawling up time and time again with bedraggled, sanguine hollers of intent – and the beady eyes cast by all manner of unlikely contenders on pop's centre stage ('We see no reason why this band shouldn't be huge') — suggests that our new proposition of an overground and underground sticks in the craw. What it means for 'us' is not so much the resurrection of 'anti-pop', but a culture of margins; a disdainful gaze upon the terrain we once occupied, a satellite relationship to a pop centre now barred to us.

It means UNKNOWINGNESS as opposed to IRONY — the afflicted voice (Pixies, Throwing Muses, et al), the white blindness of the new guitar air (Dinosaur Jr, Husker Du), or the unblinking fervour of The Young Gods. The music of the ever-receding margins, the music over which we have a claim, should be not just anti-soul (against intimations of health, the centrality of the body, straighttalking, wholesomeness) but anti-irony (the raised eyebrow, the quotation marks). Our music should be set in an outward discovery of difference and space.

Detachment, self-consciousness must be flooded out by the stream of consciousness — music caught in its own flux, a white water of dream language (REM, Muses). To hell with the GOOD TALKERS, those pugnacious interviewees all set to give 'sleepy' pop the kick in the pants it deserves — pop beauty should be the subject of dumbfoundedness, the breakdown of schematics. As for the New Boisterous, the cheery spree of custard colours and polemical beiges that are the persistently 'new' colourmotion, let's get it straight — the State of Pop is not Grey, but over-determined by a stifling, clotting *rainbow* coalition of mediocrity.

RE-MYSTIFICATION

The return to rock means the supercession of demystification by re-mystification, giving people back their sense of worship, rather than forcibly opening their eyes to the nuts and bolts of how 'myth' is constructed. Entryist pop implied the filling of every space, a tight, breathless glut of good ideas, an endless process of signification. The return to rock means a re-awakening of dub, remoteness, loss of self in a recession of space, a search for unlit rather than overlit regions. A.R. Kane and Arthur Russell skirt the peripheries, imply a distance from the centred subject of pop that is hauntingly suggested by their Plutonic, echoing surfaces of sounds. Their beauty is arbitrary, beyond grasp, gazing and gazed upon.

MY LITTLE UNDERGROUND

New pop is extrovert, forever shaping up to splash down in supposedly 'unstirred' regions, forever dramatizing itself against a torpid and shockable opposition — the grown-ups, straights, squares, 'the dullards'. The return to rock represents an abstention or introversion, a retreat (the Jesus and Mary Chain's 'My Little Underground'), a local culture rather than any doomed attempt at a global overhauling. Rebellion has imploded; the enemy is the finger-wagging parent inside your head — your own inhibitions, regular thought patterns, inflexible mental grids and perceptual blinkers. The rebirth of an underground implies induction, being drawn into shared exile, being both insider and outsider; rather than trying to break down the doors to edify the unconverted.

To 'forget' pop is to renege fundamentally upon the (over-determining) intentions of punk. No more 'resistance through rituals' (revolt into style, sartorial bricolage that confounds expectations, all of which are read, interpreted, mediatized and accommodated in a trice, these days). No more implanting the virus from within, no more attempting to gatecrash a terrain that no longer really belongs to us (whatever it may once have been, simple demographic change has turned pop into global light entertainment). No more agoraphobia (mistrust of anything longer than the classic three minutes, the squitBrit aversion to the cumulus wail). No more going public and imagining that by the gesture alone you'll be 'improving' matters. With the music we like, it doesn't matter if it doesn't 'breakthrough', if it doesn't 'happen' — because, by being created, it's happening. It's there as a choice, a reproach, and its remoteness from the secular pop world is a sign of its success. The further out, the more FAR OUT.

The return of rock means not so much a crashdown as a return towards rock, a departure from planet pop to a self-sufficiency that matches pop. A parallel universe, mutually incompatible, like matter and anti-matter. No more *Tube*, no more of your favourite bands on the telly, another dark age as regards the media. No more breaking in but breaking away, leaving and letting loose into the impending night. Goodbye, The Style Council. Goodbye, bleached pop-funk. Goodbye, the classic three-minute single. Goodbye, Janice Long. Goodbye 'wanting in' — hello THE WAY OUT. Let the fatuous sun shine by itself and let's head for the moon. Let's snuff out the short people and welcome the long shadows.

(1987)

the impossible dream
(written with Paul Oldfield)

SYLVERE LOTRINGER: 'The cause of an event is always imagined after the fact. After that jolly May we were treated to the curious spectacle of causes racing after effects.'

JEAN BAUDRILLARD: 'May '68 is an event which it has been impossible to rationalize or exploit, from which nothing has been concluded. It remains indecipherable.'

Lotringer and Baudrillard, 'Forget Baudrillard'

1988 is the year of ... 1968. The media teem with retrospectives and reappraisals. These range from elegies for a lost spirit of militancy, to post-mortems that exhume the body of revolution only to bury it the deeper in prehistory. The May insurrections are now denigrated as an adolescent rash of impractical idealism that would soon have the ground cut from under its spoilt feet by the brutal dis-illusionments of the seventies and the market forces of the eighties ('yippies become yuppies', '68 led to Thatcher'). But in pop, 1968 has been a perennial presence, through the abiding influence of the Situationists, the opportunist theorists of the May uprising. At the time, their graffiti slogans ('never work', 'under the pavement lies the beach', 'be reasonable, demand the impossible') were only a whisper in the roar of competing clarion-calls; subsequently, commentators have centred the interpretation of '68 on them.

In their celebrations of wild-cat strikes and the 1965 inner-city conflagration in Watts, Los Angeles, the Situationists had provided a convincing analysis of these apparently unmotivated and unconstructive revolts: as protests against alienation and 'the poverty of everyday life'. (In Watts, people had destroyed their own property, local amenities, cars . . .) 1968 seemed to fulfil the Situationists' prophecies of escalating discontent with consumer capitalism.

Influenced by Dada, the Paris Commune, and literary terrorists like Lautréamont and Artaud, the Situationists imagined and demanded 'the revolution of everyday life'. Where before the individual had been alienated and oppressed at work, now there was a consumer leisure culture and with it 'government by seduction'. The enemy was the commodity (substitute for real needs) and 'the spectacle' (forms of leisure like TV, cinema, spectator sport, which enforced passivity and isolation from other consumers). Their resistance was 'the construction of situations' (happenings, pranks) which breached the barrier between art and life, and demanded spontaneity, improvisation and collective participation.

For Situationism, creativity was 'the ultimate weapon'; *détournement*, the recycling of the dominant culture through collage and misappropriation, was subversive. But the Situationists recognized the power of the spectacle to 'recuperate' subversive initiatives and turn them into pacifying entertainment. Rock was a prime example of this recuperation, ultimately all the more sedative because of its seductive language of liberation/self-expression/difference.

Malcolm McLaren wanted to test the limits of the spectacle's ability to assimilate what threatened it. Both he and his artschool sidekick Jamie Reid claimed to have been present at the May Riots and had certainly been involved in King Mob, a Situationist-influenced underground cell in Britain.

Fred Vermorel: 'The whole idea of punk was for people like McLaren, Reid, Bernie Rhodes, all those ex-artschool, behind-the-scenes managers, to have their own '68. They'd been involved at the time, but had been pushed to the background by older figures like Tariq Ali.'

This time, their idea was to engender within the spectacle a series of 'situations' which would disrupt the smooth-running, tranquillizing sheen of the mass media. McLaren's pranks and scams (the notorious Bill Grundy show, EMI, the Jubilee boat trip where the Pistols played in front of Parliament) were planned, but given life by the random factor of the Sex Pistols' delinquency. Like terrorism, they were designed to provoke authority into revealing the repressive apparatus behind its façade of liberal consensus: McLaren revelled in the censorship, being fired by record companies, the police raid on the boat, even the actual physical assaults by reactionary thugs.

But McLaren's bluff was called by Branson, the ultimate liberal, who signed them to Virgin: hits followed, an irritant became entertainment, and the Pistols became a working, selling rock band trying to break America the hard way. 'The incoherence of the spectacle became the spectacle of incoherence' (Guy Debord). A desperate series of ploys to push them back beyond the pale ('Belsen Was A Gas', recording with Ronnie Biggs and 'Martin Bormann') were calmly accepted and distributed as product.

And as the liberal media was trying to sew up and explain punk, McLaren pitched in with his own, closed version of punk as a premeditated programme ('the Swindle') rather than an improvised chaos of terroristic acts, a vacuum of meaning invading the media like an embolism. Maybe he didn't want to be left out of history. But thereafter McLaren moved his role (as mastermind provocateur) to the centre.

Henceforth, he presents his own synopsis prior to its realization as a pop event: the actual process of creating situations seems redundant next to 'giving people ideas'. A series of projects — cassette piracy, gold'n' sex, techno-savagery (Bow Wow Wow). scratching, squaredancing, the hobo, Africa ('Buffalo Gals' and 'Duck Rock') — barely extend beyond their elaboration in interviews. McLaren not only reconstructs, he now pre-constructs. He boasts of his indifference to music.

Pop's danger has always been the brief interregnum of indeterminacy and uncontrol, before the youth experts rush in to explain/excuse/validate obtuse and unreadable acts like ripping up cinema seats as 'legitimate' expressions of 'healthy' teen sexuality looking for an outlet, or unconscious protest against the indignity of regimented labour. But here's McLaren, the logocrat, providing the sociological rational in advance, and in the process constituting power in himself.

McLaren imagined demystification as subversive of the spectacle. The manipulations, planning and strategy are explicit, sometimes the whole content of his pop. But what he's proved is that the spectacle can be turned inside out — with contrivance, hype and puppetry on display — and still function. Seduction can't be used to candycoat spores of disaffection: seduction can only escalate.

And yet pop Situationism is still a lingering presence in the late eighties: the incitement to DIY, the group as corporate buccaneer, glamour as a revolt against everyday life, the insatiability of desire. All these ideas persist as a diffused (and defused) residue absorbed by the likes of Sputnik, Transvision Vamp, Scarlett Fantastic, the Age of Chance school of 'dance noise terror', and ZTT. So Wendy James can prattle on about 'revolutionary individualism' and 'showing pop consumers that anyone can do it' while remaining in colourful symbiosis with the industry.

These forlorn, diminished echoes of Situationism remind us of how the Dadaist pranks of the sixties (proposing a pig as candidate for the US presidency,) degenerated into lowest-common-denominator student pranks like electing goldfish and tortoises to be student union officials.

Sigue Sigue Sputnik were at the furthest limit of depreciated pop situationism. Everything referred to earlier, exhausted signifiers of outrage (*Ziggy Stardust*, the Pistols' EMI-scam, Suicide's futuristic Elvis). But Sputnik were only fraudulent because no outrage or fraud had been perpetrated.

Both the industry and the group need the SIMULATION of power and its subversion — a swindle, or a hype, or both. Amid rumours of a £3,000,000 advance, it was uncovered that only £30,000 had been advanced. This hundred-fold inflation of the real (in which both band and corporation were complicit) was a last-ditch attempt to convince us that there can still be manipulation and/or subversion . . . 1976: EMI really are duped; 1986: EMI profit from the staged spectacle of being duped. Capitalism orchestrates its own crisis to renew itself, economically and culturally.

The legacy of Situationism in pop is the idea: 'take your desires for reality.' The Situationists fought the process by which our dreams are imprisoned in commodities and spectacles. Situationism's premises are that desire is 'insatiable' and that the 'subjective will' is the enemy of power. Everyone is supposed to be endowed with a limitless capacity to be creative, to realize their true selves and desires. It's only conditioning and inhibitions that make us bored and boring. But the Situationists simply denied the existence of deficiency, inner conflict and tragedy. For our entry into the world isn't as whole, limitlessly fecund and self-sufficient. Which is why we turn to art, or pop, or love.

Situationists did 'demand the impossible', for the impossible is to liberate all your desires, without prioritizing them. To do so would mean the dissolution of the self in an oceanic wash of undifferentiated desire — and that can only occur as an intermittent escape from 'the world', in psychedelia's momentary reversions to an unstructured state of being. This is innocence as 'unknow-ingness' as opposed to gleeful child's play, the mischief of the pseudo-Situationist pranksters.

But the fundamental flaw in Situationism is the assumption that the demand for autonomy is equivalent to the end of all power. For the individual isn't the basic unit subject to oppression, but is itself implicated and involved in the exercise of power over itself. Autonomy means literally self-rule. In the late twentieth century it could be argued that power operates by inculcating us in the art of self-policing; therapists and counsellors offer us personal regimes to realize our potential and increase our productivity at work and in our personal lives. This interface between social engineering and mental hygiene may well be the most significant terrain on which to fight power: a micro-politics of the self.

But Situationism is such a total approach to politics, culture and life that it would be surprising if something couldn't be salvaged from it. Fred and Judy Vermorel, pop theorists and (briefly) pop practitioners on Factory, are among the most interesting heirs to Situationism. They see the spectacle not as something that enforces passivity, but as something that incites action — in the case of pop, an active, uncontrollable desire.

Following Schumpeter, who believed that capitalism would be undone not by its failure to satisfy real needs, but because it encouraged a spiralling of fabricated wants, the Vermorels believe the spectacle threatens to undo itself by its own success. It must constantly police the effects (fan hysteria, obsessives who, like Mark Chapman, can turn nasty if spurned) it incites. The Vermorels challenge the traditional view of fans as pathetic and passive dupes.

Fred: 'We wouldn't use words like alienation or "manipulated masses". Fans liberate themselves through using stars, who they dispose of quite callously. The fans create their own experience of the star, and these pornographic/romantic fantasies, as we found when compiling *Starlust*, are often much more creative than anything the star has done.'

For the Vermorels the riots of '81 are as important as those of '68, because they were not 'legitimately' motivated, but copycat, media-fuelled.

'The media couldn't avoid showing people it was possible to simply take what you wanted . . . The riots were carnivalesque, like parties in the street. And the Situationists believed that every day should be a carnival.'

But historically the carnival has always been a brief intermission of topsy-turviness. Like all transgressions, it only has meaning, is only conceivable, as the other side of normality and control.

Pop Situationism (punk DIY, the new glam's 'reinvention of yourself', and the Vermorels' inflammation of mass desire) all assume that people's moments of release are ones where they are active, expressive, desiring agents, creative and self-creating. We'd argue that the supreme moments in a life, when people are most emancipated or transported, are when they are overwhelmed or undermined: the passivity of being ravished or mesmerized.

An alternative reading of the Vermorels' *Starlust* might see the case studies as instances of the star taking over someone's life and dreams, like a poltergeist. Fans use and transform the star, but their lives are annexed by the fantasy-process instigated by the star (or rather by the industry). Similarly you can be possessed — by an image or a rhythm, and yield up your autonomy to the thrall of an other. This is mysticism: the fetish stands in for all the fan/lover's unrequitable, impossible longings.

Situationism's error was to imagine that these dreams — of unbounded bliss and heaven on earth — could ever be realized. But there's another, dystopian side to Situationism that has influenced rock. Mark Stewart, for instance, has responded entirely to the critique side of Situationism, its project of negation, and largely ignores their ideas about cultural improvisation. For Stewart, 'nihilism is a way of life', almost mystical ('Anger is Holy').

Mark Stewart and the Maffia don't 'gatecrash paradise' like Scarlett Fantastic and requisition the impossible; they rage about being expelled from paradise. Like the original Situationists, Stewart looks at the world system and sees only power, deceit and exploitation; unlike the Situationists, he's given up the dream of a utopia. Stewart inhibits a hinterland of Situationist-influenced activists on the margins, groups interested in magick, altered states, conspiracy theories, pirate radio and TV, all documented in the irregular fanzine *Vague*. His kindred spirits are Psychic TV, World Domination Enterprises and Mutoid Waste Company. (The Mutoids' 'skip culture' — the détournement of refuse into art — is one of the few contemporary examples of the fun side of Situationism, their dream of a life of perpetual play.)

Jon Savage has argued that these 'media refusers, cultists, ranters, plagiarists, poets and pranksters' represent a contemporary resurgence of MILLENNARIANISM. This is the belief in an apocalyptic 'end of history', to be preceded by a short period of unrule and carnivalesque licence. Certainly, these 'alternative networks' do sustain themselves with the belief that by building up links, exchanging ideas and contacts ('networking'), they can propagate radicalism, which will snowball and fulfil some kind of 'destiny' — the dawning of a new age.

But the apocalypse has already happened, several times — 1968, the Paris Commune in 1870, many times in the sixteenth century. But always as a carnivalesque interlude, 'a holiday from life', which lasts until supplies run out and the participants accede to the re-establishment of power and with it stable production.

We'd take another line: the 'end of history' is constantly accessible, in your head, as psychedelic experience. Like the carnival, these trips out of yourself can't be turned into a new order; indeed only make sense as the inverse of (self) control.

Revolution isn't permanent and once-and-for-all, but an endless, discontinuous series of incursions and excursions. Neither revolution nor jouissance can be turned into a system. So if pop is still inhabited by the 'Children of May', they're not the directly-influenced agitators with their schemes (who are always in control, always reconstituting power). They're the despondents and *enragés* (like Mark Stewart, or World Domination, who sound like a flash riot, who recreate '68 or Watts every time they play), or the delirious and spellbound fans.

(1988)

THE END OF ME

daydream nation

New York was an inexhaustible space, a labyrinth of endless steps, and no matter how far he walked, no matter how well he came to know its neighbourhoods and streets, it always left him with the feeling of being lost. Lost, not only in the city, but within himself as well . . . By wandering aimlessly, all places became equal and it no longer mattered where he was. On his best walks, he was able to feel that he was nowhere. And this, finally, was all he ever asked of things: to be nowhere.

Paul Auster, *City of Glass*

Sonic Youth's 'Daydream Nation' is a vision of life in the schizopolis, where the border between media and reality has blurred, the subconscious come out to play. Life shatters into fragments, ultra-vivid snapshots which can't cohere into sense. Desire, unmoored from any syntax, becomes intransitive, or attaches itself only fleetingly to random objects, fetishes and figments. This limbo life can be a blissed-out daydream drift, but it's prey to dark shadows cast by the unconscious: 'There's something moving/over there to the right/like nothing I've ever seen.'

These lines are from 'Eric's Trip', perhaps the closest Sonic Youth's fractured aesthetic gets to lucidity. Every line is an urgent non sequitur, the babble of a schizo or acid casualty. 'I can't see anything at all/All I see is me . . . Hold these pages up to the light/See the jackknife inside of the dream/The railroad runs through the record stores at night/Coming in for the deep freeze . . . I breathe in the myth/I'm over the city/Fucking the future/I'm high up inside your kiss . . .'

Lee Ranaldo, who sings the song, explains. 'We're not heavy drug takers by any means. You don't need to be in this society, what with the media overload and everything. The world has taken on that kandy colored aspect just by the way things are going. The TV news will juxtapose some terrible tragedy next to some candyfloss pop item. Reality is taking on that daydream aspect, we're living in an unreal reality. Especially in New York, where you're bombarded from every side by information, 50 per cent serious, 50 per cent frivolous. You start to wander around in a kind of shell shock.'

Jean Baudrillard, renegade philosopher, has said that New York is the example par excellence of his vision of the city as desert. New York is a glimpse of the future, a state of hyperreality where the media is more real than reality, where history, 'the social', even power have silently absconded. For Baudrillard, the symptoms of this catastrophic change include: terrorism (acts that have no rationale, that are purely spectacular, whose only purpose is to commandeer media time); political campaigns that have become detached from any issues and that advertise only a command of the techniques of advertising; money transubstantiating into cybernetic data without any relation to real economic power.

The media consumes everything, every last shock effect/reality effect thrown up by the avant garde. Depth and meaning are displaced in favour of the fascination of the surface. Desire — real, dramatic relations between human agents — is superseded by seduction, 'charm' (in the true, magical sense of the word). Instead of resistance through subjectivity (which, whether it's in the name of justice, autonomy, or 'desire', he sees as the last ditch attempt to shore up an evanescent power), Baudrillard proposes 'resistance' through becoming an object. Through succumbing to the vertigo of the mass media, 'a sense of dizziness, with which you can't do anything'. 'It's suicidal, but in a good way . . . There is an art of disappearing, a way of modulating it and making it into a state of grace'. ('Forget Baudrillard', by Sylvère Lotringer and Jean Baudrillard).

Baudrillard is very much the provocateur: his nihilistic celebration of the multiple 'ends' that he says have already happened is a kind of theoretical one-upmanship. Frederic Jameson provides a not dissimilar account of late capitalism, but couched in a more elegaic and worried tone. For him, the death of narrative, linear thought, history, the detachment of signifiers from their signifieds, is not just rendering obsolete the old forms of organized oppositional politics; it is bringing about a form of mass amnesia that is close to schizophrenia. Schizophrenia, for Jameson, is caused by the failure of the infant to 'accede fully into the realm of speech and language'. What is lost in the process is a sense of personal continuity through time. With neither a past nor future projects to occupy his mind, the schizophrenic is wide open to the present: 'The world comes before (him) with heightened intensity, bearing a mysterious and oppressive charge of effect, glowing with hallucinatory energy.' But while a normal person might envy this intensification of experience, and the mystic or acid freak might aspire to it, for the schizophrenic it's a living hell. For Jameson, it's what our culture is ineluctably veering towards.

'Smashed up against a car at 3AM/kids dressed up for basketball beat me in the head/There's bum trash in my hall and my place is ripped/Totalled another amp and I'm calling in sick/It's an element of vacuum in a hyperstation/Daydream daze in a daydream nation' — 'Hyperstation'.

Sonic Youth's vision of New York life as a decentred drift is very close to the Situationist ideas of the 'derive' and of 'psychogeography'. The Situationists imagined reinventing the cities of the future as 'chaotic jungles, sparking experiences without purpose, devoid of meaning' (J. Wolman). Rather than being constructed around principles of utility (facilitating the circulation of consumers and commodities), the city would be a fantastical playground for the unconscious. In the interim, they had a provisional strategy of subversion — the derive (drifting): wandering the city in search of its zones of feeling, ignoring the official cartography of urban planning. 'The derive (with its flow of acts, gestures, strolls, encounters) is to the 'totality' exactly what psychoanalysis is to language. Let yourself go with the flow of words, says the analyst . . . But just as analysis is almost always contra-indicated, so the continuous derive is dangerous to the extent that the individual, having gone too far without defenses, is threatened with explosion, dissolution, disassociation, disintegration. And so the relapse into what is termed 'ordinary life', which is to say, in reality, 'petrified life' . . . 'In 1953–54, we drifted for three or four months at a time: that's the extreme limit, the critical point. It's a miracle that it didn't kill us' (Ivan Chtcheglov). Elsewhere, the Situationists described the derive as a 'suicidal discourse'. That's literally what it is. The attempt to recover the lost 'totality' — a total apprehension of the moment, involving the shedding of all mediations, inhibitions, and perceptual blinkers — is something that takes the individual to the edge of schizophrenia and ego-loss.

'It takes a teenage riot/To get me out of bed/Right now — 'Teenage Riot'.

To understand exactly what Sonic Youth have achieved with *Daydream Nation*, you have to understand where they're coming from: on one hand, the

New York No Wave noise aesthetic, on the other, a tradition of teen delinquent insurgency that goes back to The Stooges and the garage punkadelia of the mid sixties. And the best illustration of this is the New York group Pussy Galore, arguably the ultimate outcome of both these traditions. Pussy Galore are a critics' band. In a very specific sense: I've always thought of them as a Lester Bangs hallucination of the ultimate band, in their convergence of sixties punk's arbitrary vehemence, a trash aesthetic cartoon sensibility, and a No Wave/'Metal Machine Music' attitude to guitar cacophony. In a distant sort of way, Pussy Galore *are* a figment of Bangs's addled imagination. In 1970, completely against the grain of his times, Bangs was already elaborating a set of interconnected ideas – puerility as a way of life, the pursuit of an informed moronicism, noise-as-nirvana, the liberating power of 'crude' repetition, living on the edge, the notion that there's a certain zone of teen-rock primitivism that meets up with the far out reaches of free jazz and avant-garde noise — and using the term 'punk' as shorthand. Bangs's ideas have since become a legacy, upheld by US fanzines like *Forced Exposure* and a clutch of writers on the *Village Voice*. They've also influenced, directly or indirectly, a lineage of writers in Britain, from the adepts of 'sick noise' in the early eighties right up to today's 'acolytes of obliteration', me included. But in the States particularly, Bangs's precepts have been petrified into a little consensus as to 'what rock'n'roll is all about', ensuring that bands like Pussy Galore will always crop up, conforming exactly to a secret programme the origins of which are probably unknown to them. *Village Voice* coined the term 'pigfuck' to describe the guitar sound of bands like Pussy Galore and White Zombie, while the former's cover of the whole of the Stones *Exile on Main Street* was just the kind of act of minor delinquency — recognizing a classic by the very act of vandalizing it — that gives US crits a hard-on.

The element of fun with Pussy Galore is their raucous Demolition Derby of different trash guitar styles — rockabilly, punkadelic fuzz, Detroit wah wah, Sabbath grunge, and the moments when this quotation threatens to spill over into free noise, outside of any period or genre. But Pussy Galore never quite transcend pastiche through immolation, the phoenix of the new never quite flies free. Ultimately, they're a pointless apotheosis of twenty-five years of the teen sicko raving bloody mess-thetic. Like Mudhoney (one of Sonic Youth's fave groups) they uphold the teen tradition rather than extend or ignite it.

All this juvenile dementia is transcended by Sonic Youth's *Daydream Nation*. Here there's nothing so particular or ignoble as an urge, just the nirvana of desire dissolving. In the schizopolis, the gaze is ravished rather than the heart or loins stirred. Passion is supplanted by an enchanted passivity. Daydream nationalists are kids who aren't active enough to be exiles on main street, to be visible dissidents: instead they've disappeared.

The early incarnation of Sonic Youth was very much shaped by the US hardcore aesthetic, the quest for the hard core of reality. Hardcore's fixation on extreme acts of violence, disturbed sexuality and the macabre, stems from the conviction that these are instances of life at its realest, least phoney or prettified. This thirst for the graphic is itself a symptom of the widespread sense of reality-loss that Baudrillard analyses. Media hyperreality has stirred up cravings for ever steeper doses of stimulus that the everyday can't satisfy.

Right up to *Sister*, the predecessor to *Daydream Nation*, Sonic Youth's province was the distinctly morbid, and its musical expression angular and atonal. What distinguished them from the pack was the lengths they went to in the pursuit of noise. They used screwdrivers, drumsticks and other implements to extort new sonorities from an exhausted instrument. They called it 'reinvention of the guitar'. A Sonic Youth song at this point was frenetic and fractious, architecturally constructed from interlapping drones, and its effect was more percussive than melodic. The matter of their rock seemed forever on the verge of buckling, spraining, tearing like fatigued metal. Songs accelerated into blind alleys or subjected the listener to the vertigo of impossible gradients, inducing a hair-raising concentration, a sharpening of the senses by dread. A Sonic Youth song was, in fact, a rollercoaster trip you thought would never end.

With *Daydream Nation*, Sonic Youth still go nowhere fast, but the effect is one of suspension rather than suspense. The ultra-realism of their earlier albums gives way to irrealism. Where the serrated edges of their sound were painfully distinct, now their riffs and chords undergo 'halation': the photographic term for 'the spreading of light beyond its proper boundary in a developed image'. *Daydream Nation* sees Sonic Youth poised between its early days of urgency and the urge, and its future of somnambulist nirvana. Songs like 'The Sprawl' and 'Silver Rocket' still surge but perhaps their truest moments are when the hurtling gives way to idling, when the song is breached by a caesura of wilting and incandescing guitars, a gulf of light, a mind furnace in which all delineation disappears. 'Total Trash' starts as a ponderous punk stomp almost borne under by its own mass, but ends as a mirage of itself, an after-image lost in a dubscape of unhinged resonances and infinitely receding drones.

All rock's yesteryears are spinning inside Sonic Youth's hornet's hive of sound, but there are no specific echoes, and the upshot of 'Hey Joni' is an affirmation of NOW. 'These times can't add up/Your life's such a mess/Forget the past/and just say "YES".'

With *Daydream Nation* Sonic Youth as individuals almost disappear in the ethereal chaos of their sound. But it took a British group to go one step further, to go beyond 'reinvention of the guitar' to un-invention of the guitar, to create a sound so inchoate that the last vestiges of 'presence' or 'the player' vanish. A sound seemingly without origins in the human touch. My Bloody Valentine.

WHEN YOU WAKE YOU'RE STILL IN A DREAM

Somewhere between Sonic Youth's butterflies-in-the-stomach-with razor-blade-wings feel of barbed dreaminess, the blurred radiant surge of Dinosaur Jr and Husker Du, and A.R. Kane's delicately nuanced noise. Somewhere in between but decidedly of itself lies My Bloody Valentine's noise. Their guitars are rampant, clamorous, craving, grazed, engorged, honeyed, horny, somehow extremely oral, somehow obscurely irritable. In 1988's rock pharmacopia, My Bloody Valentine classify as a deliriant and a hallucinogen — they're hyped up and out-of-it, carnal and unbodied.

'Feed Me With Your Kiss' is a brutal, off-centre slam, whose beautiful melody is almost wilfully crushed in the melee. The chorus — 'so feed. . . me. . . with. . . your. . . kiiiiiiiss' — is a languishing swoon. As always, My Bloody Valentine sound as though their desires have put them in peril. As always, they seem to have been ravished to the point of debility. 'Vampiric' was the first word that sprang into my mind, on hearing it. And, of course, the way the vampire myth works is as sexual allegory — the rush of blood away from the head, the idea that excess brings on pallor and neurasthenia, that sex makes you ill.

What My Bloody Valentine began with the *You Made Me Realise* EP, and continue on the *Feed Me* EP and the *Isn't Anything* album, is a departure from the traditional rock musculature of riff and powerchord, towards a new and private lexicon of sounds and effects — shapeless surges, swathes, precipices, vortices, wraithes and detonations. They make the guitar sound like a windscreen shattering into a jackfrost pattern, like an airborne choir of drones. 'I Believe' is an ecstatic dirge; a surge so dyslexic, its headlong rush can seem more like an immobile, suspended ache and shimmer of sound. 'All I Need', almost dispensing with a beat, is even more directionless, a whoosh and swirl from nowhere, a trembling in the air, a little nebula of daydream. What I like is that a

THE END OF ME · 121

noise often seems origin-less, you can't imagine the physical act that brought it into being, there's just an amorphous, irresistible tide of sound, a contourless radiance.

Singer/guitarist Kevin Shields explains: 'We had this idea, it sounds pretentious, but we call it "glide guitar". That's the effect you're talking about, where the sounds just seem to be there, floating around.'

Colm O'Ciosig (drums): 'We call it the "not really there sound". I've always liked the sound of something that's been copied about ten times.'

Kevin: 'The thing is, the sound literally isn't all there. It's actually the opposite of rock'n'roll. It's taking all the guts out of it, there's no guts, just the remnants, the outline. It's like — did you ever walk around in the city on a Sunday, somewhere like the East End, or the Angel — and there's this dead, where-is-everybody feel. Nobody's about, all these millions of buildings, but not a soul around. That kind of deserted feel. Not spooky, you are not made uncomfortable. But you're not comfortable either.'

Bilinda Jayne Butcher (vocals/guitar): 'It's like that bit in the middle of "You Made Me Realise", where it just levitates. You know it's there, and you know it's coming, but when it happens, half the time you forget it's on. Your mind completely wanders, you forget it, then you remember it. When you listen to it, you don't know what's going to happen, or how it's going to end, and that's because when we recorded it we didn't know what was going to happen either.'

'Instrumental', the bonus 7-inch included with *Isn't Anything*, is their most eerie departure yet. The band more or less abscond, leaving only a hip hop rhythm track over which this ectoplasm weaves in and out of silence in a mournful, private dance. It's like something by Erik Satie arranged by Keith Levene. Imagine the ghostly echo of ancient psalms drifting through an abbey in a drowned village.

My Bloody Valentine are remarkable for reconciling the two great pleasures in rock today, apparently at odds with each other: the masculine pleasure of the oppressive, spine-crushing arse-quake, and the feminine bliss of the border-dissolving, spine-melting oceanic wash. But then both are forms of surrender to sound.

Another angle to this is the way they hark back to that sixties' combination of the brutal and the fey — groups like John's Children and The Eyes, or Love and The Velvet Underground. With the Anglo freakbeat dementia of John's Children, The Eyes and The Creation, as the object of desire slips out of reach, becomes more and more hallucinated, so the desire becomes intransitive and self-consuming. On 'I Believe', the Valentines' effete 'ooooh oooooh's disappear into the music: if Mick Hucknall was to sing this sacrament of devotion, it'd be all clenched testifying from the gut and under the spotlight, an insidious show of strength, not the sound of someone weak for love.

Maybe, by their strange working methods (recording an album in two weeks, sleeping one to two hours a night) My Bloody Valentine have discovered a natural psychedelia. Maybe it accounts for the creepy feeling of disreality that inhabits some of their songs, or the sleepy sensuality of others.

Which brings us to 'Slow'. With its monstrous sex-grind of fuzzed-up bass, unearthly guitar drones and enervated vocals, 'Slow' is a smitten, kissed-out chrysalis of bliss to rival A.R. Kane. Above all, 'Slow' sounds *incestuous*. It seems to seethe with the most illicit, buried longing of all: to drown in 'flesh of my flesh'. The lyric — 'and I got no reason . . . on top of me sugar I don't know your name . . . feeling bad feeling good/feeling like I never should . . .' — seems to be about slipping outside identities, the arbitrariness of language, into a topsy-turvy, amnesiac zone. All outlines blur in what MBV call 'the chaos of desire'.

Kevin: 'You can get so hyped up, so lustful, that you're on the edge of being really dangerous. You're carried away by lust, so that you're really irrational. You're not yourself at all. You might not be happy about it after the event.'

What's sexy about 'Slow' and 'Soft As Snow (But Warm Inside)', its sequel on *Isn't Anything*, is that they're *close*. There's a humid, humming, head-spinning stupor. And there's a near-intolerable intimacy: the songs go so close to things it's hard to see them. The normal perspective that allows us to manage time and space in a business-minded, livable way, disappears. We're in such proximity to the supremely concrete stupidity of sex, there's something hallucinatory about the experience: 'too real to feel', to quote Loop. And this is the Acid experience: the moment becomes so vivid and enhanced it threatens to engulf you, suck you outside linear time. So you flicker between immersion and detachment, 'death' and survival.

Languor has been written out of modern pop. Sex in pop is all upfront, aerobic urgency, or worse, hackneyed, exhausted ciphers of bygone raunch. What's sensual about MBV, A.R. Kane and a few other renegades from pop's athletic sexuality, is their languorous, swoony voices, and the handle this gives them on the 'voluptuous infantilism' of languor, 'the gentle haemorrhage which flows from no specific point in the body' (Barthes).

Kevin: 'I'd almost forgotten about sixties' music, but then I saw this video of sixties' stuff. And what all those bands had in common was this laziness in the way they sang. Ray Davies, Syd Barrett . . . their voices just seemed to come out of their mouths, without any kind of big put-on. The opposite of Bono, that projection of passion. In this film of The Kinks, there were millions of fans, but Davies was just letting it loll out of his mouth: there was something small and intimate about it, but something huge because of the audience's screaming. Or someone like Roger Daltrey, who started out all sloppy and untutored, but then he learnt to sing, and he got bombastic: 'Look at me, I'm using my voice . . .' A real seventies' thing, a kind of muso attitude to the voice, putting on a real performance.'

Bilinda: 'Often, when we do the vocals, it's 7.30 in the morning, I've usually fallen asleep and have to be woken up to sing. Maybe that's why it's languorous. Just got out of bed vocals! I'm usually trying to remember what I've been dreaming about, when I'm singing.'

Kevin: 'We're all heavily into sleep. One of the things that always amazes me is when people complain: you woke me up last night. I love being woken up prematurely, 'cos then you have the fun of falling asleep again.'

Maybe My Bloody Valentine's urge to savage and smother the loveliness of their melody and harmony lines is linked to the image on the cover of *You Made Me Realise*— the child-woman holding a blade against her neck. Maybe beauty is felt more keenly when it's faced by the threat of being marred or destroyed. Maybe that's why you can sometimes be possessed by the morbid impulse to think about accidents or horrors befalling loved ones, in order to enjoy each sharp spasm of anguished empathy.

Why did they choose that image of the girl with the knife?

Kevin: 'That picture was glamorous, but it wasn't something that anyone could get a sexual kick from, or at least be relaxed about enjoying on that level. In a way, the music's like that . . .'

The way you lacerate the soft, sweet melodies . . .

'It wouldn't be interesting otherwise. The whole suicide theme had a point to it, at the time: there was a lot of chaos around us. But we could never stand onstage and sing about 'suicide' with any personal knowledge. We only use the word in two songs. That song 'Sue Is Fine' — well, actually, I'm singing 'suicide' . . . It's a real pleading for attention song. The music has this jumbled up, wanting wanting wanting, gimme gimme gimme, I need it feel: it's about not knowing what you want, but wanting it desperately.'

And 'suicide' here is more a case of being brought to 'the end of me' by the chaos of unnameable, unrequitable desires.

Another preocupation is ambiguity or contradiction, the oxymoronic quality of the profoundest feelings in life: the violence of sweetness, the capacity of beauty to do damage, the hair's breadth double-edge between love and hate. The name My Bloody Valentine, and songs like 'Thorn', 'Cigarette in Your Bed' and 'Strawberry Wine' all bear this out.

Kevin: ' "Thorn" is just this idea of roses being the ultimate image of delectability, but when you reach out to grab the loveliness you get cut up. "Strawberry Wine" is a real drink – very sweet, but with a real whisky bang to it. So the song is about something that's sweet but heavy. Intoxicating, which literally means poisonous. It's about how I used to wander up and down this street where this girl lived, who I was obsessed with: my head was full of dreams of her, but all the time the reality of the situation was me tramping up and down this dirty, miserable street.

' "Cigarette in Your Bed" is a kind of play on words. You could have the stereotypical, post-coital smoke. But if you actually put a cigarette in someone's bed when they're asleep, then they're burnt alive. It's about being so close to someone, but not a very nice close. So you get a line like "scratching your eyes out/with a smile", where the other person just isn't aware of the negativity beneath the surface.'

There's a certain kind of vocal pallor that's the mark of someone who's never lived, someone jejeune: there's another kind of ashen voice that's the mark of someone who's come very close to being extinguished, who's lived to the limits of life. There are empty voices (the dinky, dainty power pop voice of The Primitives, Darling Buds, etc, ad nauseam). And there are emptied voices, drained by an access of bliss or dread. Spent ('to spend' used to mean 'to come' in Victorian slang. Now it means used up, ruined). Think of Alex from A.R. Kane, John Cale's *Music for a New Society*.

Bilinda Jayne Butcher's ballads — 'Cigarette in Your Bed', 'No More Sorry', 'Lose My Breath' — mark an outer limit in avant-rock's retreat from the vivacious, full-bodied voice. More death-warmed-up than even Kim Gordon of Sonic Youth. Bilinda's sufferings seem to have brought her to a stranded, bleached-out consciousness. Her burnt-out torch songs are set, to hugely foreboding effect, against a massive wall of acoustic sound.

' "No More Sorry" is about being used and defiled by someone, but knowing that you're all right. It's about something that happened to me, but it's not meant to be self-pitying. It's not really a pop song, or something you'd even want to listen to. It's about taking too much and not wanting to take any more. "Lose My Breath" — when I wrote that I wasn't very well, I had this migraine, and kept wanting to go to sleep. That might have something to do with the atmosphere of the song. Partly, it's about the fact that I can't breathe properly. When I'm in a state, I can't breathe or sing properly. But the other side is that my little boy Toby's got asthma. It's about my feelings about him, him being upset and not being able to cope with it, or understand.'

For My Bloody Valentine, bliss comes with the loss of agency and autonomy, (with all its incumbent anxieties of self-administration). Whether it's succumbing to the uncontrol of desire ('Slow'), offering yourself up on the altar of devotion ('I believe' pleads 'take me, take me, take me'), or sliding into the oblivion of sleep, what they look for is the moment when power slips out of their hands. Here's the female Valentines on the only experiences that have affected them as much as their music.

Debbie (bass): 'Fever. You feel as if your body's drifting, as if you're not there. Your body acts of its own accord.'

Bilinda: 'Giving birth. It happened on a motorway, when I kept being caught in snowdrifts. I was in labour while I was driving. What was it like? Horrible but ecstatic.'

CODA
The ghost of rock. The ghost town. The re-invention of the guitar. The disappearance of the player. Evanescence. Neurasthenia. Drift. Dyslexia. Somnambulism. Astigmatism. Amnesia. Absence Without Leave. Absent minds.

This is the Daydream Nation.

(1989)

oceanic rock

ROAD TO NOWHERE

If only one thing has become clear during the confused eighties, it's that rock is on the ROAD TO NOWHERE. Its Master Narrative of progress, its impulse to change the world, has petered to a standstill: all that remains of the legacy of good intentions are facile common denominator platitudes or a welter of hopelessly marginalized micro-initiatives. Gestures too broad or too local, too inclusive or too excluded, to be anything but impotent.

But there's another, less pejorative sense in which rock has become a ROAD TO NOWHERE. The forms of rock are reaching their ultimate limits just as rock's 'content' or 'use value' is withering. So bands as various as Pixies, Sonic Youth, Front 242, are about speed without trajectory, a kind of fixated acceleration. Other groups — and this is where 'oceanic' rock comes in — ascend or abscond to a no-place beyond this 'world': that's to say, outside the closed circuit of language/power.

In the late eighties, the bravest departures in rock weren't 'timely' or 'topical', didn't seize an opportune moment at all. As the decade of *The Face, Smash Hits* and the ceaseless procession of the new and urgent reached its twilight, a dissenting current made itself heard. This rock was about wanting to leave the eighties. What I've dubbed the 'oceanic' rock of the likes of A.R. Kane, Hugo Largo, or the Cocteau Twins is time-less and place-less. And, unlike some of the other consciousness-altering or heightening musics of the eighties, it's a beatific disorientation and amnesia. What this music yearns for is a gentle apocalypse (an end of history and an end of geography).

'Oceanic' is an arbitrary adjective, in many ways: 'cosmic', 'aerial', 'celestial' all have their claims. The common denominator that invites and unites this imagery is that this music is attracted to expanses (the sky, the sea, the desert, the tundra) in which self-consciousness evaporates as the borders of the self dissolve. Deep space, free fall, and the subaquatic are all mediums in which the normal rules of gravity are suspended. 'Oceanic' rock, apart from getting away from the turbulences and tantrums of pop's onward march of history, wants to liberate itself from the confines of the self, time, and the 'real' world. This rock is an attempt to rediscover lost innocence and peace. It's hypnotic, or narcotic, a fall back into the bliss-ful continuum of unconsciousness.

DREAMPOP

A.R. Kane appeared, out of nowhere, in early '87, with the single 'When You're Sad'. The initial impression was of a black Jesus and Mary Chain. But A.R. Kane claimed to be ignorant of the indie noise aesthetic, and cited the Miles Davis of *Bitches Brew* and *In a Silent Way* as their only influence: they picked up guitars only because they were the easiest and cheapest implements to make noise with. Certainly, 'When You're Sad' was less a wall of noise, more a hanging garden. 'Haunted', the B-side, was more spell-binding still, shimmering like the sun-sparks beneath half-closed eyelashes on a summer's day.

A few months later, and A.R. Kane were on 4AD, in many ways their spiritual home, with a new EP, *Lollita*, produced by Robin Guthrie of the Cocteau Twins (a group for whom they'd expressed admiration). The title track is a gorgeous haze that slowly enfolds the body, turning your nerves to frost; a lullaby split apart at the seams by a column of noise, a crystal spire veering up into the heavens. 'Sadomasochism is a Must' opens like a sandstorm on Venus, then turns into a jagged, poisoned ballad, each chord lash showering you with shards of amethyst. 'Butterfly Collector' is an icy thrash, culminating in total white-out, a saturated overload of splintered signals.

In interview A.R. Kane began to elaborate ideas that a year later they were to sully with the crassness of a slogan: 'DREAMPOP'. For singer Alex their ambition was that people 'would have dreams in which our music was the soundtrack'. His partner Rudi claimed: 'A lot of the time we're trying to transform dream imagery into sounds, which is hard to do.'

After their unsatisfactory liaison with Colourbox (the M.A.R.R.S. project, which produced a club sensation and number one chart smash with 'Pump Up The Volume'), A.R. Kane left 4AD in a cloud of acrimony. Their next record, the *Up Home!* EP, came out on Rough Trade in April 1988, and was the apotheosis of their initial ideas. *Up Home!* is the slow supernova of rock; not its burn-up in velocity, rather the supercession of riffs and even chords by a shapeless radiance of sound seemingly without origin, conceivably without end. It is rock's ice age, its Antarctica, its final petrifying spell. A sound like the chiming of a million icicles. Alex and Rudi seemed to be playing not guitars but stalactites and stalagmites. 'Baby Milk Snatchers' is a dub-cratered landscape seen from outer space. 'WOGS' is a vortex of refractions, an overload of colours cancelling each other out in a dazzling white-out. 'One Way Mirror' is almost dancey, but for the near unbearable magnesium radiance of the sound. 'Up' has an intolerably lovely melody that slowly, slowly climbs an endless, spiral 'stairway to heaven', while all around the ice cathedral resonates like a giant bell. But for all the pop lusciousness of the melodies, it isn't the songs you attend to, but the myriad harmonic refractions that soar, wilt and converge in their cloud nebula of sound.

The *Up Home!* EP took A.R. Kane's ice-floe fission to its zenith. With the LP 69 they stepped back from the full drench to locate a new sense of empty expanse, limpid and indistinct.

On 69, A.R. Kane were finding unprecedented connections between jazz, dub, acid rock, Sonic Youth-style 'reinvention of the guitar', the Cocteau Twins of *Head Over Heels*... A.R. Kane tap into our sixth sense of another realm of things aching beneath the skin of doldrum reality, something glimpsed only in those moments when the world is cracked. They take the radiance of those moments and make of them another world. 69 is a world you could wander in for centuries. It's a world where sound has different properties and obeys different laws. Everything in this music either levitates or swoons; nothing is level or even-keeled. This lack of conventional orientation is most apparent on 'Sulliday', a grotto whose acoustics are uncanny, nonsensical; it's a piece that should be listened to not as a musical or lyrical sequence but as a succession of moments. It's demanding only in the sense that you have to forget to 'read', be supine before it, let yourself be conquered in the carwash aluminium.

But 69 is no muso affair; all the songs except 'Sulliday' work as exquisite pop. Instead of hooks, though, there are 'slides and slips', swooning cadences signifying pangs or shifts between altered states. I would say that the record is deeply moving, except that what A.R. Kane are 'about' is the immobility of rapture. For them, each spasm of the gaze is a step out of time. They are petrified by beauty. Alex's voice is crucial here. He's a 'weak' singer, but one of my favourite voices. Precious, stoned, he seems always on the brink of nodding out or off, succumbing to an amnesiac numbness, beauty-as-narcotic.

THE END OF ME · 129

Sometimes you're reminded of the lazy carnality of John Martyn or Arthur Russell. It's not the pop of desires and drives, but a pop of diffused eroticism, a flux of infant sexuality, oral rather than genital. Listening, you think of bliss babies cradled in a carnal cave, a cocoon of certainty incarnate. The title 69 itself was a big clue. At first, it seemed like a reference to the year: Miles well into his submarine idyll phase, Jimi still dreaming of turning into a merman. But the album cover — mermaids making love — made it clear that they really were alluding to soixante-neuf. Why? Because it's a perfect image of mutuality, of two individuals joined in a Möbius strip of polymorphous pleasure. Sex without thrust, roleplay (active/passive), even narrative (almost an abolition of time).

But the bulk of 69 is chaster, more bodiless, than this: it's about bliss as neurasthenia, 'dizzy/like when the blood runs out'. Where most pop is about fevered fleshiness, exertion, the solid earthiness of need, A.R. Kane songs are about the vertigo of rapture, the (free) fall into love. The whole album seems to take place under conditions where normal respiration is interfered with, from the hyperventilated screams that backdrop 'Dizzy', to 'The Sun Falls Into the Sea', where the line 'I can see your breath/like cirrus' is exhaled as though crushed from the body under the duress of wonder.

'The Sun Falls Into the Sea' is just incomparable: a mermaid lullaby not so much 'accompanied' as almost drowned out by a sound like an immense quartz harp the size of a whale's ribcage, from which harmonics disperse and scatter as haywire as sunlight refracting under the ocean surface. It's not the notes played, but the untranscribable opalescence of the *stuff* of this sound that's so unbearably lovely.

'The Madonna is with Child' is another subaquatic archipelago of bliss, and gives a clue to what A.R. Kane are about. Their poignancy comes from the way they recreate momentarily something irretrievably lost: the infant's or even unborn child's oceanic oneness with the world. Poignant because we relive and mourn simultaneously. 'You said we gonna breathe together/Sleep forever.'

There are two obsessions that limn 69. The ocean — where normal laws of gravity, acoustics and breathing are eluded. And sleep — the mesmerized 'sleep' of beauty, certainly, but above all, the waking sleep of innocence, where every moment is liberated from the grid of adult forward planning, experienced full because free of traces of past and future anxiety. Where these obsessions converge is in the womb. Some people believe our very ideas of heaven stem from unconscious memories of bliss suspended in the amniotic, long before alienation constituted us as an individual and separate 'I'.

MOTHER TONGUE, MOTHER'S SONG

A few months after the release of 69, the Cocteau Twins returned after a two-year silence with the perfect lustrous surfaces of their *Blue Bell Knoll* LP. No 'progression' here, of course, but they reappeared in pop at the very moment when their wordless siren-songs were vindicated, sounded less an anomaly than ever before. The Cocteaus crystallize something that 'oceanic' rock always ends up compared with, the lullaby. The baby-talk nonsense of their song titles and Liz Fraser's vocals, which do without any hard consonants or fricatives, are all labial, take us back to the earliest love affair of all, that of mother and child. The Cocteaus are like a mother's song, all succour and softness, closeness without having to say anything at all.

The Cocteau Twins are the pop counterpart of the French writer Hélène Cixous's notion of '*écriture feminine*': poetry that echoes 'the first voice of love. . . a song before the Law, before the breath was split by the symbolic, reappropriated into language under the authority that separates.' Like A.R. Kane, they imagine song that comes before language or grammar. There's just the fluid, uninterrupted exchange between mother and child that's only lost when the father and the real world interrupt it.

For Cixous, *écriture feminine* has access to a time before time, a pre-Oedipal 'space' before the infant even has a concept of spatiality, of a distance between itself and the world. 'Voice: exhaustible milk. She has been found again. The lost mother. Eternity: it is the voice mixed with milk.'

Where the Cocteau Twins' music is by and large unambiguously halcyon, A.R. Kane have a more problematic relation with the maternal idyll they reinvoke. There are violent undercurrents, hints of misogyny, intimations of the tragic, and always a sense of the elegaic, or paradise lost rather than regained. After 69, came the *Love-Sick* EP, a record which resumed a theme first broached with *Lollita*: the pain and rage that comes from being separated from the world and having our desires bounded, vested in the single object of love.

The *Lollita* EP follows the course by which desire undoes itself, pursues the phantasm of possession to the point of madness, Mutually Assured Destruction. 'Lollita' is the idyll — 'love to go down and kiss your curl', 'when I touch your skin/something spins within', 'when I kiss your lips/Oooooh my head/Slides and slips'. But already there's the incongruous appearance of the word 'bitch', a hint of what is to come. By 'Sadomasochism', the desire for total absorption of or by the Other has degenerated into perversion. And with 'Butterfly Collector' the dread of losing the loved one (to the outside world, to time) has blossomed in psychosis: 'I'm gonna pin you down/I'm gonna keep you/I'm gonna kill you.'

What 'Butterfly Collector' implies is that violence is intrinsic to the very process of idealization itself. The living flux of a being is frozen into a series of static, consecrated images. When the flawed, fickle, changing reality of the loved one starts to play truant from the image — that's our first taste of grief, our first intimation of loss, of Death. Or rather, it's the reenactment of our first loss — our exile from the maternal haven.

The beloved is a glimpse of heaven-on-earth, a paradise that's always already lost. This maternal haven is 'atopia', a no-place before the infant has any awareness of time or of space, or of a gap between desire and its fulfilment. Properly speaking, this phase is prior to desire: the infant is not a subject yet, has not formed relations with objects, no objects have yet come to stand in for its undifferentiated longing. Desire always involves an element of desperation, the anxiety that inhabits the interval between wish and fulfilment; the infant has none of that, rather enjoys a limitless plenitude, in which nourishment, nurture and eroticism are indivisible at the nipple. This perhaps is the origin of the idea of nirvana (Buddhism's ideal state of 'consciousness', the beatitude that comes with the extinction of individuality and desires): it is also probably the source of the longing that spurs on all utopian thinkers. Moreover, this same ache, left by the memory of that 'deepest, most ancient and adorable of visitations' (Cixous), is what we call 'the heart'. The loved one is a fetish, a part that stands in for the whole (for the lost possibility of being whole). The beloved fills the wound that is the heart, but never fills it completely. The ache continues, even in the extremity of 'possession', a reminder that the loved one is always already lost, and that ache is what we call poignancy.

PARADISE LOST

Something about 69 reminds me of Van Morrison's *Astral Weeks* — the child-woman fixations, the tongue-tied murmur, the scat-nonsense whose alliteration and assonance skirt the edges of the 'more than can be said', the images of sky-gardens all wet with angels' tears. 69 is a coral reef bower, an arbour in a subaqua Arcadia.

The garden metaphor cropped up again later in '88 with Talk Talk's *Spirit of Eden*. Talk Talk first surfaced as nondescript latecomers to the 'new pop' spree of the early eighties. A few years later, *The Colour of Spring* hinted at an unsuspected ethereal potential. But *Spirit of Eden* was something else again: a pellucid, meditational, uninterrupted suite of songs, whose influences were clearly the liquid blues of John Martyn's *Solid Air*, Miles Davis's *Sketches of Spain* and *In a Silent Way*, the broken eddying folk of Roy Harper's *Stormcock*, and the aquiline, empty soundscapes of ECM's neo-jazz. Like its cover art of a drowned world in which there's just one tree left above the waters, its branches hung with marine and birdlife alike, it's a lament for paradise lost and an attempt to conjure the 'spirit of Eden' again in this 'world turned upside down'.

Talk Talk weren't alone in their quest for an oasis of serenity apart from the soiling crush of urban life. In New York alone there was Saqqara Dogs and Hugo Largo. On their *World Crunch* and *Thirst* albums, Saqqara Dogs fused primitive percussion and 'cosmic' guitar to create an ecstatic trance-rock that at times recalled Pink Floyd's *Ummagumma*. A decade earlier, guitarist Bond Bergland had been involved in the 'industrial' aesthetic with his band Factrix. 'A lot of people are still caught up in that, seven or eight years on. Noise is our natural state, sure, but to attain the supernatural state we have to go above and beyond noise, we need a new geometry and a new harmony. To reproduce that noise is reportage, journalism. And the difference between journalism and music is that music is alchemy, turning lead into gold, noise into harmony. What happens with Saqqara Dogs is that the claustrophobia and dirt of the city drives us into these open spaces. The city gives us its energy, but we go somewhere else with it.'

Hugo Largo too began as a reaction to the New York hardcore aesthetic. They distanced themselves immediately by the simple premise of abandoning drums and the driving backbeat. Where most pop proceeds, Hugo Largo songs unfurl, unwind. Their music is all veils and skeins of sound with nothing behind them. These faltering bass lines and white vapour trails of electric guitar or violin are another glimpse over the brink of being itself. On their first LP, *Drum* there are two consummate metaphors for their upsets of gravity, time, place, and (sexual) identity. Either a free fall through the sky, as if weightless in an ocean of ozone, or release from the body itself, purification by self-laceration or a plunge into oblivion, 'taking off that noisy head'.

Like so much 'oceanic' rock, it's alluring or gleefully childish AND permeated with melancholy and awe. It's irresistibly drawn to, and fearful of, letting boundaries dissolve. 'Such a struggle to unwind/Stop thinking so loud/Must be some way to give in . . .' ('So Serene'). Their music leaves you quelled and becalmed, dazed and defused, until 'you're ashamed to move'. In these cradling strings and this stratospheric cloud-chamber of light, we can be anybody or nobody, anywhere or nowhere, all at once. This is nirvana, again. It's as inconceivable as 'thinking someone else's thoughts', as they put it in 'Turtle Song'.

Their second album *Mettle* continued the obsession with drifting off. Hugo Largo music is like being taken to the brink of unconsciousness and held there. For it's only at this brink, that you reach any kind of total apprehension of 'now'. So 'Hot Day', with its heat-haze miasma of strings, is about a hiatus in the schedules of productive life: it conjures up a humid stupor in which edges blur and self-possession evaporates. 'Halfway Knowing', with its braid of indefinites and qualifications, is about being unable to make up your mind, invent yourself as any one. Hugo Largo know that to finish a sentence is to pass (death) sentence on the living world.

Singer and lyricist Mimi Goese talked of the inspiration she drew from sleep: 'I often get ideas or images just as I'm falling asleep. Someone told me that women especially are more creative around three o'clock in the morning. I don't know if it's generally true, but it does seem to apply to me. And I love dreams to death, I always try in vain to dredge up the debris and reconstruct it.'

Another of Mimi's obsessions was the ease that children and animals seem to possess: self-possession without the crippling effect of self-awareness ('children don't have so many thoughts in their head'). A state of heightened consciousness (through diminished self-consciousness), where things are so wonderfully enhanced and vivid they appear dreamlike and unreal. A state of grace, a transfiguration of the banal, to which only the child, the mystic, the psychedelic, has ready access.

Vini Reilly of the Durutti Column is such a truant from reality. A strange eating disorder has given him access to the kind of visions that holy men achieve through fasting. A Durutti Column song is a sargasso sky, a skein of sound as delicate and intricate as jackfrost, as fleeting and prismatic as dew. Each song is like those imaginary realms you dream, as a child, in cloud canopies irradiated by the setting sun, each one unique, each one mortal. Above all, this is religious music, an exaltation and a requiem to the passing beauty of the Moment.

INTIMATE IMMENSITY

Durutti Column have been doing much the same thing for over a decade now. With 1989's *Vini Reilly* album, the Durutti aesthetic seemed never more timeless yet more in synch with the times. As such, *Vini Reilly* has a profound affinity with the visionary ECM label. For twenty years ECM has been in search of 'the most beautiful sound next to silence'. Its diverse fusions of jazz, folk, Eastern musics and rock, share an uncommon spaciousness and a lambent, meditational aura. Reilly's playing recalls ECM artists like John Abercrombie and Ralph Towner, and their irradiated warp and weft of acoustic guitars, or Jan Garbarek's tundra-at-dawn watercolours.

ECM have a handle on what the French philosopher Gaston Bachelard calls 'intimate immensity'. A sense of benign space; space that isn't demarcated or geographically structured, space that hasn't yet been traversed by human relations; space that is wombing. In other words, the atopia of the uterine idyll, before the infant has any conception of space and time, or of a border between inside and outside. Earlier in the eighties, a group called Meat Puppets drew inspiration from the Arizona desert to create a psychedelic country rock with similar preoccupations. Their songs are about being overwhelmed by the immensity of nature or the weather, about the borders between the self and the world being effaced, until: 'I can't see/the end of me/my own expanse/I cannot see.' About the shock of the fact that 'We're Here'.

And Manchester's Blue Orchids, acid-freak refugees from The Fall, had sung of 'spending a year with no head', of 'feeling the flesh of the breeze', of how 'the only way out is UP'.

THIS-NESS

'We want people to look at music in a new way, not just as a blasé thing that's just there in the background. It should be like when you see a tree and suddenly it's as though you see it for the first time. You've lived with trees for twenty-five years or whatever and it's got so you don't see them, and suddenly you think: "Amazing!" Biggest shock of your life, when that kind of thing happens. I think music can help you see things freshly and can make you want to experience everything like that, as though you'd just been born.' — Alex, A.R. Kane.

In any given day, there occur maybe a hundred, maybe a thousand, moments when you could be deflected from the beaten track of your life, and be mesmerized by the SHOCK OF THE HERE AND NOW, the arbitrary this-ness of a thing or person or sensation. It's a wonder anyone gets anything done. So in order to function as social, productive beings, wonder has to be marginalized, brutally expunged from our experience. The 'divine intoxication of the moment', the child's response to the world, must be subordinated to forward planning and the logic of survival. The bands I've talked about here are visionaries who liberate the flux of experience from the grids with which we attempt to structure and manage time and reality.

'Whoever wrote the calendar was wrong/It's New Year's all year long' — Meat Puppets.

'We are not subtle enough to perceive the probably absolute flow of becoming; the permanent exists only thanks to our coarse organs which reduce and lead things to shared premises of vulgarity, whereas nothing exists in this form. A tree is a new thing at every instant; we affirm the form because we do not seize the subtlety of an absolute moment' — Nietzsche.

ANTI-SYSTEMS MUSIC

'Our music's like sculpture — there's this chaos that we chip away at until there's this beautiful shape. We love chaos, you can lose yourself in it. That's why so many people hate chaos and won't let it in. It's too vast, you can't tie it down' — Alex, A.R. Kane.

There's two impulses in rock today. One is to make systems; the other is to dissolve them. One is to bolster the self and its mastery over the world; the other is to dissipate 'I', blur the borders between the self and the world. On one side, clenched-arse agit-pop didacticism; 'punkies' like Age of Chance and Pop Will Eat Itself, with their lippy attitude, their triumph of rhetoric over both form and content; hip hop's tyrannical amplification of the self. Everybody eager to tell it like it is.

On the other side, groups like A.R. Kane, Meat Puppets, Cocteaus, Hugo Largo, suspicious of words, reluctant to spell it out, eager to be spellbound, to succumb to oceanic feelings, to go with the flow.

Two different universes: one logocentric, a world of rigid definitions; the other world, one of ambiguity, contradictions, indefinites, an infinite recession of nuances.

Two different politics of sound: one starkly produced (lots of definition) with 'in your face' vocals and a premium on clear diction; the other an illegible blur, with the voice smudged and submerged in the mix.

It's all crystallized in that line from 'Lollita' that goes: 'Oooh my head/slides and slips.' Maybe that is the thrill, that moment of teetering on the brink of oblivion, of the little death that is complete immersion in the Other.

(with thanks to PAUL OLDFIELD)

(1989)

heaven's end

Loop: Black Mysticism of Transcendental Collapse

An idle glance at Loop, and you could be forgiven for taking them to be period fetishists pure and simple, hung up on the Detroit '69 sound of The Stooges and MC5. Certainly the long hair and wah wah indicate both allegiance and indebtedness.

Loop aren't alone in this. The Stooges' debut album and its sequel *Funhouse* (regarded by some as the best rock'n'roll album of all time) remain sacred rock texts — their vision of the rock'n'roll essence as dis-inhibition attained via the cretinous and cretinizing effects of repetition, noise, and self-abasement, is one that has been subject to innumerable and widely divergent interpretations. The Sex Pistols, Black Flag, The Birthday Party and Pixies are just some of the more notable items of shrapnel in twenty years fallout.

The Birthday Party's bacchanalian seizures and Loop's seized-up mantras represent the two extremes of The Stooges' legacy. If Nick Cave took Iggy's chaotic exhibitionism and hammed it up to the limit, Loop work from the Stooges' more downered, inhibited side. Loop take the desperation of the first Stooges' album, abstract it from the specific teen kicks and aggravations that fired it, and turn it into an inchoate cosmic howl.

Ron Asheton's downered, barbiturate blues is abased even further, into a piteous, infantile wail, wah-wah as primal scream. Sometimes the guitar in Loop is an endless sub-blues solo, stunted rather than expansive. The Stooges' ballad 'Anne' could almost be the Loop prototype, with its limpid stupor and strange inertia of love. 'Anne' is a vision of love as narcosis, as capitulation: 'You took my arm/And you broke my will . . . I floated in your swimming pools/I felt so weak/I felt blue.'

But there's more, much more, to Loop than a Stooges fixation. What Loop are about is making connections between various apocalyptic moments in rock history — 1969 and Iggy's vision of 'war across the USA', the hippie dream turning to bad trip with Manson, Altamont, Vietnam; 1979 and the angst-rock and dread disco of PIL, Joy Division and The Pop Group (a cover of the latter's 'Thief of Fire' was Loop's finest moment in 1988); the paranoiac dub of the Tackhead/Mark Stewart axis. They do this not simply for the purely academic sake of joining the dots, but as a search for ultimate intensity. Loop are the colossal aggregate of the peaks of a past they surpass even as they pay tribute.

And Loop are also making links between different manifestations of trance-rock — the Krautrock experimentalism of Can, Faust and Neu, avant-classical composers like Glenn Branca and Steve Reich, Adrian Sherwood's dub odysseys, even ECM's meditational jazz.

Where apocalypse and repetition join up is that both are different routes to oblivion. Whether your mind is overwhelmed by TOO MUCH, or evacuated by focusing on too little, what happens is a kind of fall, outside linear thought and language. Loop manage to fuse together the sensory overload of apocalypse and the sensory deprivation of the mantra. Two of their favourite films, in fact, are *Apocalypse Now* (a journey through a land of fire in search of the heart of darkness) and *Altered States* (about a scientist who uses hallucinogenics and an isolation chamber in order to regress to a primal state of unbeing).

Singer Robert explains their repetition complex: 'Repetition is very much a form of psychological music. And acid's a very psychological drug. A lot of our stuff is based on the more nightmarish experiences in life. Not necessarily bad trip experiences, 'cos you can have a bummer trip whether you're on acid or not. Everyone's got their own personal phobias, stuff that really gets them. It's been said that taking acid is the closest you can come to schizophrenia. But how do the doctors know? How can you find out what being mad is like?'

Some psychanalysts see schizophrenia as a kind of language disorder, in that identity — one's sense of continuity extending from past into future — is an effect of language, of syntax. The schizoid experience is said to involve a loss of memory, and a blindness to the future. The schizophrenic lives in a perpetual present tense, which is vivid to an unbearable degree; the doors of perception are open wide to the insupportable dazzle of the Moment, whereas normal people always have some kind of focus (their minds partially occupied by forward planning or retrospection).

The parallels with acid are obvious: what for some is a highly sought after 'trip' (timeless, beyond words, transcendental) is for the schizophrenic a living hell of exile from language and any sense of purposeful continuity. Reality can no longer be interpreted, managed by being made meaningful; instead its materiality is overwhelmingly intense. But this effect is felt as a numbing loss of reality — as a Loop song puts it, 'Too Real to Feel'.

And this is one of the effects of repetition in music — a heightened awareness of the Moment, a complete immersion in NOW, which is both alluring and threatening.

Loop are part of a reaction against the hegemonic notion that rock is all about narrative — both small (the song as story) and large (rock as the Way Forward to a better world). Their name locks into a different strand in history — the repetition axis — and a different idea of what music is for: rock as a (locked) groove that takes us nowhere (to a utopia, literally no-place, outside language).

Loop have the most perfect, ultimate song titles around — 'This is Where You End', 'Fade Out', 'Fix to Fall', 'Heaven's End', 'Burning World'. Looking at the imagery, there's a preponderance of negatives — imagery of annihilation, immolation, terminal experiences, apocalypse, falling . . .

'But falling can be a totally orgasmic experience,' counters Robert. 'If I could get over my phobia, more than anything else I'd love to freefall out of a plane. I reckon that must be the most free you can ever be, and it must be overwhelming.'

That seems to be a big clue to what Loop are about — either an excess or an absence of gravity, either way a loss of orientation. And the effect of that topsy-turviness, and the unrelenting repetition, can only be described as *stultifying*. In the best possible sense. It seems that the most intelligent thing music can do is to reduce, or perhaps elevate, the listener to a state of holy stupor.

John (drums): 'Emptied is what I feel when I'm playing.'

Robert: 'It's like those old Tibetian geezers who chant the same thing over and over again. You see there's a romantic beauty about death. A lot of people are scared of death but I'm not. I'd hate to die a violent death, but to slowly slip into whatever death entails . . .'

What does it mean to talk about 'death' in this context? It's a metaphor, sure, but one with more than a grain of psychoanalytic truth. Listening to Loop you feel wombed (or is it entombed?). This is regressive rock, in a very literal sense. But

Loop don't evoke the mother-of-pearl, lambent glow of A.R. Kane's amniotic utopia. Loop are a darker, more shuddery backwards fall through the mesh of language, the circuitry of power by which we administer ourselves as productive adults, back back into the primal abjection from which we're shaped. Loop are immense but primitive. If U2 are rock as clarion call of the super ego, Loop are rock as siren song of the Id.

In 1988 Loop released the *Black Sun* EP. As a title, 'Black Sun' was perfect, too perfect. Loop's sound is the gravity's rainbow cast by a black hole — it's just that it's not a star that's collapsed under its own critical mass, but rock itself. Loop music consists of infinite refractions of black, it's a contoured void: ridges and troughs of moribund sound, like the sastrugi of deep space (sastrugi are the wave patterns left in Siberian snow by the wind). *Black Sun* says it all: Loop are an inferno that emits no light, a pyre for 'the end of me'. Catch me in the right frame of mindlessness, and I can think of no greater liberation than to be mired in the entropy of their endless end, sucked under and eclipsed.

Where did the image of the Black Sun come from?

Robert: 'The Black Sun is the heart of darkness. It's a heart. Anytime anyone talks about the heart, you have this radiant image. But to me, there's this very, very dark side to it. They say "follow your heart", but your heart can take you to the most dismal places ever. *Black Sun* is about the darker side of love for someone, where it's almost schizophrenic. One minute you feel totally radiant with the thought of someone, the next you feel very destructive to that person.'

'Follow your heart' means put yourself in thrall to stupidity, which can be glorious, or indecently asinine, like contemplating suicide when a phone call doesn't materialize. But *Black Sun* doesn't refer to black holes or anything astrophysical?

'In a way, yeah, 'cos a heart can collapse in on itself, your true feelings can disintegrate. You explode into violence, or implode into self-destruction.'

But on the second side of the EP there's an even more definitive title. 'Circle Grave', an a-rythmic mosaic of drones and resonances, provides the most perfect explication of the Loop method: they excavate the same groove, deeper and deeper, until you are entombed in a kind of living end.

For some fans, all this will have been too clinical. But maybe the only tone humble enough is that of an autopsy, an inquest into 'the end of me'. And believe me, they did it, Loop sank a vast crater in the fabric of this paltry discourse. I fell. I was void.

THE YOUNG GODS: L'AMOURIR

The Young Gods emerged from Zurich in 1987 with the best rock'n'roll name ever, and a concept: 'New Sonic Architecture'. They were the first, and, so far, the only rock group to grasp the potential of sampling, and to use it as more than a cosmetic effect. At first glance, the music appears to be magnificent, aggressive rock. Look closer and it's apparent that this 'rock' is constructed entirely from abstracted and reprocessed material — punk and metal riffs, classical bombast (flourishes from as far apart as Mozart and Varese), found and created environmental sounds (what they call 'urban sonorities'). The reconstruction of these elements as accessible and ravishing rock music is a process that brings into play Cesare Pizzi's experience as a computer programmer at Reuters, and singer Franz Treichler's conservatory training in classical guitar. The Young Gods combine rock dynamics with hip hop's unstable sense of space, use avant-garde tonality and texture within an abstract, intimidating version of pop melodrama. The result is somewhere between the musique concrete of Stockhausen and Pierre Henry and the bacchanalian insurgency of The Stooges.

There are two approaches to the mountainous debris of pop history. The playful plagiarism of the Transvision Vamp school, a 'mischievous' reshuffling of historically over-determined sounds and images. And there's what The Young Gods do: not forgery, but the forging of new compounds in the crucible of the new sampling technology. What's exciting about them is that they render impossible any forensic tracing of the origins of their noises; like A.R. Kane they imply impossible, exotic instruments. Unforeseen sounds that force the imagination to produce new mental pictures, rather than invite it to read off hackneyed, received imagery.

Franz: 'I've seen people perform who've given me such a feeling of power and joy, just by witnessing them put everything on the table. I hope we give this to people, this kaleidoscope of dazzling things, that sometimes nails you to the floor, sometimes lifts you up there. It's a celebration of life. If it sometimes disturbs, that's because it celebrates everything, not only the "I love you", "Let's have some fun" side, but also the losses, the violence . . .'

The Young Gods are a devastatingly perfect accommodation between the primitive and the futuristic: the sensual extremism of The Birthday Party or Einsturzende Neubauten (impulses to exceed the environment and the body that break loose, through desperation, in the form of vandalism or self-mutilation) enhanced and amplified by the digital necromancy of sampling. Rock'n'roll has always been about using technology to liberate savagery, about the anti-technocratic détournement of technology. The Young Gods are opening up a new frontier of pagan modernism, a new stage in the interface between the bestial and the mechanical.

The debut album, *The Young Gods* (1987) was like being engulfed. Like being cast into a maze of nightmarish Escher perspectives, where sounds no longer conform to the norms of proportion or the laws of acoustics. It was an eclipse of the mind's eye, a giant shadow passing over the soul. With 1988's *L'Amourir* The Young Gods displaced 'atmosphere' in favour of attack. The sound was stripped, condensed and converged towards a single point of impact. Instead of being enveloped, it's more like being impaled, bored through.

The title 'L'Amourir' is a play on words that condenses *l'amour* (love) and *mourir* (to die) into a single neologism. Franz: 'The two songs "L'Amourir" and "Pas Mal" go together. We're not going to have an A-side and a B-side. "L'Amourir" will be called "Face à Face", which means "face to face". And "Pas Mal" will be "side by side". This is because the two songs are about two different ways of leading a relationship. You can be side by side, and go forward together. Or you can be face to face in a head-on collision, where the relationship just goes into a circle, because you're too much concerned with the problems of all the feelings you can hardly express. Some people begin to hate themselves, some begin to hate the loved one.'

So these are the two opposed ideals of love: the late twentieth century pragmatic model of 'the relationship', and the Romantic dream of the affair. On the one hand, partnership, domesticity, contractual exchange, mutual support. On the other, the unrecoupable expenditure of passion, the impasses around intractable delusions like 'possession', 'trust', 'knowledge', whose ultimate culmination is the annihilating perfection of the suicide pact.

'In French, you say '*faire l'amour*', make love. In the song I say, "*nous ferons l'amour/nous ferons la mort*". (We will make love, we will make death.) Because love can turn into a very strange energy sometimes. It's ambivalent. You can make love and die out of making love, if you don't watch out. Loving somebody and losing yourself into somebody. Le petit mort — that's what they call orgasm, a little death. If I make love all night long, I've known sometimes that I've been very close to death. A very strange feeling. A very strange part of a relationship.'

This is substantiated by this century's great literary extremists. Céline wrote of toppling into 'those bubbling depths that cancel our existence'. Nietzsche of 'the

142 • BLISSED OUT

will to nothingness, a revolt against the fundamental presuppositions of life'. Or
Henry Miller: 'My guts spill out in a grand schizophrenic rush, an evacuation that
leaves me face to face with the Absolute.'

For Georges Bataille, the 'little death' is a lapse back into the infant's
experience of continuum — where there's no notion either of time or of borders
between things. When the infant acquires an identity (by being inserted into
language), it is condemned to discontinuity: the awareness that things change,
that we are separate. For Bataille, eroticism is the clamorous approach to the end
of our separateness and the recovery of continuity. Love is the impossible desire
to 'die without ceasing to live', to be 'always on the threshold of a swoon'. This
living end can only be reached through language, but it's the limit point at which
language dies and is replaced by silence and awe.

'Pas Mal' describes the damage-limitation situation we subsist in most of the
time, devoid of either peaks or lows.

'Pas Mal' means 'it's not bad', but also 'it doesn't hurt'. The lyrics go: 'I've got
nothing to lose/But that's all that I got'. Ha ha! Also: 'I got my whole life to die . . .
kind of, so why should I die now?'

It's the difference between the 'relationship' which enables you to do things in
this world, and the 'grand passion' which disables you from any productive
activity, sucks you through a hole in the fabric of this world.

The Young Gods' songs are in French. For Franz this is no big deal, but to me it
seems an important factor in both the sheer foreignness and the utter physicality
of their music. One's mother tongue comes deep from one's body, from the way
of breathing, of using your tongue, lips, throat, that you've been taught since
childhood. The reason people sound stilted when they speak a foreign language
is that this 'carnal stereophony' (Barthes) is coerced from following its natural
inclinations. So you are literally dis-embodied, your speech is no longer
'language lined with flesh'.

'But anyway', insists Franz, 'with The Young Gods, the words are not that
important. We're not into making important statements. What the songs are about
is all there in my voice.'

For Franz, in the words of one of his favourite authors, Céline, it's about making
'language throb rather than reason'. Like Diamanda Galas, it's about the violence
done to words by the voice.

'I used to study voice with a theatre group called Reuhart, who were very
interested in the possibilities of the voice and the different resonances you get

from your guts or head. They played me a tape of people singing five voices at the same time. Too much! I'd like to go further into controlling the body, do three voices at once, because then I could sing a chord.'

Treichler draws some inspiration from tai chi, but like the breathing exercises he does before each gig, this 'absolute bodycontrol' is a regime that liberates you from yourself. Live, he looks for those privileged moments when the music takes over. 'You completely agree with what's happening, but you go out of control, become part of the music. It happens in moments, never more than a few seconds. Time has no more importance when it happens. Complete loss of self-consciousness. Or complete self-consciousness. It's like the self flares up just as it's on the brink of extinction. There's a total possession of and by the moment.'

And this is what The Young Gods offer the listener. Total and immediate anschluss of body and soul.

ULTRA VIVID SCENE: 'SWEET SURRENDER'

Kurt Ralske of Ultra Vivid Scene has followed a similar trajectory to Green of Scritti Politti. Both began with an interest in marginal noise-making and with demystification; both decided this approach was bankrupt and embarked upon the project of deconstruction, working from within the pop format. But whereas Green chose to unsettle funk and soul, Kurt is unusual in injecting all this worry into a tradition of rock romanticism that privileges impulse and the irrational — the Velvets/Suicide/Stooges lineage. The Jesus and Mary Chain have played similar post-modern games with the same rock legacy, but with nowhere near the same degree of consciousness.

Kurt talks about wanting to combine pure pop and pure sound. It seems today that if you want to deal with the Song, you're immediately committed to playing games with iconography and borrowed signifiers — which can be done well (Prince, Nick Cave, the Jesus and Mary Chain) or badly (Transvision Vamp). But there's this realm of 'pure sound' that's beyond the iconic, that cuts under or beyond signification. Kurt wants to make music that combines the post-modern (reading pop for its references) and the post-postmodern (the illegibility of noise). A schizoid pleasure . . .

'I don't know, maybe it's kinda mystical to imagine there are sounds that are "pure" and untarnished by never having been pop currency. I'm interested in the way using a certain sound quality can put everything into quotation marks. It seems that everything has to be ironical these days, because everything's been done.'

Kurt is drawn to romanticism and its creed of the headlong, head-less leap into belief, action, passion . . . But his predicament is that he's learned too much to allow himself to fall for any kind of absolute . . .

'I'm in a position where I don't believe, but it's not particularly out of choice, I've had my beliefs knocked out of me. I used to believe music was more powerful, I used to believe in God, I used to believe in love. At the same time I don't know whether it's possible to live without absolutes or belief of any kind. If it doesn't come naturally to you, maybe you have to believe even though it's ridiculous, write songs even though it's futile.'

This makes me think of something Barthes wrote about the obscenity of sentiment — sentimental language is much more obscene than graphic sex these days because of its stupidity. Yet intellectuals seem to be drawn compulsively towards stupidity, maybe because it's an affirmation, an end to the interminable qualifications of language, a kind of amen. There's that syndrome of intellectuals who end up Catholics, perhaps because commitment to the most ludicrous form of Christianity involves the most total surrender of your intelligence.

'Someone said of the Op artist Bridget Reilly that her art was an example of the intellect destroying its own modes of functioning. I think it's necessary to be foolish. You can look at things intellectually, and see them as futile, but from another angle, they're not so futile.'

Ultimately, you have to make an affirmation, whether it's of the 'nonsense' of love, or the gratuitousness of music, an affirmation in the face of all the forces of scientific disparagement.

Does he find his own intelligence a drag, an obstacle?

'I don't think I'm so intelligent. Sometimes I credit emotion with having more 'intelligence' than intellect. Sometimes your body 'knows' more than your mind does. People can dig deep holes for themselves intellectually. You can get some perspective through some foolish act. I think a foolish life would be a good one. I find people who believe in things very inspiring. Sometimes it's ridiculous, sometimes it's really beautiful. People who have religious faith. People who believe in the possibility of a long term relationship.'

Ultra Vivid Scene music doesn't often live up to the ideas of its eloquent creator. Too often, it remains 'meta-pop', pop about pop: it falls short because it addresses ideas rather than embodies them. But if Ultra Vivid Scene are not in the same league as the British groups Ralske admires and identifies with — nowhere near as cretinizing as Loop, as dizzy and sticky-mouthed as My Bloody Valentine

— the music is never less than lovely. It sounds seduced, if not abandoned. 'Nausea', 'Mercy Seat' and 'A Dream of Love' are heavy-lidded, faintly foreboding beauties. 'Lynn Marie' is as gorgeous as a ballad off the second Suicide album. 'This Isn't Real' and 'The Whore of God' drift into narcosis, are like walking on air.

It's with the last three songs that theory and execution come closest to union. With their enfolding radiance, moonwalking feel of freedom from the surly bonds of gravity, and soft-focus anaesthesia/synaesthesia — these songs feel like heaven. The sound embodies the ideas: the search for heaven-on-earth in obsessive love, addiction, mysticism. Heaven is an endless End (that's one interpretation of Loop's *Heaven's End*.) An end to anxiety, to our travels and travails in thought, all our wandering and wondering, our interminable quest for the transcendental signified that guarantees all other meanings. An end to our homesickness.

These ideas — the yearning for a salve/salvation, an Absolute that will heal all alienation and erase all doubt, and the quest for such a 'perfect prescription' in drugs or God — have been dealt with most perfectly by Spacemen 3 on the 1989 LP *Playing with Fire*. With it, Spacemen 3 transcended their early days of drone-rock mesmerism, brought to the fore their longstanding obsession with gospel, and created a halcyon haven, an analgesic asylum. For Spacemen 3, it's as though, through sacramentalizing opiates, they've come to see God as the ultimate narcotic.

It's this serenity, reached through the abnegation of reason, that Kurt is drawn to, yet vacillates before. But why deal with the perplexity of a faithless, ground-less existence within the bohemian rock idiom?

'If you listen to the Velvets, there's at least the possibility of belief. If you listen to Scritti, there's just nothing, just surface. Maybe that's all there is. But at least with the Velvets there's at least an element of risk. They championed dangerous things. What's dangerous? Ah . . . surrender in a belief, maybe.

'Like "Heroin", that's still an incredibly chilling song. The exclusivity of the monomania. Some surrealist said something about how "beauty must be convulsive or not at all". That relates to what Barthes said about how there are texts of pleasure (that confirm your sense of your self, your place in your culture) and texts of bliss (which undo your self and your culture). Maybe it's kinda mystical to invest so much in this convulsive jouissance, but at least it's not something that can be commodified.'

Kurt isn't interested in the pleasure of tyranny (whether exerted over others — as with hip hop; or over yourself — Euro body music), but in the bliss of vassalage. Like My Bloody Valentine on 'I Believe', he wants to give up the ghost, be en-thralled.

'Maybe it's my own psychology, but I think an act of surrender can be as liberating as an act of gaining control. The idea of surrender is connected to mysticism, giving in to a visitation of God's will. And it's very unfashionable.'

Hence 'Lynn Marie 1': 'Lay me down upon your bed/hold my hands behind my head/there is no world/there's only you/all of me belongs to you/you could could hurt me if you would/you know I'd do the same for you.'

'I guess people will be wondering if I'm some kind of pervert! But I just thought it would be funny for a man to sing a love song of complete dependency and surrender.

'A standard subject in pop songs is power relationships between people: "Oh, I love you, but you don't love me." And if you take it to its logical conclusion, the most extreme and self-conscious expression of power relations between people is the S/M relationship. It's dominance and submission taken to its illogical conclusion. It's just exaggerated. I'm not talking about actual S/M practices. It's a metaphor, and one that works really well for me. There's dominance and submission at so many levels of life: in career struggles, in love relationships, and at a more mystical level, in someone's attitude to life: whether they're trying to dominate life, trying to use their will to make life submit to their whims, or whether they have a Buddhist total acceptance of, and submission to life.'

Some would say that it was a male luxury to let go of the reins. Suzanne Moore, for instance, has castigated this kind of flirtation with being 'feminized' on the part of postmodern writers as mere 'gender tourism': safe little trips into the 'other', followed by a return to masculine privilege and power.

'Sometimes it's hard to say what power is. You could say that, in a psychological sense, women are more powerful than men. It's not as though the ability to dominate others makes anybody happy. Whereas the ability to take control of some situations, and lose control in others, might make somebody happy. Strength isn't always in trying to control situations.'

I remember Julian Cope ranting about Green's cowardice in placing quotation marks around 'The Sweetest Girl', his stepping back from the brink. And for once, the nincompoop was right — the quotation marks, the distancing effects, have to be shed, in life. Being committed is the only way of attaining asylum from discourse's interminable, neurotic churning. You have to succumb to stupidity, affirm 'nonsense', fill your head with sweet nothings. Love's lore is the last heretical reservoir of superstition and enchantment in a demystified world.

THE PIXIES: 'MY MIND SECEDES'

The hollering is all. The Pixies are what's left when all the obstacles and absences that once prompted rock'n'roll into being have faded away or been catered for, and all that remains is the urge to holler, shriek and whoop it up for the arbitrary, unnegotiable hell of it. They're a poltergeist whose restlessness can never be pacified, the ghost of rock'n'roll. They throb with an obscure randiness it's difficult to imagine what would ever satisfy. A Pixies song is that primal, that post-postmodern.

The Pixies are about . . . no, the Pixies plain are, the disfigurement and degradation of language. A Pixies song consists of gnashing, obscure imprecations, rabid interjections, palsied reveries, and the occasional lurch into lucidity: 'You're so pretty/when you're unfaithful to me.' Like their Boston neighbours Throwing Muses, they provoke emotional responses you can't pin down: is that seven feelings at once, or a new, as yet unnamed emotion? They run strange gamuts and achieve peculiar juxtapositions of feeling, one minute haggard, the next luscious.

A casual listen and you'd take them for a garage group. But this garage is like Dr Who's Tardis: there's a supernatural amount of space in this rough-hewn, scrapping sound, a wilderness across which Pixies songs careen like tearaway mustangs or stampeded wagons shedding everything but their chassis. Along with space, there's a deformed sister to conventional rock geometry.

It's as though the acid-crypt punkadelia of bands like The Hombres or The Groupies has been possessed by the spirit of Dada. It's Pere Ubu meets The Gun Club. They rock crooked. Rampaging ruins. 'Wit', 'playfulness', 'quirky', 'kooky' are all offensively paltry and misleading words to use in connection with The Pixies. It's altogether less suave, more spume-flecked than that. Spooked is a bit better.

Surfer Rosa (1988), their second album, was not so much produced as abased by Steve Albini from Big Black. The sepulchral, impossibly foreboding 'Break My Body', the deranged shriek-whine 'uh-huhn uh-huhn' that kick-starts 'Broken Face', the truly gargantuan, holy horny 'Gigantic', the strange soaring and wilting guitars of 'River Euphrates', 'Where Is My Mind' with its crass but genuinely eerie harmonies and its chorus recited in a strange alloy of rueful puzzlement and mild irritation (as though Black Francis has simply mislaid his sentience somewhere round the house) . . . all these and more have encouraged a drastic loss of cool around these parts.

In person, the Pixies seem too placid to be responsible for such ruffled music. They appear to be neither acid-fried nor psychopathic. But there are more than a few hints of the radical loose-mindedness that lies behind their music. (The Pixies put a lot of thoughtlessness into what they do.) Mere transcription cannot do justice to the array of stresses, inflections, manic touches, weird characterizations, in a Pixies conversation: the dismembering of syntax, the jaywalking and lane changes within language, the abandonment into inarticulate noises and gestures that are more expressive than conventional eloquence. People have celebrated America as a non-verbal, demonstrative culture, and compared with someone like Green of Scritti Politti (where the voice is corseted and coerced by the precision of what's being said), what the Pixies do, in their music and their conversation, is to liberate the sensuality, the breath of the voice. What they want to 'say' will come out, despite the resistance of language: like a voluptuous geyser, like talking in tongues.

You don't learn a great deal through interrogating the Pixies. Singer Charles (a.k.a. Black Francis) has his influences. Surrealism is one, both direct ('Debaser' raves about slicing up eyeballs and being '*un chien andalusa*') and mediated through heirs like David Lynch. 'I like Lynch's movies, like *Eraserhead* and *Blue Velvet*: that attitude where you don't always explain everything, you just come up with stuff that looks and sounds good, and you go with it.'

Religion is another 'influence', though it's more like something that seethes in his bloodstream, something congenital rather than of his choosing. 'There's a certain attitude, that — although when you analyse it, it's all baloney, just volume and entertainment — that "yeah, THIS is what I have to say, everyone else has what they have to say, but THIS is what I have to say, it doesn't make a lot of sense, but it's all I have, and THIS is it." I've been affected by the charismatic Pentecostal thing, which my family was into when I was a kid in California. I grew up exposed to a lot of preaching and righteous rage, and though I've since rejected the content of all that, the style has left an impression on me. It certainly left me fucked up, that's for sure.'

Your mind will collapse/If there's nothing in it — 'Where is My Mind'. In *The Powers of Horror*, Julia Kristeva expands upon her theory of revolutionary poetics, with an analysis of 'abjection' as it has figured in literature. Kristeva's theory is that poetry is subversive when it makes manifest the materiality of the body in the text; when the rude, unruly presence of 'the semiotic' intrudes into the realm of the symbolic. 'The semiotic' is linked to the pre-Oedipal phase, and its primary oral/anal processes. These semiotic 'pulsions' make themselves heard in discourse through rhythm, intonation, figurative and musical effects; everything that disarranges the perfectly-formed sentence structure of correct syntax; everything that vents emotion and makes language closer to music than a clean exchange of data.

'Abjection' is the name Kristeva gives to everything the individual ab-jects, out-casts and expels in order to constitute itself as separate. 'Abjection' is everything that blurs the borders between me and not-me, inside and outside: the excremental, the cadaverous . . . What is found abject varies (just like what is found erotic) from culture to culture, and individually, according to your personal psycho/somatic history. (Kristeva describes how her whole body revolts against the viscous film on the surface of a cup of coffee.) Abjection threatens, but it also beckons: its lure is that in it we recover momentary access to the maternal body, a bliss-ful body we had to reject in order to participate in the symbolic order, in order to be.

For Kristeva, religion, with its demarcation between the abominable and the sacred, the unclean and clean, as tabulated in rules about diet, bodily hygiene, proper sexuality, is a way of apprehending and making present this realm of 'maternal horror': a realm characterized above all by viscous fluids (mother's milk, menstrual blood, uterine waters, mucus, afterbirth . . .) that are both loathsome and delectable, precisely because they dissolve the edges of our autonomy. A conflagration devoutly to be wished.

It is the lure of abjection, then, that raves and rages in the Pixies music; it's this loathing/longing that accounts for the recurrent images of incest, devils, whores, broken bodies and faces. Abjection is a fever that breaks over the body of Pixies music, breaks up the syntax of the classically proportioned pop song, breaks out in the scream, the sharp, shuddered yelp of werewolf bliss that is Charles's last-ditch attempt to utter the unutterable, apprehend and fuse with the un-speakable.

Doolittle, the devastating third album, is the Pixies' most lucid disquisition on the horror and ecstasy of 'bestial unreason' ('if we could talk like the animals/be like the animals . . .'). Words fail, words flail, in the face of the facts of life. 'Uh/Said the man to the lady/Uh/Said the lady to the man she adored/And the whores like a choir/Go uh all night . . . uh/is the sound that the mother makes/when the baby breaks/We're chained' ('Hey'). There's nothing to be said: 'Prithee my dear/why are we here/nobody knows/I go to sleep/as breathing flows/my mind secedes/I bleed' ('I Bleed'). These facts of life, the base denominators that unite us with each other and all creation, are simultaneously life at its most material, and the void upon which discourse founders. The Pixies are drawn again and again to this nothing-to-be-said which, in the end, is all that there is: a nothing they simultaneously recoil from and affirm, in hysteria.

(1989)

I-AND-I SURVIVE
the masculine deconstructed

This essay is about the peculiar lure of certain kinds of ultra-masculine pop that have emerged in the eighties — rap, speedmetal, and European electronic body music. Why does their heady brew of triumphalism, combat postures and paranoia, appeal to people like myself who otherwise like to think of themselves as liberal and feminist?

Suzanne Moore, in an essay entitled 'Getting a Bit of the Other' has attacked my vicarious pleasure in rap as 'gender tourism'; along with other more distinguished post-modernist writers I'm guilty, she argued, of toying with 'optional feminine subjectivity'. But if this is the case, my 'gender tourism' is a trip into masculinity. But why make excursions into this men-only hellzone, anyway? There's four facets to the fascination. First, there's a substantial element of simple voyeuristic pleasure: the vicarious enjoyment of the adrenalin high of danger and confrontation. Second, there's the fact that the uncaring brutalism of rap etc. provides a blessed reprieve from the suffocating altruism and maturity of eighties' mainstream pop. Third, there's the undeniable fact that the most musically progressive and avant-garde music of the eighties (rap, acid house, hardcore) has been the most emotionally regressive. Finally, I'd argued that you can 'learn' something from this ostensibly male supremacist music. Hip hop, metal and Eurobeat can function as a deconstruction of the masculine psyche, drawing you into the VOID at the desperate centre of the male ego. This essay, then, is both an apology for and a celebration of eighties' pop forms that are simultaneously reactionary and radical, beyond the pale and far out.

hip hop

Hip hop's shock, hip hop's pleasure, lies in its nakedness. The music is stripped, fleshless, free of frills or plumage, streamlined for efficiency. In terms of motivation, too, there's a minimalism or nakedness. Hip hop reveals straight values and aspirations, but as in a kind of distorting mirror, one that strips away the veils of protocol and ideology, the cant about freedom and enterprise and choice. Hip hop reveals the impolite reality of capitalism — dog eat dog struggle.

Hip hop is about a strange kind of unity: it's a community that responds to oppression not with a dream of solidarity and equality, but with a pathological individualism. A brotherhood bound in ruthless competition with each other. At a hip hop concert there's a resonance that comes because the star lives out the fan's megalomaniac fantasies in a theatre of cruelty and triumph.

Most writing about hip hop celebrates it as the authentic voice of the street; the assumption being that the 'truth' of the street is somehow identical with some kind of proto-socialist solidarity, or at least a defiant 'pride and dignity' in the face of a system that dehumanizes by valuing people according to their economic status. But it's important to problematize this 'pride', see it as it really is: not the harbinger of revolution, not resistance through self-belief, but something almost psychotic in its denial of vulnerability, dependence and tenderness.

Listening to hardest-core hip hop, like Schoolly D, we are confronted with what the system does to people. Victims fight back by victimizing others. Schoolly D has reduced himself to nothing but armour, masks, the capacity for massive retaliation. And millions live like this. This is what free market society does to people.

Hip hop is a hyperbolic reflection of the system — capitalism/patriarchy. Inevitably, those who are excluded from full status in society, only want that status and its material trappings, more severely. Look at the macho lore and mega-acquisitive norms of the other traditional escape routes of the working class — sport, crime.

In its more extreme manifestations, the hip hop imagination is drawn to the language of criminality — Schoolly D, Run DMC's gangster pose, Public Enemy's talk of Uzis. Crime isn't a subversion of capitalism, but its caricature: an alternative means to the symbols of status used by those for whom conventional channels are blocked by inequality.

Criminality is part of hip hop's fantasy vocabulary because it's a metaphor of total possibility. In this, hip hop reminds me of nothing so much as punk's anti-social individualism/anarchist-Antichrist attitude. Hip hop can represent an epic solipsism, an arbitrary and aggressive will, comparable with that which animates a Sex Pistols or an Iggy and The Stooges song. Hip hop, like punk, nihilistically inverts values — 'bad', 'wicked', 'ill', 'damage', 'treacherous' are all good terms — but this is also an exposure of what it takes to get on in 'free market' society. Value and meaning have absconded, the only authority is the self, there are 'so many ways to get what you want'.

LL Cool J is the apotheosis of hip hop's delusions of omnipotence. Think about LL's comparisons of himself to Napoleon and Hitler, about lyrics like 'they call me Jaws/My hand is like a shark's fin', and 'I'm an executioner/I should wear a black hood'. Consider that voice — bug-eyed, Tyson-veined, clenching you up inside taut and murderous, making you want to stomp victims. Or how his face has a vague resemblance to a Nazi helmet — that sleek, matt finish, that dull glans sheen. And does he really say, in one song: 'I'm the Nietzsche of rap'?

There's truism that under a pop persona lies a real person, flawed and vulnerable and human. But maybe there is no 'real' LL Cool J, just a shell, an aggregation or accretion of claims and fantasies. Empty vessels make the most sound. Maybe being larger than life is LL's truest being, maybe when he's impossible, he's most himself: as he raps it, 'even when I'm bragging/I'm being sincere.' Only 'when I'm bragging'?

For what LL excels at is 'talking on myself', which involves a paradox — rap is about being proud of your pride, striving to be the best at saying you're the best, becoming somebody through an art whose message boils down to the simple assertion 'I Am Somebody'. The message is the mode of utterance (articulating

154 • BLISSED OUT

the relationship between rapper and fan as despotic monologue) and that message is simply: 'I'm telling you.'

LL Cool J: 'It all goes back to when you start rapping in the park. You want to make a name for yourself. You want to be better than the guy who went before you. You've got to talk about how *baad* you are better than he talked about how cool he was. That street attitude of wanting to be recognized, that eye of the tiger attitude . . .'

'Eye of the Tiger' — a song by a heavy metal group called Survivor. From a film about the boxer Rocky Marciano. LL Cool J himself identifies obsessively with Mike Tyson. It's a universe where nothing exists but the stamina to hang on in there, the ability to take and to deal massive punishment, an autistic strength that exists only to flex itself aimlessly and intransitively.

For the rapper's megalomania is a monomania. Rappers have nothing to say, they just want to prove themselves, prove they exist. There's no meaning, just assertion, a scream in the face of eternity. Hip hop intimidates because its motor is fear — the fear of anonymity and failure, of death. There's something tragic about the rapper, about his victories in a vacuum. These are people who can only feel they exist when they're doing somebody down.

BLACK ROCK'N'ROLL
Public Enemy's Chuck D adheres to the Def Jam party line: that rap is black rock'n'roll, that it's based around rock'n'roll's 4/4 beat rather than disco's pulse beat, that its renegade, vandalistic attitude is the antithesis of the showbiz aspirations of 'Urban Contemporary' (US radio's euphemism for black pop).

'My thing is I don't like house music. I first heard it as a DJ, when I was doing radio shows, and I said then that I thought the beats lacked soul. Certainly you could move to them, by choice, but they don't move you like a 4/4 beat does. And I dislike the scene that's based around house — it's sophisticated, anti-black, anti-culture, anti-feel, the most ARTIFICIAL shit I ever heard. It represents the gay scene, it's separating blacks from their past and their culture, it's upwardly mobile. People see the music as a luxury item, a social status thing, something to "elevate" me from all that B-boy shit I was into when I was a teenager — and I hate that shit, I HATE it. That attitude of "don't speak loud".'

Trad-rock objections to disco, these, but the point is that this magical dissolution of origins, of class, race and sexual differences, is what the dancefloor is all about. House constructs its ideal consumer as a biracial androgyne, lost in a swirl of polymorphous sensuality and fantasy glamour, lost for words and lost to the world. Immediately outside the club, the world and all its differences impinge: people kill each other on the doorsteps of (the) Paradise (Garage).

THE BLACK CLASH

They try, oh but they do try. Whenever Left-inclined subcultural theorists encounter a black pop culture, they always follow the same syllogistic reasoning. Black people are oppressed. Such-and-such is a music of black origin. Therefore, such-and-such a music must be animated, at however sublimated and submerged a level, by currents of resistance to the way-things-are. Often the desperation to locate such micro-resistance, to uncover a subtext of cultural dissidence, results in bizarre interpretations. So Paul Gilroy can argue that Eric B and Rakim's *Paid in Full* is a 'demystification of their means of production'.

Demystification, eh? The guys are on the make, they want in, they're counting their money, and if they're not as cynical as Schoolly D (who won't put out unless he's paid in full, IN ADVANCE), it's still hardly worth celebrating. So much for all the cant about hip hop serving a community. The trouble with hip hop is that, no matter how you juggle the subcultural arithmetic, the end product is not going to be a clearly defined 'contribution to the struggle'.

The politics of hip hop occupy a different space altogether. Take Public Enemy. Chuck D's political orientation derives from the inspiration of the Black Panthers, the sixties activists. 'What the Panthers did was to structure and organize a force that represented order and strength to the community. They started off peacefully, but as they encountered opposition, they grew more militant.

'We're trying to revive their project, rebuild the self-respect and identity that got eroded in the seventies. What we need is to build a sense of community and a sense of business. We're in a capitalist society, we can't overthrow this government, so we must learn to use the system.'

So your vision of how to change things isn't socialist or collectivist . . .

'Only among ourselves, black people. I have socialistic ideals, but I also have an awareness of what's real and feasible. Obviously, for America to survive it'll have to become socialistic, ultimately, 'cos the system's crumbling. But in the meantime, we have to stand on our own feet, raise ourselves, because nobody else will do it for us.'

The meantime is a mean time. Compare seventies 'political' soul with Public Enemy. With 'What's Goin' On', 'Love Train', 'Why Can't We Live Together', 'We Gotta Have Peace', as well as pristine woe, you also got a glimpse, in the angelic purity of the harmonies and arrangements, of a utopian vision of how things should be — a rainbow coalition of love and equality. Compare the plaintiveness of 'Backstabbers' with the vengeful 'You're Gonna Get Yours', Public Enemy's metal-motored anthem. With Public Enemy, there's no vision of the perfect world that is the goal of struggle. Public Enemy are hooked on the glamour of the means of militancy and mobilization, barely aware of the vague halcyon end. Would Chuck D even like it if there was integration?

'Once again we're talking fantasy, man! Of course I'd like it if everybody white married somebody black, and then the next generation were all black. But this integration is never gonna happen. So people should stick to their own. Without a strong sense of black consciousness, there's no cohesion, and no survival. The Chinese, the Jews, they stick together, deal with each other, but blacks don't.'

Doesn't hip hop just reflect that lack of cohesion, all the rivalry between rappers, and between possees, all against all?

'But inside each and every rapper there's something that's saying: "I am yelling out loud for shit that ain't right." Now he don't know what, 'cos he's uneducated. A rapper speaks out loud, and really he's asking for help. 'Cos for the last fifteen years no information has been given to him about the system.'

We're back with subcultural theory again — daily life as rife with acts of micro-resistance, pre-conscious skirmishes with bourgeois ideological hege-mony, unarticulated rage — if only it could be channelled into revolution. The Black Panthers tried to do just that, taking the fact of young black male street. criminality, and trying to radicalize it. And the Situationists dreamed that all you needed for a revolution was a federation of teenage delinquent gangs.

SOUL ON ICE

Throughout popular culture, being black is being installed as a signifier for being more human. From the histrionics of George Michael and Mick Hucknall, to the Kronenbourg ads (New Man who plays saxophone is tutored in reaching into the depths of his soul by a wizened black master of the instrument called Earl Page — the slogan: 'A Different Kind of Strength'), blackness is being elaborated as a model of oneness with your body, of being in touch with your emotions, of a new, more acceptable kind of masculinity. The cluster of ideas here have quite a genealogy — the depth that comes with a history of Suffering; the idea of the black as warmer, looser, less hung-up than the white; the offensive notion of 'natcherel riddim'.

While white pop bases itself entirely around the form and ethos of black passion, what's fascinating is that black pop has gone in the opposite direction, becoming colder, more inhuman. In the case of hip hop, more wound-up, heartless; in the case of house, dispassionate, inexpressive, plastic. Hip hop is (to abuse Eldridge Cleaver's fine phrase) — SOUL ON ICE — a survivalist retreat from engagement with the outside world or other people, back to the frozen shell of a minimal self. There's a new kind of relation to the body, not the slow suffusion of 'getting in touch', but more domineering a regime, a priming of the machine in readiness for self-defence.

This is the DISS TOPIA. An eternal now forever teetering on the brink of extinction, a world without narrative (that's why 'Rebel Without a Pause' is like a locked groove): the hip hop ego traverses a 'treacherous' soundscape, constantly faces sonic ambush or mined terrain, always overcomes, can never rest.

Klaus Thewelweit, in his book *Male Fantasies*, takes the Freikorps — First World War veterans who formed into rightwing militia in the post-war years in order to suppress proleterian uprisings, and who later became a substantial component of the Nazi's streetfighting cadres — and examines their correspondence, diaries, poetry and favoured literature in order to psychoanalyse their attitudes to women and femininity. He notes a startling consistency in the imagery used: women, female sexuality, emotion (the feminine side of men), and popular communism, are all described in terms of floods, lava, 'streaming', unstanchable flows of fluid. Thewelweit suggests that masculinity is constructed around a chronic terror of being swept away on a tide of desire, of being swallowed up by oceanic feelings, of the borders of the self being dissolved, and this fear goes back to the original moment of being severed from the mother and her suckling breast. The moment at which the male ego was constituted.

Men can only consolidate their selves by trampling again and again on femininity, both inside, and outside themselves.

The relevance of this to hip hop should be fairly obvious. If soul singers like Al Green and Prince melt sexual divisions into a world of fluid, androgynous bliss, then hip hop freezes sexual divisions, hard. In more senses than one, hip hop is not a fluent music.

Chuck D says: 'Rap is like psychology — you can see people's insides.' Are they a pretty sight? Where do women fit into the Public Enemy picture? Do they?

'Of course, they have a place. Man is husband and woman is wife. You can only go to that point with me. You can even have black women leaders to a degree. But I think that, where America has elevated a few women in a process of tokenism, in order to keep the black man down, as we pointed out in "Sophisticated Bitch", then I think it's maybe time to go back to some kind of original structure.'

You seem to be into firm, fixed borderlines — between races, between sexes, between straight and gay.

'Borderlines have to be set, because borderlines are there. If ten whites and ten blacks go to an interview, and ten jobs are available, you can bet your life it ain't gonna be five/five, it'll be nine white jobs and one black. For us there has to be cohesion. And men should be men and women should be women. And there's no room in the black race for gays, a black gay can't raise a kid, the kid's gonna be confused enough as it is being black. Lines have to be set. There has to be guidance. The shit has to be stable.'

So uncertainty is a privilege, a luxury for white middle-class people.

'Uncertainty is bullshit, as far as black people are concerned . . . Right now, the black race needs leaders. We're the only people who can raise ourselves. I don't think anything will be achieved in my lifetime, but a start can be made, and maybe by the next century we'll be so strong and independent that only overt aggression, a new wave of lynching, can stop us. Right now, they don't need to destroy us, 'cos we're doing it to ourselves.'

Finally I get to talk to Griff, leader of Security of the First World, Public Enemy's security force and . . . well, it turns out to be rather more complex and peculiar than I'd imagined.

'The name Security of the First World reflects our belief that Africa and Asia are not the Third World and that America is definitely not the First World. If you look at history you see that mathematics and science and all kinds of culture began in Africa and Asia. So our job is securing the knowledge of that history. Our job is the Preservation of the Young Black Mind. We have meetings and discussion groups where we educate ourselves in our history and culture, or we discuss the present conditions of blacks in America and Africa.

'But our main function is to attend concerts of Public Enemy. Onstage, we're there to project images of strength and order, send signals to our people that these are young black men who are standing up, who ain't gonna back off. We're not trying to control their physical behaviour, we're trying to control their mind, not their physical safety. We want to indicate to them that there is an ability to bind and conform in a chaotic situation.

'We wear paramilitary uniform, because everybody wears uniform today – look at Khadaffi. Everybody who joins gets involved in physical training. Martial arts. Because if you know yourself mentally and physically, you're better able to deal.'

(N.B. The Americans often use the words 'to deal' intransitively — a sure indicator of the survivalist mindset of the nation.)

'We do drill, it's called the Fruit of Islam. It brings about harmonious totality among ourselves. Sixty guys all in one step.'

Rectitude in the face of chaos. An admiration for Colonel Khadaffi ('blacks in America didn't know who to side with'). Harmonious totality. No faggots. Uniform and drill. It all sounds quite logical and needed, the way they tell it. And it's all very dodgy indeed.

If there's one thing more scary than a survivalist, it's a whole bunch of survivalists organized into a regiment. It must be that when a group of young men band together in a tight unit and around a very channelled mindset, a particular structure develops, and it's pretty much the same structure, or 'desiring machine' that's behind communist youth groups, the Freikorps, any army anywhere in the world, and fascism.

Fortunately, Public Enemy and Security of the First World are sufficiently powerless ('fifty-two and growing') to remain fascinating to us pop swots, rather than disturbing.

Chuck D: 'A lot of the critics pick up on the violence element, but they don't understand that it's an analogy. It's like "my Uzi weighs a ton". No gun weighs that much, it's a metapahor, a strong image, 'cos you got to grab people, wake them up. It's like if I hit you over the head with this stapler, you'd give me 100 per cent attention, maybe even 150 per cent! So what I'm doing is cracking heads, but verbally, and with NOISE!'

POSTSCRIPT

Public Enemy have made the single most concerted attempt to politicize hip hop. They took on the first person plural, the 'we' of protest rock, but there was only so far they could extend hip hop's premisses beyond 'talking on myself'. The hip hop ego is the male ego in extremis, that's to say, paranoid schizophrenic. Paranoid schizophrenia combines delusions of grandeur with a feeling of being under siege from all sides: the survivalist mentality in a nutshell. With their first album, *Yo! Bum Rush the Show*, Public Enemy rubbed our faces in some truths about the world. By the time of the second album, *It'll Take a Nation of Millions to Stop Us*, and the single 'Don't Believe the Hype', their subject matter had contracted to the media shock waves generated by their own impact. They disappeared in a miasma of self-righteousness and fantastical conspiracy theories. They dramatized themselves in a perpetual state of imminence, the eve of apocalypse, with the huge clocks around their necks permanently fixed at a minute to midnight. As with so many rock messiahs — The Clash, The Jam, Dexy's Midnight Runners, U2 — eventually, there was nothing to communicate but the fact of remonstrance, the aura of weighty utterance and mass rally itself.

But their third album, *Fear of a Black Planet* was an unexpected reaffirmation of Public Enemy's importance. *Fear* was both a major musical advance, and provided vital insights into what lay behind the more perplexing and distressing aspects of the Public Enemy worldview. The best way to understand Public Enemy is to realize that they're *chaos theoreticians.* Their loopy racial and historical theories may seem risible and offensive, but for Public Enemy they are steel handrails in the hour of chaos, a way of mapping the confusion of the contemporary political landscape and *forcing* it to make 'sense'.

Fear contained its fair share of acute fingerpointing, but its lyrical bulk consisted of a livid, febrile jumble of self-aggrandisement, rallying cries, cryptic slogans, and turbid stream of consciousness. Textually and texturally, the album was a work of unprecedented density for hip hop, its claustrophobic, backs-against-the-wall feel harking back to Sly Stone's *There's a Riot Goin' On* or even Miles Davis's *On the Corner.* Overall, what *Fear of a Black Planet* showed was not how singleminded Public Enemy are, but how *confused.* Public Enemy remain important, not because of the thoroughly dubious 'answers' they propound in interview, but because of the angry questions that seethe in their music, in the very fabric of their sound; bewilderment and rage at the damage done to Black America, and the damage Black America inflicts upon itself.

(1986–90)

euro body music – front 242

With the bloodcurdling electronic efficiency of their sound and their emphasis on the spectacular effects of lights, lasers and samples (regarded by rock traditionalists as 'alienating'), Front 242 could easily be mistaken for an 'inhuman' experience, and condemned as such. But they aren't inhuman so much as supra-human. Front 242's 'masterhit' is the thrill of mastery, of self-overcoming. Their 'music' and bodymoves put me in mind of the automatized reflexes and clinical grace of the martial arts. There's no margin for error, no flaws or frailty, in their impregnable, marauding sound. There's no nuances, inflections or flexibility, just the flexing of muscles and psychological armature. Front's sound is all girders and girded loins, tension and the tensile. 'Never Stop' indeed; this is music that can never find a point of rest, that envisions an eternity of anxiety and sublimation.

What thrills about a song like 'Headhunter' is that Front 242 feel of impeded but implacable motion, of progress through hostile, slightly viscous territory. The predatory beat carries a cybernetic chassis that's all glistening armature and steel claws, but there's no guiding soul, no redemptive consciousness, just a programme, a 'nature' it can't escape. The lyrics of 'Headhunter' — 'I'm looking for a man/To sell him to other man/At ten times his price at least' — are ripe for all manner of *Blade Runner/Angel Heart* analogies: the hunter in flight from or in pursuit of himself, men turning themselves into machines, masculinity as machine . . .

But unlike The Young Gods, Front 242 don't reinvoke a new paganism or envy the noble savage of the pre-Modern Age. As 'Headhunter' reveals, Front 242 see the Nietzschean 'values' of rapacity, singlemindedness and will at large today in the corporate jungle. It's a vision of *Übermensch* in business suits stalking the corridors of late capitalism with portable phones and electronic filofaxes instead of swords and shields. Front 242 have an amoral fascination for this future now of information war, cybernatic hacking, computer viruses, industrial espionage and sabotage. They envision capitalist society, correctly, as a barely disguised state of total war, the war of all against all. But they offer no critique, rather show not revulsion but relish for the primal energies seething behind the technocratic façade.

Front 242's name, dress (black leather, cropped hair and paramilitary goggles) and slogans (determination, persistence, assimilation, infiltration) are all facets of an ambiguous but unashamed flirtation with terrorist chic. But, explains Patrique, Front 242's sampling expert, they use terrorism as a metaphor, 'Terrorism is about a group of people, a disciplined unit, working against other people. And that's how we feel in relation to pop music. We use the idea of terrorism because it conveys a very strong impression of power and energy. But we consider power in itself to be neutral. It's like sport. We're interested in the means, not any real, violent ends.'

In fact, Front 242 see discipline and singlemindedness as essential defensive strategies in the face of the 'terrorism' of advertising and media brainwashing in general. 'This has a lot to do with the specific geography of Belgium. It's bombarded with media from all over Europe. There's an absolute saturation of information, images and stimuli. But we're not necessarily saying that this is a bad thing. There are positive aspects: these days it's possible to compress a lot of information into a short space, and young people are able to assimilate much more data than their parents. But the media overload can also confuse and pacify people.'

'Welcome To Paradise' is a typically objective presentation of our contemporary panic culture, where we're going nowhere faster every day. It's a centre-less mediascape in which those who are trying to relocate the thread of life — the TV Evangelists, the counsellors — are mischievously reduced to blipverts, just more interference in the media blizzard.

Front 242's samples simulate the chaos of the media, whose disconnected images of terrorism and catastrophe stupefy and paralyse people in appalled fascination. But the rigour and precision of their rhythms literally embody a survivalist response to chaos, a dance discipline that galvanizes and primes the listener in readiness for trouble.

'For us it's a question of wanting to make the music of our time, reflecting life today, rather than judging whether it's good or bad. We never take positions. That's because as individuals we all have different political ideas. But collectively, we're all conscious of how Front 242 must be presented, and that's strong and emphatic. We spend as much time in coordinating our marketing and presentation as we do in making music.'

Like Nietzsche, and after him Foucault, they see no end to power. All there is is power and resistance, in itself a manoeuvre that replicates power. Front 242's form of survivalist resistance is what has been dubbed 'micro-fascism': disciplining your own body and soul along military lines, maximizing efficiency, erasing doubt, mechanizing your responses in order to achieve infallibility. No wonder, then, that Front 242 have succumbed to a disinterested admiration for the very brainwashers and despots they're organizing themselves against: Swaggart, Khadaffi, the advertising moguls, all the great masters of puppets. Front 242 understand the 'seduction' of strong images, regardless of their content or context. They make me think of a recent episode of the US Max Headroom spin-off, where a terrorist group realize it's futile to stage real acts of destruction, and instead jam the media with images of blown-up buildings they've simulated in a studio with models and special effects.

Packed with ideas as they are, Front 242 aren't thoughtful; the ideas aren't 'communicated' so much as embodied (in the sheer visceral putsch of their rhythms) and emblazoned (in the sheer spectacle of their show). Their version of dance music isn't a groove but a grid, doesn't involve but subjugates. It's Dionysus turned into a diagram. One song cuts from the inquiry 'do you like to party' to the imperative 'we must be obeyed'. They turn the dancefloor into a gulag, in which the crowd work with a will, happily turn themselves into appendages of flesh attached to the machine-beat. This wilful subordination, this deliverance from self-rule and all its anxieties, is the paradoxical bliss that Front 242 offer us. Their live show ends with an uproar in which the screams of an apeshit crowd mingle with the 'blood and soil' bombast of Carl Orff's *Carmina Burana*: music inspired, I believe, by poetry from the Middle Ages, and as such deeply revealing of the Mediaeval matrix of desire inside Front 242 futurist surfaces.

millennarian metal — metallica

Righteous violence is the delusion that motors a certain kind of metal, that comic-book vigilante idea where sado-masculinism is absolved by the justice of its cause. It allows the fan to get off vicariously on the viciousness, but to feel it's warranted, purified by honour. Hence, the fantasy of violence as hygiene. Of course, this is nonsense: violence is messy, and gooey, it smells, it putrefies. But it's precisely this flesh-hating, sensuality-fearing fantasy that underlies metal's economy of pleasure, its S/M matrix of sublimated desire.

When writing about metal, about hip hop or hardcore, it's easy to lapse into the lexicon of sadomasochism, and appraise things in terms of how 'punishing', how ear-deflowering, they are. So these terms must be volatilized by an awareness of what they're rooted in. And that's the male fear of flesh, fear of one's own vulnerability/mortality, ultimately fear of nature and its laws of growth and decay. The survivalist solution is to deaden your nerve endings, automatize your reflexes, suppress the woman within. In other words, to beat death, you enter a living death. All this is particularly resonant for male adolescents because it's then that the body's growth is at its most virulently repulsive, then that the flesh is at its most fearful. For these unhappy boys, the mushroom cloud is a kind of orgasm-in-negative, a holocaustic act of hygiene.

This makes a band such as Metallica all the more intriguing a paradox. Like Anthrax (but unlike Megadeth, who exult in their vision of apocalypse), Metallica are sincerely anti-war. But their music is a perfect analogue of modern techno-cratic warfare. Like Anthrax, Metallica fiercely defend the individual. But their music embodies and in effect celebrates the unitary and singleminded: each player is a cog in the killing machine, rather than someone 'expressing' himself.

For me, metal (like rap) can function as a perfect deconstruction of masculinity. On ' . . . And Justice for All', Metallica verge on doing this explicitly. 'The ultimate in vanity/Exploiting their supremacy/I can't believe the things you say/I can't believe the price you pay/Nothing can save you/Justice is lost/Justice is rape/Justice is God/Pulling your strings/Justice is done/Seeking no truth/ Winning is all.' This almost seems to be an attempt to dismantle the myth of righteous violence, smash and break free from the cage of a male psychological armour. But all the while the music makes that psychology, that ethic of retaliation and vigilance, seem intoxicating.

But it's the very seduction of the imagery that allows for a deconstructive effect. Metal and rap place me, as a pleasured listener, in an ambiguous relation to the music: as masochist victim of its devastating effects, and as sadist, merged as one with its violence. A parallel to this induction into reactionary psychology is *Taxi Driver*, where you're with Travis all the way, until Scorsese's vertiginous camera pan makes you linger on the carnage that is the consequence of righteousness.

It's all very mediaeval, this worldview, something Metallica compound, consciously or not, by strange little pastoral interludes that sound like minstrels strumming lutes and psalteries. Titles like 'Harvester Of Sorrow' hark back to the mediaeval idea of the world as a vale of tears, and of the absolute visions of Rasta music, anarcho-punk, and hardcore, where society is Babylon, we're all wholly subjugated to a system that wrecks and rapes, and the only hope is the apocalypse. In the mean time, there is only the brotherhood of exiles on main street: I-and-I survive.

Musically, the key word is hygiene. This is completely sublimated rock, on a quest for a purity of form, light years beyond raunch or blues rock. Metallica turn heavy metal's melodrama into algebra. This isn't thrash, but thresh: mechanized mayhem. There's no blur, no mess, not even at peak velocity, but a rigorous grid of incisions and contusions. Everything depends on utter punctuality and supreme surgical finesse. It's probably the most incisive music I've ever heard, in the literal sense of the word.

Metallica are austere, but they're also generous. Their songs are epic constructions, that use up and discard hundreds of riffs that other bands would give their eye teeth for. At its best, there's a concentrated complexity that suggests the almost stellar beauty that mathematicians claim is to be found in the higher reaches of pure maths. The tempo shifts, gear changes, lapses, decelerations and abrupt halts, play unnerving games with your sense of time. Nothing flows, everything is severed from itself. This kind of metal is at the opposite extreme from the oceanic, border dissolving, continuum rock of the moment (A.R. Kane, Cocteaus etc): this gulf is precisely the divide between masculine and feminine sensibilities in music.

Some find it almost wilfully frustrating to listen to (it certainly forestalls any kind of oblivion or forgetfulness), but for me the constant jar on the system induces a hyper-wakefulness, an almost painful alertness. The eternal vigilance of the survivalist.

THE END OF MUSIC

sampling
(written with David Stubbs)

'Piracy'. 'Plunder'. 'Pillage'. 'Steal it!'. 'Fairlight Robbery'. Please feel free to yawn. Media approaches to sampling have been uniformly couched in this shopworn, predictable language of 'irreverence' and 'subversion'. Sampling is invariably treated as an issue in terms of the politics of the music industry — a challenge to specific property rights, but also a shift in the struggle over who 'owns' our music culture. A struggle between the industry and 'the people'. What's barely considered is the formal possibilities and aesthetic implications of sampling: the way it makes difficult, time-consuming techniques hitherto the preserve of the conscientious, 'engaged' avant-garde musician, accessible to ordinary rockers; the personal rather than public destabilization (of sensibilities, of states of consciousness) that these facilitated techniques promise.

Sampling has been pounced upon by a rock culture/music press desperate for a new threat to shore up its beleaguered faith in the seriousness of popular music: since punk this frantic scurrying has fastened first on the dream of a politicized, positivist funk, then on rap (seen as a proto-socialist street protest) and now on sampling. As always, threat is directed outwards, seen in terms of shocks and blows to the record industry, 'the establishment', the straights and squares. 'We', of course, are insiders, in the know, in control: it's never a question of disrupting our value scheme, outstripping our ability to manage sounds, interfering with the political structures inside our own heads. Sampling allows an equivalence to be read between the 'violence' of a jarring edit and the 'outrage' of a flaunted musical theft.

The legal status of sampling is in flux at the moment, with various suits in the offing. Most critical of these is one undertaken by Stock Aitken Waterman against

M.A.R.R.S. over a tiny snatch of the former's 'Roadblock' that appears on 'Pump Up the Volume' (one of thirty samples). Stock Aitken Waterman's argument is that plagiarism (which they admit regularly doing) is radically different from outright theft (to copy demands musical expertise, whereas sampling requires mere gall). They also claim that M.A.R.R.S. broke new ground by sampling from current releases. (In fact some recent hip hop and house records contain lifts from white label pre-releases, 'quote' from records before they've even entered the dance culture!)

Sampling has been championed as a new punk — both a repossession of control from the industry, and a liberation from the inhibiting effect of notions of expertise. Even less need to pay your dues than in the days of punk's one-chord wonders. And no need to make a virtue out of not being as good as John Bonham, because with a sampler you can appropriate Bonham's prowess, his unique drum sound. Commentators often link sampling with groups like Culturcide, Pussy Galore and Sonic Youth's alter ego incarnation Ciccone Youth (all have recorded catastrophic versions of classic songs — in Pussy Galore's case, a version of the whole of *Exile on Main Street*), seeing both piracy and parody as acts of détournement, local insurrectionary gestures against global pop hegemony. But there are some problems with the idea of sampling as the consummation of punk's DIY ethos. Sampling may well produce a groundswell of bands making their own music (as with punk) but those individuals will still be buying music-making technology from companies that are vertically linked to the major record companies (as with punk). Also, although sampling makes certain effects more attainable to the impatient, it can't democratize the unequal distribution of brilliance. As with punk, after an initial unsettled period (favouring the quickwitted) we can expect that the people who will prosper will be those with a sense of rhythm and architecture, i.e. the ones who would have always got on, whether sampling had existed or not.

What seems likely is that the 'threat' to the industry will either be crushed in a series of test cases (forcing sampling into the underground, where the price of being untrammelled is impotence) or it will be emasculated just as surely by being allowed. Which is to say that the situation will revert to the state of play pre-M.A.R.R.S., where petty larceny was already a commonplace, unremarkable happening. When everybody does something, meaning evaporates. The only way to recharge sampling as an issue is by perpetual aesthetic innovation. The sure proof of this is the case of Art Of Noise: their clarion calls and broadsides are still being reheated and revamped by bands, even though their repertoire of noises has ossified, ending up as the funny voices on the Bols commercial. Typically, the rock press would still prefer to deal with attitude rather than sound, text rather than texture, subversion rather than topsy-turviness.

The real 'politics' of sampling may lie in the effects on consciousness of formal futurism. Sampling facilitates the techniques of cut-up and bricolage (long practised by the likes of Cabaret Voltaire, but using tape loops). In the work of Mark Stewart, cut-up signifies the psychic state of being cut-up: the technique's a tool of his project of destabilizing the listener's values, common sense perceptions. Stewart's nihilism in many ways just reflects — in a more sinister light — what's already happening in popular culture: the death of the Song, to be replaced by the decentred, unresolved, in-finite house track; the brain-rotting vortex of quick-cutting in video and TV; the supercession of narrative, characterization, and motivation by sensational effects. Blip culture means the death of sequential, linear thought, an erosion of people's ability to plan and manage their lives. There is only a NOW that is either blissed-out, or dread-ful (dread is a kind of jouissance-in-negative, a slow subsidence into uncontrol and panic).

In hip hop, discontinuity and juxtaposition can induce both jouissance or a sense of impending doom. A producer like Herbie Azor (Salt 'N' Pepa, Kid'n'Play) or a group like De La Soul create a kind of dance psychedelia, disrupting consciousness by rupturing stylistic integrity. Splicing together grooves, beats and chants, licks and stray murmurings from unconnected pop periods, they create a friction, a rub that's both sensual and uncanny. Different auras, different vibes, different studio atmospheres, different eras, are placed in ghostly adjacence, like some strange composite organism sewn together out of a variety of vivisected limbs, or a Cronenberg dance monster. In *The Recording Angel*, Evan Eisenberg argues that 'phonography' bears the same relation to live music that cinema bears to theatre. What a record documents is not an event, but a phantasm constructed out of different takes. It never 'happened'. Sampling takes the fictitious nature of recording even further, creating events that never could have happened. 'Deconstruction of the metaphysics of presence', or what?! Public Enemy, Eric B and Rakim, Mantronix and The Young Gods each achieve their own 'balance' between fusion/fission, between the organic/machinic, between seduction/alienation.

The Young Gods are worth extracting from this little list because their use of sampling has been exemplary. Their approach to their sources is not ostentatious collage, all cut-ups, disjunctures that state no more than a spurious 'nerve', with their joins flapping in the wind of their outmoded rhetoric. Rather, their use of sampling is incendiary, genuinely reproductive. They cast all that old rock into a furnace, cook them up rather than peep at them, opt for molten purification rather than an aesthetic based around the notion of a cultural junk heap. The Young Gods are remorselessly Futurist. They are an implicit reproach to the underlying pessimism (often lazy cynicism) which you'll often find among samplers, the sad idea that we've reached the end of pop's book, and that all that's left to do is to flick back through the pages, let the brassiest moments flash before our eyes. The sound of The Young Gods is unmistakeably rock, a mechanical reversion to its 'natural' state, as opposed to a Luddite degeneration to basics. There's a ghostly, savage feel to their noise, a sense of reinvocation, perhaps of a lost paganism. The Young Gods have used sampling to point to the structural possibility of a post-postmodernism, a music that refuses to lapse into differentiation and wistful intrigue. Subtly, The Young Gods have reconstructed rock but haven't concealed too well the joins. A feeling of depthlessness and impossible angles indicate a New Method at work here, but the overall impact of songs such as 'Jusqu'au bout' is gnarled, visceral, spectacular.

The Young Gods are as expansive as sampled sound ought to be. They have resolved the existential crisis posed by the new machine which is still too much for some. In many cases, sampling in pop has proven to be a rather modest affair, subordinated to the role of simulated brass section or drum lick. Pop structures aren't tampered with or called into question — all that's expanded is an increased sense of airtight efficiency, exuded like deodorant.

The most conspicuous practitioners of sampling, who most clearly dismantle their surfaces, display a curious fear of straying beyond an agreed-upon cluster of sources. What is heralded as a vast empire of accessible noises, a sonic mine, is discovered, upon inspection, to amount to little more than a few rare groove licks, hip hop samples, Led Zep drum rolls or Sabbath guitar splashes. When these vast reserves run dry, they then sample each other's records. The reason for this absurd symbiosis in the face of the infinite is that the vast majority of the current wave of samplers are more concerned with identity (if white, to be black hip-hoppers, if black, the same), fetishism and orientation than with staring into the endless universe of possible musics. Furthermore, cut-up culture is closely linked with club culture, which has its own established norms and textural requirements, with the technology largely in the hands of DJ's. This perhaps explains the lack of a glut of amorphous, remotely beautiful samples of Bartok and the Ramayana Monkey Chant (in mitigation, we should point that Was (Not Was) did sample George Antheil on their recent 'Dad, I'm in Jail!').

Of course, what the likes of Eric B and Public Enemy do to their (albeit often predictable) sources is stunning. James Brown and Bobby Byrd are put through the machine, their grunts or peals of ecstasy clipped and frozen to emerge the other end as sheer metal, impenetrable components in the cold exteriority of hip hop. Some regard this sampling as a kind of tribute to the old soul masters, and maybe in some way it's intended as such — but the effect is far from soulful. With one push of the button, black heart becomes white noise, detached from its original context, a piercing bleep in your cranium, an abstraction. This is one of the inevitable, Futurist effects of sampling that occurs in spite of all intentions to the contrary — the death of soul, the irrelevancy of an author's passion, the birth of a New Sonic Architecture.

Sampling can only be welcomed. What's the point in resisting? But what's yet to be welcomed is a concomitant breakdown of entrenched attitudes. The sampler is not a kidney-machine to give new life to the punk values of groundswell, breakthrough, subversion, a merry street dance of egalitarianism. (So often, the cry goes up that 'everybody' is 'out there' fooling around with their cheap samplers, thus somehow constituting a 'groundswell'. But even if they are, so what? Are the pavements cracking? Is a state of collapse imminent?) Samplers will certainly not be suppressed by the Industry. The 'raging debate' about copyright laws will simply drag on at its current level for years and years, a bit like home-taping — remember the home-taping debate? The real 'crisis', or challenge to rock and pop posed by sampling concerns aesthetic possibilities and the fearsome prospect of the future and the infinity of sounds imagined by precursors such as Varese and Schaeffer.

Sampling should not be the cue for pop to eat itself so much as to breach itself. Sampling can mean disorientation, expansion, the disruption and death of the song, sonic architecture, futurism. Who is brave, willing or capable enough to embrace these prospects?

mantra-onics

1987 was a year when 'black' values ruled supreme in Pop. Terence Trent D'Arby was so feted because he was one of the few black perpetrators of this suffocating hegemony. D'Arby parroted back to the soulboys their own discourse of 'pride and dignity', eagerly presented himself as candidate for the vacant mantle of Soul Statesman, and was immediately hailed as a new Marvin Gaye, all set to tell us 'what's goin' on' in the troubled eighties.

D'Arby is one of those pop phenomena that seem vaguely called for, demanded into being by pop's climate of desire. In this case, a hankering for 'ye olde' 'real soul' is married to the requisite eighties' designer-socialist sense of image; soul and gospel classicism is relocated to the new world of Filofax self-management.

The title of his debut album, *Introducing the Hardline According to Terence Trent D'Arby*, is a claim to have suffered the kind of inspirational tribulations that fired up the soul greats. His biography (an aborted career in boxing, a spell in the army, followed by desertion and court martial) seems rich in character-building experience. The lyrics propound a vision of soul as a crash-course in fortitude-in-adversity and self-belief against all the odds. Terence Trent D'Arby showed how thoroughly soul — once the music of breakdown — had become a component in a personal regime of narcissism and self-realization.

D'Arby is a reactionary, literally, a reaction to state-of-the-art modern pop. It's a peculiar pop time that has produced and elevated D'Arby, a time marked by a failure of nerve and a falling back to simplistic notions of 'real music'. There's a lot of vintage referencing going on; a pining for a lost 'organicism' in pop, for real musicians interacting with one another, that's reflected in the fads for go go (pub

THE END OF MUSIC   •   173

rock for soul boys) and 'rare groove'. And there's a hunger for roots: a sense of place, community and shared history that we British seem only able to experience vicariously, voyeuristically, in American roots music, or Third World musics (Sting/Gabriel/Kerr's pan-global concern, U2's arbitrary location of their 'roots' in US country, gospel and blues). Above all, 'real soul' is about the desire for narrative: there's two levels here — the song as story, with a moral, or at least a wisdom we can draw from; soul as a music with origins and destiny, a grand canon, extending into the future.

Narrative is the way we structure and manage time. What's interesting about modern black dance music is that it's abandoned narrative: both hip hop and house exist in a kind of eternal present. In the case of hip hop, an unstable, threatened, tense present. In the case of house, a utopian perpetual now of polymorphous pleasure. Hip hop and house are the latest phases in an unwritten (because unwriteable) history of black pop: a history determined not by sacred cow artists but by producers and backroom technicians; a history conditioned not by individuals and their notions of the meaning and purpose of music (as with rock) but by changes in technology, in what it's possible to do with sound.

In every way, modern black dance contravenes the definitions of 'real soul'. Take house. House is disco ultimate, assembled not born; an extraction of the most dance-effective elements from Hi-NRG, Moroder Europop, English synthipop, and early eighties electrofunk: the gimmicks, special effects and extended breaks once added to spice up disco, have become the whole body of house. House music is neither the result of individual self-expression, nor is it the collective voice of a community. It's the ultimate pure pleasure product, churned out in cottage industry conditions. The product is more or less interchangeable, becomes rapidly obsolete, resulting in an endless turnover of new beats. Instead of the song (like the novel, supposedly a whole work created by a whole human being) there's a kind of terrain, a shifting dance environment without borders or destination. There's no charismatic centre to this music either: the singers are puppets, cruelly treated by the backroom boys (who vivisect the outpourings of their soul, reducing them to inane zombified gimmicks, inhuman effects). The mixing doesn't foreground the vocal, instead there's a kind of democracy of sounds, provoking 'intoxicated hearing', where one's attention wanders around the mix. Rather than the satisfaction of soul narrative, with its dynamic progression, resolution and catharsis, house offers an interminable seduction, the teasing intermittance of dub (intermittance is almost a definition of the erotic, according to Barthes). In place of 'communication', there's a depthless doggerel of catchphrases and buzzwords. Rather than the organicism of musicians grooving off one another, house is the sound of machines talking among themselves. Above all, this music is shallow, an array of surfaces and forces that engage the listener through fascination (what was that sound?!): there's no depth, no human truth or social content to be divined, no atmosphere even, just an illegible, arbitrary alteration of torques, vectors, gradients, whose opacity is endlessly resistant to the attempts of white rock critics to read anything into it.

A good example of the British media's attempts to salvage meaning from the music, is the excitement about the arrival of British house, with groups like M.A.R.R.S., Krush, S'Express and Bomb the Bass. 'Upsurges' of 'homegrown' versions of black American musics are vaunted with tiresome regularity in the music press. We've had Brit-funk, British jazz, British hip hop . . . Why this strange residual patriotism in an age where the pop networks of distribution and reciprocal influence have made national boundaries irrelevant?

A noise band in Manchester can have more in common with a peer group in Austin, Texas than with one of its 'neighbours' two blocks away; house music 'originates' in Chicago, but British northern soul fans have responded to it more fervently than almost any US city. The very fact that house is massive over here proves how irrelevant questions of nationality and location are in pop, yet still the media tries to rally an obsolete patriotic allegiance to 'our' bands, a kind of positive discrimination.

Partly these reflexes derive from punk, which inculcated an emotional commitment to the idea of things 'breaking out all over', 'our manor', 'the kids on the streets': the continued recourse to the language of 'upsurges', 'waves', 'onslaughts' allows nostalgic writers to cast whatever's happening in the same vaguely combative, oppositional light as punk. Another factor is the unease felt over Britain's tributary relationship to American pop culture: it rubs up against 'soul-cialist' anti-Americanism and fear of 'passive' consumerism. The hope is for some kind of musical self-sufficiency, or the grafting of a distinctive Britishness into imported genres.

A really close listen to house indicates how singularly unsuited it is to be the subject of punk-style clarion calls. It's difficult to imagine a genre more place-less or hostile to an infusion of ethnicity. Although it comes from a place (Chicago) it does not draw anything from its environment. House departs from the old organic language of music — roots, cross-pollination, hybridization.

Nor is biography, the other standby of the inadequate critic, at all relevant as an approach to house music. Producers like Mantronix and Todd Terry are not authors, but engineers, architects. Their music is not an expression of the soul, but a product of expertise. The signature is superseded by the trademark. A Mantronix track isn't a song, a finished work, but a process, a space capable of endless extension and adaptation, a collection of resources to be re-arranged and re-structured.

The strangest twist is that house is hugely influenced by the pop era that, for the Campaign for Real Soul, is the dawning of the Dark Ages. 'Brutal house', 'Acid', and other variants like 'Detroit Techno' and 'Belgian New Beat', take a lot of their tonal and textural repertoire from early eighties synthipop like Depeche Mode, Human League and New Order. Kraftwerk's glistening vistas and Art of Noise's fleshless, faceless, soul-less and sense-less techno-symphonic fantasia are big influences too. House has moved so far beyond 'real soul' it's jettisoned 'warmth' and 'flesh' in favour of cold plastic and the moderne. Time to chill out.

acid over
(written with Paul Oldfield)

House music is so impersonal, minimal and repetitive it seems to take effect beneath the level of conscious hearing, sweeping you up by a process of 'molecular agitation'. Acid house is the purest, barest distillation of house, the outer limit of its logic of inhuman functionalism. With acid, black music has never been so alien-ated from traditional notions of 'blackness' (fluid, grooving, warm), never been so close to the frigid, mechanical, supremely 'white' perversion of funk perpetrated by early eighties pioneers like D.A.F. and Cabaret Voltaire.

Acid house is not so much a new thing, as a drastic, terminal culmination of two tendencies in house: the trance-inducing effects of repetition and dub production; a fascination for the pristine hygiene and metronome rhythms of German electronic dance. Pure acid tracks like Tyree's 'Acid Over' recall the brute, inelastic minimalism of D.A.F. — it consists of nothing but a bass synth sequencer pulse reiterated with slight warps and eerie inflections. Other tracks parallel the obscure innovations of bands like Suicide, TVOD ('Warm Leatherette'), Liaisons Dangereuses (very big in Chicago), Die Krupps (proto-metalbashers and an early incarnation of Propaganda). Ex-Sample's 'And So it Goes' combines cut-ups ('Heroin Kills'), unidentifiable bursts of distorted, sampled sound, and human cries torn from their context (agonies of ecstasy or distress), in a manner not unlike Front 242. Reese's 'Just Want Another Chance' sets a guttural, Cabaret Voltaire monologue of desire over the spookiest of Residents synth-drones, an ectoplasmic bassline four times too slow for the drum track. 'Strings Of Life' by Rhythim-Is-Rhythim (a.k.a. Derek May, a prime mover on the acid scene) takes the sultry swing of Latin disco and clips into a spasmodic tic that's deeply unsettling; his 'Move It' is a perimeter of trebly rhythm programmes that restlessly orbit the black hole where the song should be, and strangely recalls one of those lost, desolate Joy Divison B-Sides.

Weirdest of all is 'Acid Trax' by Phuture, the record that started the whole fad off. The 'Cocaine Mix' starts with a treated voice midway between a dalek and the Voice of Judgement that announces, 'This is Cocaine Speaking'; spectral eddies of a disembodied human wail (reminiscent of nothing so much as PIL's 'No Birds Do Sing') simulate the soul languishing in cold turkey; then we're launched on terror-ride that again reminds me of PIL's 'Careering' or 'Death Disco'. 'I can make you lie for me/I can make you die for me/In the end/I'll be your only friend.' If disco was always meant to be about escapism, acid is about no-escapism.

In this, acid house takes after the white avant-funk of the late seventies/early eighties, its concept of disco as trance, a form of sinister control or possession. The flash and dazzle of disco classics like Chaka Khan's 'I'm Every Woman', Michael Jackson's *Off the Wall* album, or anything by Earth Wind and Fire, is replaced by a clinical, ultra-focused, above all inhibited sound. Expansive and expressive gestures are replaced by a precise and rigorous set of movements, *demands* on the body; flamboyance and improvisation by a discipline of pleasure. Perhaps there's a kind of 'liberation' in submitting to the mechanics of instinct, soldering the circuitry of desire to the circuitry of the sequencer programmes.

As for the connotations of 'acid', all involved in the Chicago scene deny that hallucinogenics have anything to do with the sound. The name comes from the slang term 'acid burn', which means to rip somebody off, steal their ideas (i.e. sample their sound). However many club-goers do take Ecstasy, a drug related to LSD which provides its euphoric sense of communion (and aphrodisiac effects) without causing hallucinations.

House has been bordering on the psychedelic for some time anyway, with the spaciness of its dub effects, its despotic treatment of the voice and its interference with the normal ranking of instruments in the mix (encouraging 'perceptual drift'). On one mix of Nitro Deluxe's 'On a Mission', a single phrase of female voice is vivisected, varispeeded and multitracked into a psychedelic babble of sub-phonemes and vowel-particles, becoming an airborne choir of lunatic ecstasies, a locust swarm of placeless peaks and plaints spirited free of their location in the syntax of desire.

On the Kenny Jones mix of Ralphi Rosario's 'You Used to Hold Me', stray sibilants from Xavier Gold's vocal flake off to bob inhumanly in their own parallel slipstream, until her vocal is absorbed into the backing track, with one spasm of passion turned into a jack-knifing rhythm effect. On the 'Devil Mix' of Master C&J's 'In The City', Liz Torres's voice is distorted and distended in a manner uncannily akin to The Butthole Surfers!

With pure acid house, however, it's not really a question of acid-rock's 24-track technicolour overload, of a dazzling, prismatic opening of the doors of perception, but more like a contraction or evacuation of consciousness. Not a matter of being saturated by TOO MUCH but of being compelled to focus on TOO LITTLE, reduced to a one-track mind. If people do drop a tab or two to 'acid house' they must have strange digital visions, enter Mondrian phantasmagorias, Spirograph inner orbits.

What the berserk strobe-flicker of acid house is most reminiscent of is an episode from *Star Trek*: miscreants are punished by being subjected to a strobe-like flashing lightbox which clears the brain, leaving them suggestible and capable of being literally re-formed. But one deviant is left in the machine, brainwashed but unprogrammed, lost in a terrifyingly blank catatonic limbo.

Like D.A.F.'s new savagery, like psychedelia's orgiastic utopianism, house incites a superhuman/inhuman insatiability. With the jettisoning of the song/ storyline, sex loses narrative and context, becomes asocial and fantastical. There's no sense of trajectory (courtship/seduction/foreplay/union), no sexual healing, no communication, no sense of 'scene' in the Baudrillardian sense (dramatic relations between human agents). Instead there's an ob-scene explicitness, a graphic depiction of a fantastical algebra of pornotopian configurations. Sex turns into a series of quadratic equations, flesh becomes spectral. Nothing is ever resolved: house is the beat that can never satisfy or be satisfied. The stutter-beats, the costive basslines, sound neurotic: the music's a repetition-complex, a symptom of some unstaunchable vacancy of being. Every bar of the music becomes an orgasm, making the idea of climax meaningless.

And where acid rock imagined utopia as a garden of pre-modern innocence, acid house is futuristic, in love with sophistication and technology. Acid house imagines a James Bond/Barbarella leisure paradise of gadgetry and designer drugs. House is a kind of pleasure factory (an orgasmotron, in fact) and as Marx wrote, the factory turns human beings into mere appendages of flesh attached to machinery.

If house, acid, new beat, etc, are radical, it's a radicalism that's inseparable from their simple effectiveness, pure pleasure immediacy. Here's a pop culture based around the death of the song, minimalism, repetition, departure from the stability of the key and harmonic structure in favour of sonority and sound-in-itself. No need for interpretation, context or rhetoric, all the things that people turn to the music papers for. No delay, no mediation, but a direct interface between the music's pleasure circuitry and the listener's nervous system.

Nobody even cares who made the music, which is why the personal appearances of the 'stars' are so farcical (most clubgoers continue to dance with their backs turned to the stage, while the band mimes to the record). Does this make the scene dehumanized and impersonal? You could argue, as some do, that it's a realization of one interpretation of punk: not 'anyone can be a star' so much as 'no more stars', a deconstruction of stardom (most new beat or house 'stars' are merely fronts for the producer). There's a similar kind of deconstruction to that wreaked by seventies glam: the gestures and iconography of showbiz are exaggerated, amplified and disconnected until nothing is signified but a style that can only be sustained here . . . There's just intensity without pretext or context (just like the music).

And this is a blank generation if ever you saw one, sucked into house's void and left adrift, prettily vacant. But if the scene is 'democratic', it's with a capitalist inflection; the music is pure product, consumer-tested on the dancefloor, with an inbuilt obsolescence factor. Some tracks are monumental constructions, Brutalist ziggurats you could gaze at in wonder for a lifetime. But in a club, it's compatibility rather than difference that rules, with a seamlessness that has you as happy as a nodding dog.

where 'now' lasts longer

Noise Or Not (NON) are the production team behind *Jack the Tab*, the first volume in the 'Acid Tablets' series of compilations of original UK acid dance freakbeats. NON are Richard Norris (press officer for Bam Caruso, the psychedelic reissue label, DJ and journalist) and Genesis P. Orridge of Psychic TV and the Temple organization.

Jack the Tab had to happen. Acid house has taken on so much of what was originally proposed by industrial music (Throbbing Gristle, Cabaret Voltaire) and brutalist Euro-electro (D.A.F., Liaisons Dangereuses, Front 242) that it was inevitable the original avant-funkateers would respond to what house has made of their innovations. But there's another point of convergence — figures like Orridge have moved from the demystification of Throbbing Gristle to an interest in acid rock, magick and mystique, at roughly the same time that acid house has revived the slang and cosmic imagery of psychedelia (if not the sound).

What links acid rock, Euro-electro, avant-funk and acid house is a fantasy of primitivism as un-repression and release. This record is where twenty years of flirtation with ritual and ecstatic music converge in the ultimate trance-dance, the ultimate techno-pagan bacchanalia. But this isn't a synthesis, it's fission rather than fusion, a multiple pile up at the end of the road to nowhere. Nothing really gels. The sound is organized around implacable oppositions. Between the entrancing monotony of the beat (the locked groove as stairway to bliss-out) and random, arbitrary effects (samples, jolts of indecipherable sound, which like the images of terrorism and catastrophe that bombard us via the media, we can no longer make sense of, can only respond to with appalled fascination).

And between the hygienic precision of the drum and sequencer programmes, and the chaos of treated sounds (all these strays sounds are warped into gibberish, whether it's the phased and flanged guitars, the accelerated/ decelerated voices, or the speaking-in-tongues of the ecstatic/ethnic singers. There's either a maniacal exactness of syntax, or a lunatic dereliction of syntax.

'Terminate' by Over the Brink is perhaps the stand-out. It's a simulation of war as histrionic and ambiguously pitched between horror and glorification as *Apocalypse Now.* Sky-razing guitar swoops and soars like massed dive-bombers, becomes indistinguishable from the samples of machine-gun fire and explosions, until the air itself catches fire. Snatches of military voices are interpolated — terminate with extreme prejudice, praise the Lord and pass the ammunition — but there's no real commentary, no stance, just a vertigo beyond orientation.

When did NON first become aware of acid house?

Genesis: 'In 1987 I was already on a personal quest for a hyperdelic form of dance music. Hyperdelia was the idea Psychic TV had of taking psychedelic music further by taking its attitude to mutating technology, and squaring that, in order to cube the mindwarp on the listener. It seemed inevitable that a form of dance music would occur that was contemporary but also psychedelic.'

Richard: 'And somehow the term 'acid' came over last year, before the music arrived. *Jack the Tab* was our interpretation of the term, before we actually heard what it referred to.'

When I first heard the term 'acid house' I imagined something a lot closer to what you're doing, than the hyper-minimal, suppressed, sub-D.A.F. sound that acid turned out to be. Like a lot the best music of the moment (A.R. Kane, Skinny Puppy, Eric B) *Jack the Tab* is based in the collision of mess and precision, spillage and rigour, a chaos of (mis)treated sound and an inhuman rhythmic discipline.

Genesis: 'We were using the phrase "acid dance" before the term acid house appeared. Richard was talking about freakbeats, which is a term Bam Caruso invented to describe sixties beat music gone weird, mod music on LSD, groups like The Creation, The Eyes and John's Children. A lot of our terminology comes from phone calls at strange hours. Like we'd decided on *Jack the Tab* as the title, and then the next day he rings me up and says: "What if someone asks what the 'tab' refers to?" So in a flash I said: "Techno Acid Beat."

'One of the things that's universal in all interpretations of acid house is a revival of the original idea of psychedelia, which is to take whatever technology is current — back then it would have been the wah wah, the mellotron — and try to find the weirdest, most irrational thing it can do. That's what Throbbing Gristle were into. We had a machine called the Gristleizer, which we built ourselves. We bought a computer and converted it to do sampling way back in '76, long before sampling was invented. Six tape decks in sequence, throwing sounds out at random, creating rhythms and conjunctions.'

Richard: 'It's weird how it's gone. The post-punk electronic experimental thing influencing the Chicago scene, and then us listening to what they're doing and going "oh yeah" in recognition.'

Genesis: 'At last all the different dreams and different threads that have gone in strange meandering patterns for about fifteen years have all converged, WHOOMPH! And what's so great is that it's all so open-ended, there are no rules. There are purists who try to say acid has to have a Roland drum track, a Roland bass line, about two samples of a voice, preferably from an old soul record, and so forth. But I think even the people who use that format in Chicago would feel insulted by such a simplistic view.'

Richard: 'What's different about us is that we're not purists, we don't feel the pressure of the dictates of club culture. And I think that's why the British scene as a whole will start to produce much harder and weirder sounds than Chicago.'

Genesis: 'It's gonna be like what happened in the sixties. We took US R&B and tried to imitate it, and in the process peculiarized it, got it a bit wrong, made it British, and re-exported it to the US on a massive scale. I think there's gonna be a new British beat invasion. So that's why we use the Union Jack sign, combined with the upside-down peace sign.

'The Mods used the Union Jack sign (which relates to the freakbeat thing, 'cos that was the Mods going psychedelic). The punks used the torn-up Union Jack. Now we're using it, but upside down, 'cos everything's reversed.

'I love the way the music allows sarcasm and disrespect and experiment to become a credible way of life again. We were doing all that anyway, because it's our nature. But for once, circumstances have conjoined with us. All the best ideas are inevitable. Nobody owns them.'

Richard: 'And they seem to happen at the same time, everybody thinking along the same lines.'

Genesis: 'And the right drugs arrive too. In the sixties, LSD: in the eighties, Ecstasy.'

Is Ecstasy an essential part of the subculture/experience?

'Not as regards making the music. But it's an essential catalyst for a lot of people to alter their behavioural perceptions. When you've been conditioned into using death drugs like alcohol and speed and barbiturates, and you've inherited a snobbery about psychedelics and hippies, you pooh pooh those things without any real idea of why people do it. But because, with Ecstasy, there's a different name and the effect is more benign and less out-of-control, people have experimented.

'Basically they've put themselves through psychotherapy, which is what Ecstasy was originally used for. It was claimed that three sessions with Ecstasy was the equivalent of three years deconditioning. But the drug's effect has been to open people up into accepting the mutation of old and new ideas, old and new technology.'

Richard: 'The experience in a club like Joy is very trance-like — strobes in perfect synch, smoke, minimal music. You just go on for hours and hours. But the British thing is really an extension of a European approach that's been going for years, that relates back to Neu and Can and Kraftwerk.'

Aciiieeed was a figment of the British imagination, a fantasy of what was happening in Chicago: like all British subcultures it staged a remotivation of an American music, by misrecognizing it.

Genesis: 'All popular culture has become a fair target for reworking, stealing whatever bits you need. Not just music, but TV, political speeches, cartoons, movies. Nothing is immune and nothing is sacred. And I've always wanted to live in a world where nothing is immune and nothing is sacred. And no one could tell you what was the correct way to do something.'

But it's the reworking that counts, not the fact of theft: what's done with the new options, not the cheek and subversive irreverence of petty pilfering. Sampling has been presented as a new punk, a democratization of the means of musical production, an "anyone can do it" bonanza. But like punk, sampling opens up things only for the emergence of a new kind of musical intelligence. Those who endure will be those who would have got on anyway.

Genesis: 'You're right. This initial burst will involve a lot of mimicry and second-hand ideas. And as Burroughs said: "People think it's easy to do a cut-up, and physically it is. But the trick is choosing what to cut up. That's when the artist's brain comes into play, the choosing, ordering, discarding." That's the aesthetic in sampling — recognizing the conjunctions of sounds that work.

'Obviously, the ones that push it further will be the ones who survive. We just want to make it more extreme, more absurd. To stimulate ourselves. To confuse ourselves. You get jaded. Richard's been studying, reissuing, playing, writing about music since . . . forever. I've been involved in deconstructing culture and music for nearly twenty years! So what's shocked me is that I actually get excited by this music, by the sound in itself, at this late hour. I can listen to it over and over, get fresh ideas every time . . . about what new jarring connections, what stupid but funny commentaries can be made by juxtaposing sounds, word and personality.'

How did you and Richard get together?

'With the whole *Godstar* project, I embarked on an historical investigation of psychedelia; the hypnotic colours, costumes and gestures; the strange noises, like overdone phasing and ludicrously exaggerated wah wah, that sounded so much more exciting than what we hear nowadays. That's how I started buying Bam Caruso records. In such huge numbers that Richard noticed, came to interview us, and we linked up.

'It was like two units of commandos fighting in the jungle, slogging away in parallel lines, then all of a sudden appearing in the same clearing and deciding to join forces and go down the same path. Because it'll be more fun, and we'll get more done.'

Richard: 'Really, the idea of psychedelic dance has been on the cards for years.'

Why has it cohered around house rather than, say, hip hop?

'Rap is more an ego-boosting thing. House is more about losing your ego.'

Genesis: 'Acid house has no vocals, there's no ego being projected. Or if there are vocals, they're very short, clipped phrases, or they're conflagrations of words. The vocals are deadpan, in the tradition of Kraftwerk and Eurorock. That's what you want when it comes to trance-music. You don't want to hear a soul singer expressing himself all over the shop.

'Also, it's got something to do with the speed of the beats. It's hypnotic, tribal and primal. That particular speed has worked for thousands of years, which is why you can spin in Arab music, Bhangra music, Aboriginal music . . . You can take all these different cultures and find the same beat, between 125-130 bpm. It's there in ecstatic, trance music, where people shake and spin until they reach a state of hyperventilation and psychedelic alpha-wave experience. In a sense, acid is regressive music. You're going back to the roots of why music was invented: to reach ecstatic and visionary states, in a communal tribal celebration.'

This is like the Saqqara Dogs' idea of leaving the twentieth century (where music is subordinate to words, is merely a kind of journalism or surrogate literature) and going forward in order to go back to the primordial function of music. Noise Or Not allude to this idea of House as ritual, communal release by the extensive use of field recordings of ecstatic, tribal music.

'I've got a huge collection of field recordings, documentary programmes, and

I've made tapes myself, and I've scrounged off people like Dr Alan Presence who did a programme on Tibetan music.'

Richard: 'The sampling trend is mostly focused on speech now, but I definitely think it's going more towards sound, passages of noise. That's where we're heading. That whole musique concrete idea as exemplified by Stockhausen, Cage, Pierre Henri.'

Genesis: 'The other thing we sample from is video, which is another unexplored area. Think about it — listen to *Apocalypse Now!* or *Star Wars*, and there are noises that the director probably spent millions of dollars getting. The sound of people disintegrating in *Evil Dead.* The sound of a flame-thrower. All these can be yours for the couple of quid it costs to rent a video from your local store. You can take a million dollar sound and use it in such a way that it's unrecognizable and basically no longer that sound.

'We've started collecting old Analogue equipment, because it has a particular sound digital studios have lost. Same reason we use CDs and old 78s and videos. There's the subtle alteration in texture depending on the medium you use. That's why someone like Derek Jarman will use Super-8 and 35mm. You get grains and colours you cannot get with the 'best', up to date technology.

'Now, when we go to a flea market, we don't look for rare psychedelic records anymore. We hunt for spoken word albums, John F. Kennedy, the US army in the Rhine . . . There's this theory that if you take a bit of a record, you take with it something of the whole of that record, of the people who make it, even of the era it was made in. You make a statement about a whole era, and that's taken further when you juxtapose it with a sample containing another whole era.'

Is it really about 'making statements', though? My pleasure in it is disorientation, not coming away with any stable units of sense.

'I don't mean there are "messages", but that the music itself is a statement about information explosion and the acceleration of experience which is what the effect of the mass media is.'

Do they agree that there's a disparate tendency at work in rock, right now, that wants to liberate music from words? Something you can see right across the spectrum, from A.R. Kane and the Cocteaus' consonant-free continuum of baby babble, through Pixies visionary gibberish, to the coerced, mantric chants of Euro Body Music.

'I think you're right, that's one of the really significant things at the moment. The disassociation from a need for language. For whatever reason, narrative lyrics are just pointless. There's not really anything to "say." Maybe I'm a moron, but I just can't think of anything to say to people at the moment. Except that there are ways to express yourself that are non-verbal. Of course, there's this disgusting singer-songwriter revival at the moment, but that's a kind of rearguard action.'

It's the opposite tendency: instead of a depth of sound to drown yourself and meaning in, there's almost nothing but the meaning, only the most negligible, scanty smear of sound as a backdrop.

'What value have words got in this society anyway? We're pummelled daily by millions of bloody words. Words are ten a penny. But noises arranged in odd ways can still jar or captivate.'

It sounds like the approach has infinite possibilities. Is this the End of Music, an End that will extend into eternity?

Richard: 'That's why we're trying to lose the house tag, because house will die, but our kind of music will live on.'

Genesis: 'Techno acid beat is the best label, but ultimately who cares what it's called? It's got a lot of people out of a hole. Whatever comes out of it — and there are going to be a lot of fly-by-night dross merchants — the residue of expanded minds is going to be worthwhile.

'I think a lot of people are underestimating the implications. Even this first wave hasn't washed everywhere around the globe yet, hasn't got to Japan and Europe and South America. Even if it stopped progressing now, it's BIG . . .'

Tales are filtering back of a dance scene in Goa, India, at the crossroads of the drug trade routes, where the freaks go to huge beach parties on the edge of the jungle, and get out of their heads on cheap LSD and the brutalist electro of Skinny Puppy and Front 242. Someone who's been there tells me, 'It's the end of the journey, man. Apocalypse Now.'

(1987–9)

BIBLIOGRAPHY

Auster, Paul. *The New York Trilogy.* London: Faber and Faber, 1987.

Bachelard, Gaston. *The Poetics of Space.* Translated by Maria Jolas. Boston: Beacon Press, 1969.

Bangs, Lester. *Psychotic Reactions and Carburetor Dung.* Edited by Greil Marcus. New York: Knopf, 1987.

Barthes, Roland. *The Pleasure of the Text.* Translated by Richard Miller. New York: Hill and Wang, 1975.

    A Lover's Discourse. Translated by Richard Howard. New York: Hill and Wang, 1977.

    'The Grain of the Voice', in *Image-Music-Text.* Edited and translated by Stephen Heath. London: Fontana, 1984.

Bataille, Georges. *Visions of Excess: Selected Writings 1927–1939.* Edited by Allan Stoekl. Translated by Allan Stoekl with Carl R. Lovitt and Donal M. Leslie, Jr. Manchester: Manchester University Press, 1985.

    Erotism: Death and Sensuality. Translated Mary Dalwood. San Francisco: City Lights, 1986.

Baudrillard, Jean. 'Forget Baudrillard', an interview with Sylvère Lotringer. In *Forget Foucault.* New York: *Semiotext(e),* 1987.

Cixous, Hélène and Clément, Catherine. *The Newly Born Woman.* Translated by Betsy Wing. Minneapolis: University of Minnesota Press, 1986.

Cleaver, Eldridge. *Soul on Ice.* New York: Dell Publishing Co., 1968.

Cohn, Nik. 'Awopbopaloobop Alopbamboom'. In *Ball the Wall: Nik Cohn in the Age of Rock.* London: Picador, 1989.

Eisenberg, Evan. *The Recording Angel: Music, Records and Culture from Aristotle to Zappa.* London: Picador, 1988.

Foucault, Michel. *Power/Knowledge: Selected Interviews and Other Writings 1972–1977.* Edited Colin Gordon. Translated by Colin Gordon, Leo Marshall, John Mepham, Kate Soper. Brighton: Harvester, 1980.

    The History of Sexuality – Volume One: An Introduction. Translated by Robert Hurley. Harmondsworth: Penguin, 1981.

Gray, Christopher (editor and translator). *Leaving the Twentieth Century: The Incomplete Work of the Situationist International.* London: Free Fall Publications, 1974.

Hebdige, Dick. *Subculture: The Meaning of Style.* London: Routledge, 1979.

    Hiding in the Light: *On Images and Things.* London: Comedia, 1988.

Hoskyns, Barney. *Prince — Imp of the Perverse.* London: Virgin Books, 1988.

Jameson, Frederick. 'Postmodernism and Consumer Society'. In *Postmodern Culture.* Edited by Hal Foster. London: Pluto Press, 1985.

Knabb, Ken (editor and translator). *Situationist International Anthology.* Berkeley, California: Bureau of Public Secrets, 1981.

Kristeva, Julia. *Powers of Horror: An Essay on Abjection.* Translated by Leon S. Roudiez. New York: Columbia University Press, 1982.

The Kristeva Reader. Edited by Toril Moi. Oxford: Basil Blackwell Ltd, 1984.

Kundera, Milan. *The Unbearable Lightness of Being.* Translated by Michael Henry Heim. London: Faber and Faber, 1982.

Lasch, Christopher. *The Minimal Self: Psychic Survival in Troubled Times.* London: Pan, 1985.

Marcus, Greil. *Mystery Train: Images of America in Rock'n'Roll Music* London: Omnibus Press, 1977.

Lipstick Traces: A Secret History of the Twentieth Century. London: Secker and Warburg Ltd, 1989.

Moi, Toril. *Sexual/Textual Politics: Feminist Literary Theory.* London: Methuen 1985.

Moore, Suzanne. 'Getting a Bit of the Other: The Pimps of Postmodernism'. In *Male Order: Unwrapping Masculinity.* Edited by Rowena Chapman and Jonathan Rutherford. London: Lawrence and Wishart, 1988.

Morley, Paul. *Ask: The Chatter of Pop.* London: Faber and Faber, 1986.

Nietzsche, Friedrich. *The Birth of Tragedy.* Translated by Francis Golffing. New York: Doubleday, 1956.

Savage, Jon. 'City: 68/77/88/2000'. In *Vague 21: Cyberpunk.* London: Vague Publications.

Thewelweit, Klaus. *Male Fantasies — Volume One: Women, Floods, Bodies, History.* Translated by Stephen Conway. Minneapolis: University of Minnesota Press, 1987.

Vermorel, Fred and Judy. *Starlust.* London: W.H. Allen, 1985.

Fandemonium. London: Omnibus Press, 1990.

SELECT DISCOGRAPHY

ABC
The Lexicon of Love (Phonogram LP)

JOHN ABERCROMBIE
Characters (ECM LP)
(with RALPH TOWNER):
Sargasso Sea (ECM LP)
Five Years Later (ECM LP)

ACID HOUSE
PHUTURE — 'Acid Trax' b/w 'Your Only
    Friend' (Trax 12″ single)
NITRO DELUXE — 'On A Mission' (Cutting 12″
    single)
REESE — 'Just Another Chance' (Incognito
    12″ single)
ROYAL HOUSE — 'Party People' (Idlers 12″
    single)
RHYTHIM IS RHYTHIM — 'Strings of Life' b/w
    'Move It' (Transmat 12″ single)
MASTER C & J — 'In The City' (State Street 12″
    single)
RALPHI ROSARIO — 'You Used to Hold Me'
    (Hotmix 12″ single).
THE IT — 'Donnie' (DJ International 12″
    single)
VARIOUS ARTISTS — *Jack Trax: The Third
    Album* (PRT LP)
VARIOUS ARTISTS — '*Jackmaster Volume One*'
    and '*Jackmaster Volume Two*' (DJ
    International LPS)

ACT
'Snobbery And Decay' (ZTT 12″
    single)

AGE OF CHANCE
'Kiss' (Fon 12″ single)
One Thousand Years of Trouble (Virgin LP)

A.R. KANE
'When You're Sad' (One Little Indian 12″
    single)
Lollita (4AD EP)
Up Home (Rough Trade EP)
69 (Rough Trade LP)
Lovesick (Rough Trade EP)
I (Rough Trade LP)
(as M.A.R.R.S.):
'Pump up the Volume/Anitina' (4AD 12″
    single)

BEASTIE BOYS
Licensed to Ill (Def Jam LP)

BIG BLACK
Atomiser (Blast First LP)
Songs About Fucking (Blast First LP)

BLUE ORCHIDS
The Greatest Hit (Rough Trade LP)

BUTTHOLE SURFERS
Rembrandt Pussy Horse (Blast First LP)
Locust Abortion Technician (Blast First LP)
Hairway To Steven (Blast First LP)

NICK CAVE AND THE BAD SEEDS
From Her to Eternity (Mute LP)
Kicking Against the Pricks (LP)
Your Funeral . . . My Trial (Mute LP)
Tender Prey (Mute LP)
(as THE BIRTHDAY PARTY)
Prayers on Fire (4AD LP)
Junkyard (4AD LP)
The Bad Seed (Mute EP)
Mutiny (Mute EP)

THE CHRISTIANS
The Christians (Island LP)

COCTEAU TWINS
Head Over Heels (4AD LP)
Sunburst and Snowblind (4AD EP)
'Pearly-Dewdrops Drops' (4AD 12″ single)
'Aikea Guinea' (4AD 12″ single)
Blue Bell Knoll (4AD LP)

TERENCE TRENT D'ARBY
Introducing the Hardline According To . . .
(CBS LP)

DE LA SOUL
3 Feet High and Rising (Big Life LP)

DEXY'S MIDNIGHT RUNNERS
Searching for the Young Soul Rebels (EMI)

DINOSAUR JR
You're Living All Over Me (SST LP)
Bug (Blast First LP)

DURUTTI COLUMN
Valuable Passages (Factory LP)
The Guitar and Other Machines (Factory LP)
Vini Reilly (Factory LP)

EINSTURZENDE NEUBAUTEN
½ Mensh (Some Bizarre LP)
Haus der Luege (Some Bizarre LP)

ERIC B AND RAKIM
Paid in Full (4th & Broadway LP)
Follow the Leader (MCA LP)

FLIPPER
Gone Fishin' (Fundamental LP)

FRANKIE GOES TO HOLLYWOOD
Welcome to the Pleasuredome (ZTT LP)

FRONT 242
'Masterhit' (Wax Trax 12″ single)
'Headhunter' (RRE 12″ single)
Front by Front (RRE LP)

JAN GARBAREK
Dis (ECM LP)
'Paths, Prints' (ECM LP)

HAPPY FLOWERS
My Skin Covers My Body (Homestead LP)
I Crush Bozo (Homestead LP)

HAPPY MONDAYS
'Squirrel and G-Man . . .' (Factory LP)
'Bummed' (Factory LP)

HEAVEN 17
Penthouse and Pavement (Virgin LP)

HUE AND CRY
Seduced and Abandoned (Circa LP)

HUGO LARGO
Drum (Land LP)
Mettle (Land LP)

HUSKER DU
Zen Arcade (SST LP)
Flip Yer Wig (SST LP)
Warehouse: Songs and Stories (Warners LP)

JACK THE TAB
Jack the Tab (Castalia LP)

JESUS AND MARY CHAIN
Psychocandy (Blanco Y Negro LP)
Darklands (WEA LP)
Barbed Wire Kisses (WEA LP)

LL COOL J
Radio (Def Jam LP)
Bigger and Deffer (Def Jam LP)

LOOP
Heaven's End (Chapter 22 LP)
'Collision/Thief of Fire' (Chapter 22 12″ single')
'Black Sun/Mother Sky/Circle Grave' (Chapter 22 122 single)
Fade Out (Chapter 22 LP)
The World in Your Eyes (Chapter 22 compilation LP)

MALCOLM MCLAREN
Duck Rock (Epic LP)

MANTRONIX
The Album (10 LP)
Music Madness (10 LP)

MEAT PUPPETS
Meat Puppets 1 (SST LP)
Meat Puppets 2 (SST LP)
Up on the Sun (SST LP)

METALLICA
Master of Puppets (Music For Nations LP)
. . . And Justice for all (Vertigo LP)
MORRISSEY
Viva Hate! (His Master's Voice LP)
(in THE SMITHS):
The Smiths (Rough Trade LP)
Hatful of Hollow (Rough Trade LP)
Meat is Murder (Rough Trade LP)
The Queen is Dead (Rough Trade LP)
The World Won't Listen (Rough Trade LP)
Strangeways, Here We Come (Rough Trade LP)

MY BLOODY VALENTINE
'Strawberry Wine' (Lazy 12" single)
You Made Me Realise (Creation EP)
Feed Me With Your Kiss (Creation EP)
Isn't Anything (Creation LP)

PET SHOP BOYS
Actually (Parlophone LP)
Please (Parlophone LP)

PIXIES
Come on Pilgrim (4AD mini-LP)
Surfer Rosa (4AD LP)
Doolittle (4AD LP)

PRINCE
Dirty Mind (Warners LP)
Controversy (Warners LP)
1999 (Warners LP)
Purple Rain (Warners LP)
Around the World in a Day (Paisley Park LP)
Parade (Paisley Park LP)
Sign o' the Times (Paisley Park LP)
Lovesexy (Paisley Park LP)

PSYCHIC TV
'Godstar' (Temple 12" single)

PUBLIC ENEMY
Yo! Bum Rush The Show! (Def Jam LP)
It'll Take a Nation of Millions to Stop Us (Def Jam LP)
Fear of a Black Planet (Def Jam LP)

PUSSY GALORE
Right Now! (Product Inc LP)
Dial M (Product Inc LP)

THE REDSKINS
Neither Washington Nor Moscow (Decca LP)

REGRESSIVE ROCK
NME C86 (Rough Trade compilation LP)

ARTHUR RUSSELL
'Let's Go Swimming' (Rough Trade 12" single)
The World of Echo (Rough Trade LP)

SALT 'N' PEPA
Hot, Cool and Vicious (Next Plateau LP)

SAQQARA DOGS
World Crunch (Pathfinder mini-LP)
Thirst (Pathfinder LP)

SCHOOLLY D
Schoolly D (Rhythm King LP)
Saturday Night (Rhythm King LP)

SCRITTI POLITTI
Songs to Remember (Rough Trade LP)
Cupid & Psyche 85 (Virgin LP)

SIGUE SIGUE SPUTNIK
Flaunt It (EMI LP)

SKINNY PUPPY
Mind the Perpetual Intercourse (Play It Again Sam LP)

SONIC YOUTH
Evol (Blast First LP)
Sister (Blast First LP)
Daydream Nation (Blast First LP)
(as CICCONE YOUTH):
The Whitey Album (Blast First LP)

SPACEMEN 3
The Perfect Prescription (Fire LP)
Playing With Fire (Fire LP)

MARK STEWART AND THE MAFFIA
Mark Stewart (Mute LP)

THE STYLE COUNCIL
Our Favourite Shop (Polydor LP)
The Cost of Loving (Polydor LP)

THE SUGARCUBES
'Birthday' (One Little Indian single)

SWANS
Cop (K.442 LP)
Greed (K.442 LP)
Children of God (K.442 LP)

TALK TALK
Spirit of Eden (Parlophone LP)

THROWING MUSES
Throwing Muses (4AD LP)
Chains Changed (4AD EP)
The Fat Skier (4AD mini-LP)
House Tornado (4AD LP)

TRANSVISION VAMP
Pop Art (MCA LP)
'Born to be Sold' (MCA single)

ULTRA VIVID SCENE
Ultra Vivid Scene (4AD LP)
Joy 1967–1990 (4AD LP)

WORLD DOMINATION ENTERPRISES
Lets's Play Domination (Product Inc LP)
Love From Lead City (Product Inc LP)

THE YOUNG GODS
The Young Gods (Product Inc LP)
'L'Amourir' (Play It Again Sam 12" single)
L'Eau Rouge (Play It Again Sam LP)